FLASH® PROFESSIONAL CS6

ESSENTIALS

CERTIFIED ASSOCIATE
Approved Courseware

FLASH® PROFESSIONAL CS6

ESSENTIALS

CERTIFIED ASSOCIATE
Approved Courseware

William (Bill) Heldman

WILEY

John Wiley & Sons, Inc.

Acquisitions Editor: Mariann Barsolo
Development Editor: Kim Wimpsett
Technical Editor: Richard Hauck
Production Editor: Eric Charbonneau
Copy Editor: Judy Flynn
Editorial Manager: Pete Gaughan
Production Manager: Tim Tate
Vice President and Executive Group Publisher: Richard Swadley
Vice President and Publisher: Neil Edde
Book Designer: Happenstance Type-O-Rama
Proofreader: Nancy Bell
Indexer: Ted Laux
Project Coordinator, Cover: Katherine Crocker
Cover Designer: Ryan Sneed
Cover Image: © William Heldman
Additional images in the book used courtesy of Art Explosion® Nova Development, Copyright 2004.

Copyright © 2012 by John Wiley & Sons, Inc., Indianapolis, Indiana
Published simultaneously in Canada
ISBN: 978-1-118-12965-4 (pbk)
ISBN: 978-1-118-22566-0 (ebk)
ISBN: 978-1-118-23844-8 (ehk)
ISBN: 978-1-118-26306-8 (ebk)

For general information on our other products and services or to obtain technical support, please contact our Customer Care Department within the U.S. at (877) 762-2974, outside the U.S. at (317) 572-3993 or fax (317) 572-4002.

Wiley also publishes its books in a variety of electronic formats and by print-on-demand. Not all content that is available in standard print versions of this book may appear or be packaged in all book formats. If you have purchased a version of this book that did not include media that is referenced by or accompanies a standard print version, you may request this media by visiting http://booksupport.wiley.com. For more information about Wiley products, visit us at www.wiley.com.

Library of Congress Control Number: 2012935364

10 9 8 7 6 5 4 3 2 1

Dear Reader,

Thank you for choosing *Flash Professional CS6 Essentials*. This book is part of a family of premium-quality Sybex books, all of which are written by outstanding authors who combine practical experience with a gift for teaching.

Sybex was founded in 1976. More than 30 years later, we're still committed to producing consistently exceptional books. With each of our titles, we're working hard to set a new standard for the industry. From the paper we print on to the authors we work with, our goal is to bring you the best books available.

I hope you see all that reflected in these pages. I'd be very interested to hear your comments and get your feedback on how we're doing. Feel free to let me know what you think about this or any other Sybex book by sending me an email at nedde@wiley.com. If you think you've found a technical error in this book, please visit http://sybex.custhelp.com. Customer feedback is critical to our efforts at Sybex.

Best regards,

NEIL EDDE
Vice President and Publisher
Sybex, an Imprint of Wiley

To those who have always wanted to learn more about Flash and have decided to take time out of their busy days to do just that. I was one of you, and I'm glad I made the journey. You will be too.

ACKNOWLEDGMENTS

Thank you especially to all of the people at Sybex who have been so supportive, friendly, and professional with me in the years I have been writing for this superb publisher. Neil Edde—thank you for taking a chance on me years ago and for being patient with me over the years. You are and always will be *the man*. I hoist a virtual glass of '00 Bordeaux in toast to you my friend.

Thank you as well to everyone on the staff who worked with me in some way on this book: Pete Gaughan, Mariann Barsolo, Kim Wimpsett, Eric Charbonneau, and Richard Hauck. Gentle spirits, amazing people all. Books are not written by one person but by teams who help authors make sense out of what they're doing and saying. Without you, it would not have been possible.

I would also like to thank my family: my wife, Kim, and my son, daughters, and granddaughters. When you are writing a book, there are lots of times you have to "put your family on ignore." Fortunately for me, my wife is the author of the *Project Management Professional (PMP) Study Guide*—a long-running Sybex best seller—so she gets it when the headphones go on and I'm checked out into the virtual world of letters and sentences. But when your kids come to the door for Thanksgiving dinner and your wife has to answer because you're getting that last sentence knocked out, well, that takes extra patience from your loved ones. And that's what they demonstrate day in and day out.

Thanks also to my students, who have unwittingly been the fodder for many of the ideas in this book. "Just in time curriculum development" means that you have an idea while you're driving to school for the day that will hopefully entice your kids into wanting to delve more into the world of technology. All of the examples in this book were used in the classroom before they made it into this book. They're tried and tested, mmm good. A big hats off to one of my students—nicknamed Ginger—for his odd and strangely beautiful gift for design. He was the inspiration for the cow abduction section of this book.

ABOUT THE AUTHOR

William (Bill) Heldman is the author of several Sybex books, predominantly in the technology certification exam space, the most recent of which is the *CompTIA Project+ Study Guide*. During the day Bill is a computer science and game development instructor at a Career and Technical Education (CTE) high school in Lakewood, Colorado, called Warren Tech (www.warrentech.org).

Teaching is Bill's third career. Having come out of an information technology path of increasingly responsible roles, Bill has found his passion in helping 11th and 12th graders explore the world of information technologies and make decisions about potential college and career paths.

Bill lives in Lakewood, Colorado, with his wife, Kim, and toy poodle, Nutmeg. In his spare, spare time, Bill is the director of a big-band jazz and swing group called William and the Romantics (www.williamandtheromantics.com). Bill also enjoys writing blogs (educationgenesis.blogspot.com and blog .billheldman.com) and pursuing various hobbies, including reading, movies, music, and wine. Oh, and now that they've built a store in Denver, there's his need for a nearly weekly IKEA fix, but that would take up too much space.

You can read more about Bill at www.billheldman.com. You can contact him at billheldman@gmail.com.

Contents at a Glance

CONTENTS

CHAPTER 3 Drawing Shapes in Flash   51

CHAPTER 4 Getting Started with the Timeline   81

CHAPTER 5 Adding Flash Text and Fonts to Your Creations   109

INTRODUCTION

Welcome readers. This book is for those who are new to Adobe Flash Professional and who may be considering taking the Adobe Certified Associate (ACA) Rich Media Communication with Adobe Flash Professional exam.

First of all, you will learn a lot about Adobe Flash, and I believe you will be glad you did. It is a tremendously important web development tool, one that will greatly enhance your skills and provide you with bountiful new ways to express your ideas. But also, by using this ACA Approved Courseware, you will be more than adequately prepared for the ACA exam. I have taken it, passed it, and enjoyed it a great deal. And you can too.

Who Should Read This Book

Anyone who is new to Adobe Flash or who has dabbled in it a bit and wants to know more will benefit from reading this book. If you're a Dreamweaver developer interested in expanding your skills in Flash, this book is for you. If you've always wanted to have more tools in your kit for expanding and enhancing your ideas and expressing yourself, this book is for you. If you're looking for ways to make yourself more employable, this book is for you as well. And of course, for those who are reading this as a study guide for passing the ACA exam, I believe you will find this book to be of invaluable assistance.

If you're interested in more information about the ACA exam, this book can be a great resource to help you prepare. See `http://www.adobe.com/education/resources/certificate-programs.html` for more certification information and resources.

What You Will Learn

You will learn how to use Adobe Flash at a granular and productive level. You'll learn about the Flash interface, how to create graphic objects on the Flash stage, how to create animations and use the timeline, how to build tweens (amazing little tools that blend one shape into another or move an object over time), and how to write ActionScript code to enhance your creations.

All of the Flash subject matter you need to pass the ACA exam you will find in this book. But I've tried to go beyond the exam a bit and give you more insight and information so that you feel comfortable leveraging the tool in your work-day environment.

What You Need

You will need to have Flash Professional installed on your computer. All of the examples in this book will work with Creative Suite 5.5 or higher. No other software is required. Flash can be a resource-intensive application when you're in the throes of a development cycle, so a fast processor and plenty of RAM are both going to help you have a better experience when working with Flash.

What Is Covered in This Book

Flash Professional CS6 Essentials is organized to provide you with the knowledge needed to master the basics.

Chapter 1, "Before Jumping into Flash: Rich Media Design Principles and Practice," This chapter deals with some of the exam elements that you will use in Flash but that also have broader context. The chapter starts out defining what is meant by the term *rich media*. The chapter also has a section in it on accessibility issues—a big issue for exam takers—as well as a section on project management, also a topic about which exam takers will need to know.

Chapter 2, "Getting Acquainted with Flash," Beginners who open up Flash for the first time may be taken aback by its daunting user interface (UI). This chapter will provide you a thorough overview of the Flash UI so that it will be scary no longer. You will be able to navigate Flash quickly and easily.

Chapter 3, "Drawing Shapes in Flash," In this chapter, you will learn how to use the Flash shape tools to begin creating your designs in the Flash environment. Just as you can sketch with different shapes and textures to create more complex designs, so you can use Flash's shape tools to do the same thing with your rich media designs.

Chapter 4, "Getting Started with the Timeline," You will learn the basics of how to use Flash layers and the timeline to create complex rich media documents. For people familiar with Photoshop or Illustrator, the layers concept will be easily accessible. But for those who've not worked with animation, the timeline may be an unusual new twist. Fear not! This is the chapter that will work you through to the happy combination of layers *and* the timeline.

Chapter 5, "Adding Flash Text and Fonts to Your Creations," Text is an important part of your rich media storytelling, and Flash brings a variety of ways for you to create text environments that are inviting and compelling. You still have to craft the story, but Flash brings you the tools to show your text in a better way.

Chapter 6, "Working with Flash Symbols,"   Flash symbols—graphics, buttons, and movie clips—are the geniuses behind compelling rich media environments. You will learn how to use these clever little elements to heighten your work to stunning levels.

Chapter 7, "Developing Simple Flash Animations,"   Flash allows you to create nearly any kind of animation you have in mind. In this chapter, you will begin to learn how to create these animations using a little story I like to call "Cow Abduction."

Chapter 8, "Using Tweens,"   Tweens are nifty little algorithms that calculate the difference between one shape and another or the motion of something from one place to another. You need tweens in your animation efforts, and this chapter shows you how to build them. You'll learn how to tweak your tweens (say that three times fast) to make them work for you. Got clouds that you need to move slowly across the screen compared to other faster moving objects? Parallax scrolling is your answer, and that's one of the things you'll learn in this chapter.

Chapter 9, "Techniques for Creating More Technical Animations,"   Now that you've got the basics down, you will learn how to create more technical animations. You'll take your tweens and put them on steroids—combining them to form a delightful whole. In this chapter, you'll find out how to do this by creating a bicycle scene, replete with moving pedals and wheels.

Chapter 10, "Creating Characters with Inverse Kinematics,"   Inverse kinematics (IK) is the process of putting bones into your Flash objects so that they can move. In this chapter you'll take your bicycle scene to the next level, learning how to cartoon yourself, put bones into your virtual body, and then make your cartooned self ride that bike through town. You'll also use parallax scrolling to make the buildings and clouds roll along.

Chapter 11, "Working with Audio,"   Bang a drum! No really, bang a drum! In this chapter you'll learn how to use sounds in Flash, and what better way than taking what you've already learned about creating complex objects using the Flash shape tools and creating a cool set of drums that, when hit, actually play sound?

Chapter 12, "Working with Video,"   Now that smartphones have made video so accessible, videos must be included as part of your rich media repertoire. This chapter will show you how to quickly and easily snap in any video you want using Flash's built-in video management tools.

Chapter 13, "Working with ActionScript,"   Are you afraid of those folks people call under their breath coders? Does the very use of the word *code* send shivers down your spine? This chapter will take you gently into the world of

ActionScript, the coding environment that, behind the scenes, takes your rich media work from great to amazing.

Appendices   Appendix A provides a table of the objectives and in which chapters you can find those objectives covered for the Rich Media Communication With Adobe Flash Professional exam. Appendix B deals with the things you should think about next, now that you have a solid dose of Flash in your system.

CHAPTER EXERCISES AND COMPANION WEBSITE

Solutions are provided for most of the exercises in the chapters; you can download them from the book's companion web page at www.sybex.com/go/flashessentials.

The Essentials Series

The Essentials series from Sybex provides outstanding instruction for readers who are just beginning to develop their professional skills. Every Essentials book includes these features:

▶ Skill-based instruction with chapters organized around projects rather than abstract concepts or subjects.

▶ Suggestions for additional exercises at the end of each chapter so you can practice and extend your skills.

▶ Digital files (via download) so you can work through the project tutorials yourself. Please check the book's web page at www.sybex.com/go/flashessentials for these companion downloads.

Certification Objective   The certification margin icon will alert you to passages that are especially relevant to Adobe Certified Associate (ACA) Rich Media Communications With Adobe Flash Professional certification. See Appendix A and www.adobe.com for more information and resources.

How to Contact the Author

Bill Heldman can be contacted via email at billheldman@gmail.com.

CHAPTER 1

Before Jumping into Flash: Rich Media Design Principles and Practice

Well-crafted rich media experiences rapidly draw viewers into your scene. Rich media tools such as Flash allow designers to bring action to a scene and provide ways to tell the viewer more than what they can simply read on a page.

When creating rich media, you need to consider your client—their intended audience and the purpose for the media they want you to create. You'll also need to pick the media type relevant to the content's purpose and master basic project management techniques so you can keep your efforts on track. Other up-front considerations are the accessibility issues some users face and copyright and publishing rules.

▶ **Working with clients to create rich media projects**

▶ **Addressing accessibility issues in rich media**

▶ **Understanding project management 101**

▶ **Understanding copyright issues when using others' work**

Working with Clients to Create Rich Media Projects

Your rich media design experiences will likely start with your clients. While your customers have probably had the pleasure of experiencing rich media environments for themselves, they most likely want you to make rich media content for them because they don't have the expertise in tools such as Flash. In fact, when asked how to create rich media, most people don't have the slightest idea where to start or even know what the term entails.

What Is Rich Media?

Depending on whom you query, you will find that the basic definition for rich media sounds something like this: Rich media tools serve as a way to provide the viewer with more interesting methods of garnering information than just a static web page with infrequently changing text.

Rich media can include streaming video, rich Internet applications (RIAs) created with Adobe AIR that do some job for the viewer, buttons, music, mouse cursor changes, color variations, animations, games, cartoons, banner ads, floating ads, tickers, special effects, and much more. Flash isn't the only rich-media publishing method. You can use Flash to publish Adobe AIR apps as well. AIR apps can be published to iOS or Android devices, or do the desktop.

Rich media also has the ability to use well-crafted designs to get at a variety of subtler elements. For example, you may be interested in the age of your viewers, their affluence (or lack thereof), the kind of work they do, their educational level, various demographics such as ethnicity or urban clustering, and so forth. You can even adapt your rich media to non-computer-literate types: neophytes to the web. For example, Flash has found a fantastic foothold in creating games for young children—teaching them to garner the tools needed to be computer literate long before they ever take a computer class in school.

The user interface (UI) for Flash is easy to learn and yet amazingly powerful. Moreover, all the other products in the Adobe Creative Suite (CS), such as Illustrator, Fireworks, and Photoshop, have been designed to easily interact with one another.

Beginners can accomplish many great things using the native Flash UI, but there is also a scripting language associated with Flash called ActionScript (currently in version 3.0; we typically refer to it as AS3). When the Flash UI meets AS3, some pretty sophisticated things can begin to happen. There is also a formal integrated development environment (IDE) for AS3 programmers called Flash Builder (formerly called Flex), but that topic is way out of scope for this book and for the Adobe Certified Associate (ACA) exam for Rich-Media Communication using Flash, which I will heretofore call simply the "ACA Exam." (There may be some very minor AS3 questions on the exam, so I'll cover some AS3 basics in Chapter 13, "Working with ActionScript.")

Although rich media isn't limited to websites, in the majority of cases the Web is where you will find rich media content, and it is most likely the place where your customer will want you to do your work. That said, all Flash creations can be easily copied onto USB drives or CDs or DVDs and installed on local computers. The name of the working file you'll use while you're developing your Flash rich media content has the extension `.fla`, but once you publish it, the content is converted into a movie with the filename extension `.swf` and can be run from any computer with Flash Player installed whether or not Flash itself is installed on the computer. There are other file types with different filename extensions that can be created with Flash, but `.fla` and `.swf` are the most common. Rich media designers building content for the web, mobile or AIR apps should be highly cognizant of download and overall application speed, as well as general design principles.

With Flash Player installed, a SWF file (pronounced "swiff file") can run on a variety of platforms—a very cool feature. Flash also includes robust tools for developing applications for other devices such as Android or Apple (e.g. iOS) smartphones using the built-in templates for creating AIR for Android or AIR for iOS. Because Flash is capable of so many things, designers need to be always cognizant of how quickly the viewer will be able begin viewing the content.

Viewing Great Rich Media Examples

Flash is in use all over the globe, in a plethora of environments. All you need to do is Google "best Flash websites" and you'll have more than you can look at in a week. Let's take a look at a few Flash-based sites that have been recognized for their excellence in design. As you look at these sites, think about what makes them interesting and at the same time informative because this is the nexus where rich media lives:

Certification Objective

Otoko Music www.otokomusic.com/web/main.html   One of the interesting things about this site is its lack of a progress bar. Instead, there's a subtle notification to the viewer that there is some program loading going on. Another important feature of the Otoko site is its 3D feel. By displaying one piece of paper over another (Figure 1.1), the site gives the viewer a sense of dimension and depth. This kind of display is easily handled using layers in Flash (covered in Chapter 4, "Getting Started with the Timeline."

FIGURE 1.1 The Otoko music site: The viewer can see progress without a progress bar!

Canturi Perfume   www.canturi.com/#/home Stefano Canturi is a jewelry designer who has branched out into the perfume business. The site's features include a well-crafted short movie that provides an overview of Canturi as well as some beautiful jewelry designs, a perfume section, and even a section on Barbie. While I'm not usually a big fan of all black sites, this one works well because of its simplicity (Figure 1.2). Things seem to float in and out of space, a technique easily accomplished using Flash's ability to adjust the transparency (called the *alpha value*) of objects (covered more in Chapter 7, "Developing Simple Flash Animations").

FIGURE 1.2 The Stephano Canturi site

Leon Vanrentergem www.leonvanrentergem.be/#/welcome/ This site's owner, based in Bruges, Belgium, has done a fabulous job of creating a curiously interesting place to visit. It's playful, with lots of different things happening all at once. The progress bar loads on the site of the main page, a great way to handle the loading yet display some of the essence of the page at the same time. On the main page (Figure 1.3) there is a banner as well as a photo montage. Click the Guestbook button and you travel diagonally upward to a page with a completely different look and feel, and yet it's harmonious with the home page. Click to go back home and a pair of bare feet follow you. One does not need to understand the owner's native language to appreciate what this site is about.

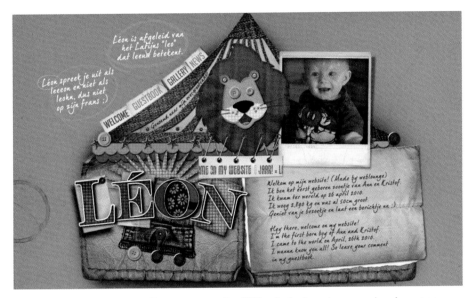

FIGURE 1.3 The Leon Vanrentergem site: Whimsical, charming, amusing, language translation almost unnecessary

Monoface www.mono-1.com/monoface/main.html When you view this site, you're immediately struck with a sense of playfulness, whimsy, and fun. The loading bar is nothing more than a white sheet dropping down to expose the actual screen, which is clever because the scene is hidden from the viewer until it explodes in front of their eyes (Figure 1.4). Click any part of the face and a replacement for that section of the face is brought in from another image.

FIGURE 1.4 The Monoface site: Clever, simple, fun

Right-clicking in any of the sites produces the context menu shown in Figure 1.5. This is a Flash menu telling you that you are viewing the site's content using Flash Player. This single context menu easily tells you when you're viewing a Flash-based site and when you're not. It also tells you your Flash Player's current version (versions are covered in Chapter 13. One of the things that makes Flash such a great rich media product is the ubiquity of Flash Player. See Adobe's "census" site for more Flash Player ubiquity information:

```
www.adobe.com/products/player_census/flashplayer/version_
penetration.html.
```

Settings...
Global Settings...
About Adobe Flash Player 10.2.153.1...

Download This Video To RealPlayer

FIGURE 1.5 Flash Player context menu in a website

If you take a second look at the sites listed, what is one element that sticks out? It is the use of ample space on the site. The designer's term for this is *white space*, and it is every bit as important as the site's content.

Certification Objective

The old literary adage advises writers to "show, don't tell." Using the power of video, audio, and animation, when coupled with your creative imagination, Flash equips you to bring visualization to the message. This is incredibly powerful stuff because once you have the viewer hooked, you can take them anywhere you want—so long as your creativity is consistent, consuming, and provocative.

ABOUT SYMMETRY

Designers worry about a concept called 'symmetry.' The idea is this: How are things positioned on the page relative to one another, and are they pleasing to the eye? There are various kinds of symmetry to which one must pay some attention: horizontal, vertical, and diagonal symmetry are the most common. For example, Figure 1.4 above is a great example of vertical symmetry: the menu items are all properly aligned. There is also radial (i.e. circular) symmetry: how things logically flow around a circle. Figures 1.2 and 1.3 illustrate the use of circles in a symmetric setting. Circles are pleasing to the eye and attract the viewer back to the center of attention the designer wants for the viewer. A unique concept some designers purposely use all the time is asymmetric symmetry: things are out of whack, but purposely (and pleasingly) so. Figure 1.1 is a good example of asymmetric symmetry. Other design elements include emphasis, balance, unity, alignment, line, the rule of thirds, proximity, rhythm, proportion, and several others not covered here: color, form, shape, space, texture, value, contrast, movement, pattern, and others. Using your favorite search engine and the string "graphic design principles" will result in numerous pages with helpful explanations of each.

What NOT to do

The above sites show great design examples, but what is it that designers shouldn't be doing? These are probably intuitive to you, but here's a small list: extraneous graphics, site/scene inconsistency, overcrowded layout, distracting colors, use of numerous outrageous or garish fonts, providing lots of information in paragraph rather than bulleted- or numbered-list form, and not providing navigation cues.

Identifying Your Content's Purpose and Audience

Whether you're aware of it or not, whenever you develop rich media, you have a client. It may be the end users of a game you're developing to upload to a site such as Kongregate (www.kongregate.com). If you're a working designer and you (rightly) believe you can attract more by assimilating rich media skills, you will definitely have a client sitting in front of you describing the work they want you to create for them.

Certification Objective

Given Flash's sky-is-the-limit capabilities for even newbies to the tool, you may be so excited about your task that you're inclined to provide your client with something different than they had imagined. Your client says "water," and with your newfound Flash skills you immediately start thinking about oceans, rivers, waterfalls, infinity pools, and other beautiful moving sources. But in reality what they they have in mind is an attractive ice-cold shimmering glass of water with droplets tantalizingly dripping down the outside. It's the same water but two different stories.

The disconnect comes about for a couple of primary reasons:

▶ You have not listened carefully to your client, which means even though your client may be a poor communicator, the onus is on you to gather the appropriate requirements for the job.

▶ You have assumed you know what the client wants.

It's important to apply the technology to the customer, not the customer to the technology. Develop great listening skills, ask probing questions, and garner information about what your customers really want from you. But it's not enough to simply hear what your customers are saying; it's important that you *process* what's being said—that you get at the nuggets of detail your customer is trying to share with you. There are two salient questions you can ask that will cause your customer to give you more detail:

What is your purpose?   What is it that you want to do or accomplish? Given a successful rich media campaign, what does success look like to you?

Who is your audience?   Whom do you want to talk to? More important, given a specific audience, *how* do you want to speak to them?

The last item is important because it speaks to the client's core business. If you're doing work for a bank, you probably don't want to send a message about being colorful, playful, and fun loving. Not that these aren't traits a bank may exhibit. But the conservative notions that people have about banks and their money stored therein don't lend themselves to those descriptors. On the other hand, a children's clothing store may very well want to convey such notions. So, understanding the customer's audience is quite important.

When you're dealing with rich media, it's important that you go beyond thinking about the descriptive text and begin cultivating a visual, audible, and animatable feel for what your client wants. It's wise for you to first meet your client, hear them, ask the questions that give you more detail and information, and *then* begin sketching out some ideas. You should take the ideas you draw while sitting in front of your client back to your office where you can work on more formal storyboards. A *storyboard* is a hand-drawn, painted, or digital rendition of how you imagine the scene or scenes playing out. Storyboards are the first draft of how you plan on turning into rich media what you thought you heard your client saying. I'll cover storyboards more in Chapter 7.

DON'T SHOW YOUR PORTFOLIO!

It's not wise to show a customer your portfolio of past work and say something like, "Here's what we did for Acme Widgets, and I think your ideas are similar." Most customers want something new and fresh (else they wouldn't have consulted you, right?). That doesn't prevent you from utilizing your other stuff back at the ranch, out of sight of the customer, but it does keep you from an embarrassing faux pas in front of your customer.

Along with the two basic questions listed earlier, you have some practical questions to ask:

▶ Why do you want to do this? You want to understand their motivation. Is it money? Time savings? Connectivity options? Getting more customers?

▶ On what media sources would you like to have this material presented (e.g., Web, game, applet, iPhone or Android app)?

▶ When are you requiring this work to be finished (e.g., what's my deadline)?

▶ Do you have a certain budget in mind?

▶ Can you give me ideas about some of the things that have worked for you in the past?

▶ Are there certain topics or ideas I should stay away from?

▶ May I see some of your products or services in use by your customers?

▶ If you had to tell me in one minute or less what you want done, what would you say?

Your efforts here are in getting the client to compartmentalize their thoughts and to use words that point to targets they're thinking about. At the same time you're listening to this, you can be thinking about how this translates into animated storylines.

The bottom line is that you should get to know your client and find out the reason they want to do this project and the audience it will reach. Write these things down, print them out, and tape them to your desk where you can see them as you work on the project. Hit the targets the client gives you and you're likely to be successful and also obtain more work from them in the future.

Choosing the Best Media Types

Certification
Objective

Once you determine what your client wants to say with the rich media content you're creating—basically, what its purpose is—you can then determine the media types that are best for the content. Flash can host a variety of media types that may be relevant for your client's content:

Text   Flash's text editing and display tools are quite granular, providing you many options for displaying text. Flash's new Text Layout Framework (TLF) format for putting text in your rich media content provides all kinds of sophisticated text controls (covered in Chapter 5, "Adding Flash Text and Fonts to Your Creations"). Adobe also kept the text editing tools used in previous editions, called Classic Text. Additionally, you have the ability to embed any special fonts you use in your rich media right into the Flash document so you don't run the risk of the viewer not having access to a special font you used.

Photographs   Flash easily imports standard digital photos (covered in Chapter 10, "Creating Characters with Inverse Kinematics [IK]"). In addition to simply displaying photos, Flash allows you to do extra work with them. For example, you can break apart a photo into its pixels or you can use Flash's Swap Bitmap capability to turn the photo into a kind of cartoonized version. You can turn a photo into a movie clip—a special flash symbol we'll talk about in Chapter 6, "Working with Flash Symbols"—and then do all kinds of work with it. For example, you can use Flash to modify the picture's transparency level (called its *alpha* value). You can use animation techniques to
create moving photo montages, scrapbooks, and other photo display devices.

Audio   Flash has built-in audio controls that allow you to present a sophisticated audio player that has full controls with very little technical knowledge. You can also programmatically stop and start audio using AS3. Figure 1.6 shows the Code Snippets panel in the Flash UI. *Code snippets* are prewritten pieces of AS3 code that you simply double-click to add into your content. This sounds like it's fairly plug and play, but there's a little bit more to it than that, as you'll see in Chapter 11, "Working with Audio." Flash supports a variety of audio formats when performing audio importation including MP3, WAV, AIFF, and Adobe Audition.

FIGURE 1.6 The Code Snippets panel in Flash

Video   Flash also provides built-in video player technology with a variety of controls that can be used to stop, reverse, and play video (shown in Figure 1.7). You can also apply different prebuilt skins to your video player so it more closely matches your site's design (Chapter 12, "Working with Video"). Importation video formats are numerous; see `http://kb2.adobe` `.com/cps/402/kb402701.html` for more information.

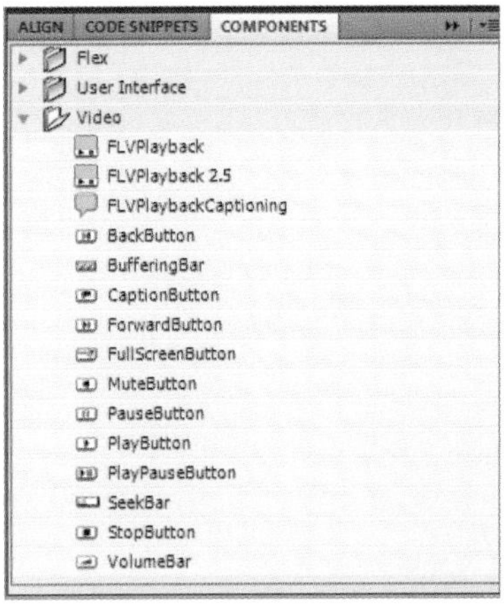

FIGURE 1.7 The Components panel in Flash

Animation   When coupled with Flash's robust set of drawing tools, the Flash timeline allows you to craft interesting and provocative animations without resorting to other environments (Chapter 2, "Getting Acquainted with Flash," and Chapter 4). However, in those cases when another tool can bring more precise capabilities to the table, Flash has integrated support for other tools in the Adobe Creative Suite (CS), including Photoshop, Illustrator, and Fireworks. Flash's slick importation procedure can grab a file built in these other environments and natively bring it into the workspace. In the case that you used layers in another CS tool, Flash gives you the option to keep the layers intact and still be able to use them in your rich media creation or convert them to Flash frames.

Inverse kinematics (IK)   Flash gives you the ability to animate separate elements of a drawing by using bones connected to linear or branched armatures that exist in a parent-child relationship (Chapter 10). This provides you with the ability to bring realistic movement to your drawn objects.

NOTE   "Even though Flash provides amazing capabilities in the pursuit of interesting rich media documents, the designer must remain cognizant of download speeds. The more assets added to the document, the more time it will take for the end user to retrieve it. There is a balance to be struck between wonderful rich media design, and the user experience."

3D   A couple of 3D tools included with Flash—the 3D Translation and Rotations tools—allow you to create animations that are convincingly 3D in action (Chapter 9, "Techniques for Creating More Complex Animations").

Your ultimate goal is not only to make the new deliverable pleasing, but also consistent. Buttons look alike, pages behave the same, there are no unexpected elements with which the viewer must grapple. Consistency not only improves your viewer's experience, it also helps you churn out cleaner work in a more efficient, timely manner.

Addressing Accessibility Issues in Rich Media

Certification Objective   It's important to design for all potential viewers of your page, and Flash has significant built-in tools for providing accessibility to people with disabilities.

FLASH ACCESSIBILITY TEST QUESTIONS YOU MIGHT EXPECT

The ACA Flash exam and associated practice materials located on the Adobe website (see www.adobe.com/education/resources/certificate-programs.html) don't go into tremendous detail about what accessibility is or what users might have accessibility issues. However, the expectation is that you understand at a functional level what the Accessibility panel in Flash looks like and how it is utilized. Moreover, Adobe is quite cognizant of the viewers who require accessibility options and has gone to great lengths to make rich media accessible on its own site. You will encounter at least one accessibility question on the Flash exam.

The following categories of people require accessibility options in their rich media experience:

Blind   People who are blind will not be able to view any text you include in your rich media content. Screen reader software such as Jaws, IBM Home Page reader, or Window-Eyes will probably be in use.

Low vision   Individuals who can see a little bit, but not very much, may benefit from the use of special accessibility software and equipment to help them view the content. These people will not be able to see the text you include in your rich media content without difficulty. Screen reader software such as Jaws, IBM Home Page Reader, or Window-Eyes may be in use.

Hearing impaired and deaf   Some people are not completely deaf, but their hearing is profoundly impaired. These people will likely not be able to hear very well any sound clips you include in your rich media content. Others do not have the ability to hear at all and therefore won't be able to hear any sound clips you include.

Physically impaired   These individuals may not be able to use a computer keyboard and/or mouse the way others do. For example, someone with a crippling disease such as multiple sclerosis (MS) may have lost the use of their hands or at best suffer from extremely diminished capabilities.

Cognitively impaired   People with cognitive impairments such as autism may be able to read and hear the information just fine but may not be able to intellectually process it in the same way others do.

Photosensitive epilepsy   The people who suffer from this have a form of epilepsy in which seizures are caused by visual stimuli forming patterns in time or space. Examples include flashing lights, bold and regular patterns, or regularly moving patterns.

You shouldn't diminish Flash's rich media capabilities for your able users just to provide accessibility to your less-ably-equipped users. On the other hand, you should be completely cognizant of those users with accessibility needs and understand (as best as you can) how they'll access your content. In some ways this concept represents the dividing line between good design and great design.

Moreover, there may be rich media projects you create in which you or your clients simply don't think there will be much interaction by those requiring accessibility options. For example, a rapidly paced first person shooter (FPS) game in Flash probably won't get a lot of hits by blind users. In cases like this, you may make just cursory use of Flash's accessibility tool.

From a client perspective, the accessibility question arises when you're determining who your client thinks their audience is. It's quite likely your client hasn't even considered accessibility issues with the content they'd like to present. Conversely, they may simply assume that you'll automatically cover that angle since you're the expert. In either event, it's up to you to ask about accessibility and make sure this topic is discussed.

Designing for People Who Are Blind

Screen readers are software products—whether built into the operating system or stand-alone, commercially available for a price, or free—that read aloud the screen's content for blind (and vision-impaired) users. The verbosity of the output can be controlled in the software so users aren't barraged with audio content. Screen readers can also read the labels on buttons or other labeled objects. It's important to note that with screen readers, blind users don't even necessarily need a display hooked up to be able to utilize computers. (Some blind readers also have equipment that translates the computer's text into Braille.)

The essence of the screen reader idea is similar to having someone read a newspaper to you. It works well in static text environments where nothing changes but could become confusing and clumsy in rich media environments.

Some of the more popular Windows-based screen readers are Freedom Scientific's JAWS, GW Micro's Window-Eyes, and IBM's Home Page Reader. In addition to the commercial products, Windows includes its own screen reader called Narrator (shown in Figure 1.8), and the Mac has a built-in screen reader called VoiceOver. There are also open-source screen readers for our Linux friends.

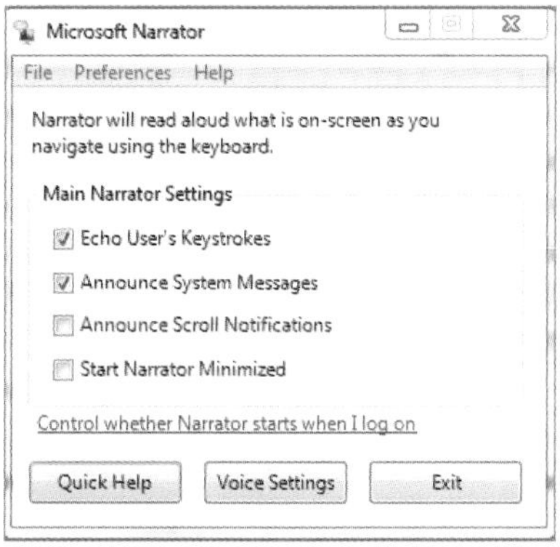

FIGURE 1.8 The Windows 7 Narrator

While screen reader software is a really cool idea, you should turn on Narrator and work with it awhile to see what the experience is really like. If you're like me, you'll find the verbosity to be both annoying and confusing, and it probably won't take you long to turn it off. To start it in Windows 7, make sure your computer's speakers are on and then just click the Start button. In the Run box, type **narrator**. Windows 7 will show you the Narrator icon. Just press Enter or double-click the icon to launch the program. Work with it awhile, surfing the Web, hitting a Flash site or two, launching Word—you'll come away with a new appreciation for the difficulty our vision-impaired friends go through daily when trying to work with computers.

When developing accessibility options for rich media content, Windows users will (unwittingly) use Microsoft Active Accessibility (MSAA; see www.microsoft .com/enable/). MSAA is bundled into the Windows operating system (OS) and is able to talk to commercial screen reader software. MSAA reads text inside Flash movies when they are playing. MSAA frees you from having to worry about the complex interactions of rich media software and your own code—the screen reader software simply retrieves from MSAA the audio version of the text on the screen. Because MSAA comes with Windows, Flash movies and screen readers are able to play nicely in the sandbox together.

However, even with MSAA, screen reader software may have a difficult time accurately reading aloud to the user what's going on in the Flash movie. Suppose, for example, you have an animation on the stage showing a string of letters making up a word, each of which is randomly dancing and jumping around on the stage—say for a children's activity page. This is quite easy

Certification Objective

to accomplish in Flash, but it creates havoc with screen readers because they don't know how to react to each individual letter of the animation. It's likely the screen reader will attempt to read aloud each succeeding letter on the screen, which of course will be nonsensical to the listener.

There are several workarounds for this kind of problem, but you must consider the options and integrate them into the design before the work proceeds. Flash rich media designers can overcome issues with screen readers in three ways:

Make sure flash content is natively accessible.   When programmers use the word *native*, they're talking about the idea that the current combination of software and hardware doesn't need anything else for it to work properly. When you hear "make sure the Flash content can natively access the screen reader," it should mean to you that the user doesn't have to go through any extra effort to be able to consume your content. For designers who are interested in making sure their content is natively accessible by vision-impaired or blind users, purchasing some screen reader software may be in order to accomplish this goal. You should also consider performing your accessibility testing of the content on both a PC and a Macintosh computer and in the most popular browsers: Internet Explorer, Firefox, Opera, Safari, and Chrome. You have learned that MSAA hands off the Flash content to the screen reader, but testing your content in a real-life situation can easily help you find the accessibility-poor holes in your structure.

Some users have disabled their browser's ability to view Flash content. Their screen reader won't even try to access your content, which means your content is, by definition, not accessible.

Make the flash content self-voicing.   The way to handle this is to use the Flash Accessibility panel, found by clicking Window ➢ Other Panels ➢ Accessibility. For any movie clips, buttons, or other dynamic content, you should use the Accessibility panel to assign a name to the object and any descriptive text. Screen readers will read this alternative text in place of the text within the object (and will also read any ordinary text on the page).

Let's use the example I talked about earlier of putting separate letters on the Flash stage. In Figure 1.9, you see the letters scattered all across the stage. I've turned each letter into a movie clip (more on that in Chapter 6) and then Shift+clicked each letter so you can see that I've got them all selected. Thus, the stage contains *five* separate objects. Depending on the tab order—the order in which the objects are accessed when using the Tab key—the screen reader software will read the letters aloud: first the *F*, then the *L, A, S,* and *H.*

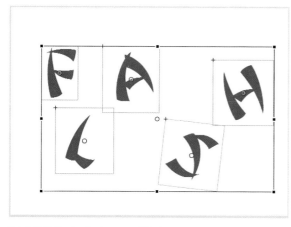

FIGURE 1.9 Inaccessible letter array

The way to fix this is to group all letters together into a single movie clip so that only one entity is on the stage. Finally, you edit the Accessibility panel to alert screen readers that there is alternative text for the movie clip, as shown in Figure 1.10. The screen reader will not only read the name Flash, it will also read the accompanying descriptive text: "The product we're using is Flash!"

Text and objects that are not relevant to impaired users (such as decorative bullets) can be hidden from screen readers. Go to Window ➢ Other Panels ➢ Accessibility, and uncheck Make Object Accessible.

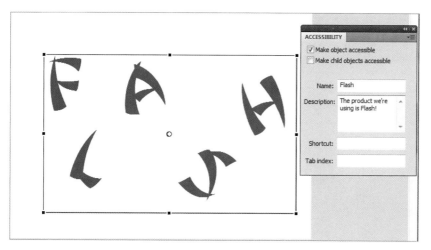

FIGURE 1.10 Converting an inaccessible letter array using the Flash Accessibility panel

Provide an alternative. Another method is to simply make a separate alternative for the Flash content in a different environment. Got a beautiful Flash site that you've spent months creating, but now that you know about accessibility options you're worried about your vision-impaired viewers? You might consider spending some more time creating a separate text-based site strictly for them.

SEPARATE VISION-IMPAIRED-ACCESSIBLE SITE?

I think creating a separate text-based site strictly for vision-impaired users is a last-ditch effort because there are lots of creative ways to make the content accessible without having to give up Flash. However, it does bring up a good discussion point: Should designers be *so* concerned about accessibility that they create a variety of projects all with the same content but with different accessibility requirements? For example, should you create a Flash project for your more ably equipped viewers, a high-contrast site for your vision-impaired viewers, an all-audio site for your blind users, a site with simple navigation tools for users with physical disabilities, and so forth?

It's all about the audience. If a corporation wants the public's business and disabled users are a key component, then maybe it's in their best interest to think about accessibility at all levels.

Designing for Low-Vision Viewers

Certain viewers have some vision, but it is quite limited. They can read content on the screen, but it has to be displayed in ways that make it accessible to them. In fact, your users may or may not have access to screen reader software. But you can be sure they have the screen resolution set very high so they can read the letters on the screen. How to best meet the needs of these users? Here are some simple solutions:

Use high contrast.   Using high contrast means differentiating two or more things so they are obviously unique. This is easy to do with Flash because you have access to drawings, photographs, icons, buttons, animations and many other ways to differentiate elements of your rich media.

However, viewers with limited vision will have a difficult time sorting through such detail. Imagine, for example, looking at your screen with fonts 6 inches tall. As you use your mouse and/or arrow keys to move around the screen, you run across a tangle of lines and colors, but you can't make out what they make up: The view makes no sense to you. Consider Figure 1.11 as an example. You can clearly make out the difference in colors, but the jagged bold strokes make no sense. This is what an image might look like if you were someone with highly restricted vision. But anyone with normal eyesight can clearly see that the designer has included a piece of clip art showing a young girl holding a satchel and accompanied by her dog (Figure 1.12).

FIGURE 1.11 What the person with low vision sees

FIGURE 1.12 What average sighted people see

Flash provides a really cool tool to view the stage in a super-sized way. Near the upper-right corner of the stage is a drop-down menu that provides you with a way to enlarge or shrink what you're viewing. You're not limited to these choices: You can simply type in the amount you want to enlarge or reduce and Flash will carry out your instructions. This is a great way to help yourself imagine what low-vision users will be seeing when they view your content. In Figure 1.11, I simply enlarged the stage size to 1600% and then snapped the shot.

Mind your colors.   You also want to use high contrast in your colors. One of the biggest gripes I have with designers is when they use a font color that's similar to the background color. For example, a dark red font on a black background is incredibly hard for me to read because I'm red/green color-blind. No matter how cool the designer thinks the scene looks, or how interesting I think the topic is, I lose interest in the content because I have to work so hard to read it.

According to `www.hhmi.org/senses/b130.html`, nearly 10 million American men are color-blind, and the majority of them suffer from red/green color-blindness.

Bottom line. Don't assume your viewers can easily see the colors you're putting on the screen, especially when it comes to the red and green spectrums. Make sure those colors are vivid so they're easily discernible and that they're highly contrasted, don't play around too much with soft-toned colors, and keep font sizes a little larger than the usual 10-points. Once you think you've got your content viewable for color-blind people, grab someone who happens to be color-blind and have them test the content for readability. It's possible some viewers have their screen display adjusted for strictly black and white. As you test your rich media content, it might be interesting to temporarily adjust your own display to see what your content looks like in a high-contrast black-and-white environment.

Use vector-scalable objects   Objects that are made up of individual pixels that cannot be altered are called *bitmap objects*. (Another term you might see in place of bitmap is *raster*.) All photos are bitmaps. A photo on the screen might look great in one size, but when it's sufficiently blown up, you'll see what we call pixelization—all those little boxes that make up the photo start to show up, and the picture looks grainy and squared off around the edges of the elements inside it. This has to do with the amount of pixels a digital camera uses when a photograph is taken. Generally speaking, the higher the camera's resolution, the more pixels make up the photo and the more easily enlargeable it becomes. There's more to it than that: For example, you can change your camera's settings for various resolution settings, and you can determine the file type the camera will save to when taking photos; file type has a lot do to with the amount of pixels in the photo.

Some artwork is also bitmap oriented. Older versions of the Windows Paint program would save drawings the user had created only as bitmap (`.bmp`) images.

Thus, the image could only grow so large—we call this *task scaling*—before that pesky pixelization started showing up.

Figure 1.13 shows the Flash logo that appears in the Start box when Flash first runs. The logo has fidelity—it's nice and crisp and you can easily make out the letters. However, in Figure 1.14, I've blown up the logo to the point where you can begin to see the pixelization. It is especially prevalent at the bottom loop of the *l* and does not retain its crisp clarity and sharpness.

FIGURE 1.13 The Flash Logo: normal size

You can use Flash's trace bitmap feature to change a bitmap-based object into a vector-scalable object. After bringing your bitmapped object into Flash and putting it on the stage, just select it then select Modify ≻ Bitmap ≻ Trace Bitmap from the Flash main menu.

FIGURE 1.14 The scaled Flash logo

Most if not all Flash objects are scalable. They are given this characteristic by virtue of mathematical algorithms that recalculate the size of the object, allowing it to be redisplayed with equivalent clarity and sharpness. Objects such as this are said to be *vector scalable*. Most fonts in use today are vector scalable. If you put an *f* in 10-point on the screen and then change it to 120-point, the fidelity of the *f* will be the same, with no loss in sharpness.

Figure 1.15 shows the letters *Fl* on the stage in Arial, 40-point. Figure 1.16 shows the same text object enlarged to 120-point. You can clearly see there's no loss in fidelity upon enlarging the object.

Fl

FIGURE 1.15 *Fl* text object in 40-point Arial

Fl

FIGURE 1.16 *Fl* text object in 120-point Arial

There is a hitch to providing your viewers vector scalability: Without some relatively significant AS3 coding, you cannot put objects on the screen that viewers themselves can simply drag to enlarge—though the vector scalability of such objects would support larger viewing with continued fidelity.

But with a little bit of sleight of hand you could provide your low-vision users with the ability to see a scene with larger fonts in it. There are a few options:

▶ You can provide a button that vision-impaired users can click to take them to a scene with much larger font detail and minimal artwork. This will require you to understand how to place a button on the screen, give it an instance name, and add code in the form of an event listener and a function that takes the viewer to the new scene. Fortunately, Adobe has automated much of the work for you so you don't need to stay up late at night reading tutorial sites on how to create buttons that work in Flash. The Code Snippets panel contains lots of prewritten code that you can easily put into your content for purposes such as this.

▶ You can make text items clickable so viewers can click them to enlarge them. This would involve turning text objects into button objects. Buttons are essentially movie clips that have four separate action sections to them, called *hit states* (see Figure 1.17): Up, Over, Down and Hit. What this means is that different scenes can happen based upon what the viewer is doing with the button. When the button is up (e.g., it's not being clicked right now), it displays one way, but it displays another when the user hovers over it or clicks it. (Hit is a special hit state that can be used for buttons with complex shapes). By simply turning a text object into a button, you can set the Over hit state to greatly enlarge the text's font so it's easily readable. As soon as the viewer navigates away, it goes back to its normal size.

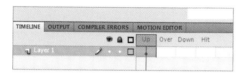

FIGURE 1.17 Flash button hit states

The thing that's really cool about buttons is that they don't have to appear as your garden-variety conventional button most users have become accustomed to using. While buttons do have to have a shape, they don't even need to be visible in Flash! The fact that they're on the stage means the mouse cursor will change shape when the user hovers over a section where a button is residing. This turns out to be fiendishly useful for designers—many clever things can be done using this technique.

Watch those fonts! As the baby boomers age (see `www.bbhq.com/bomrstat` `.htm` for more data on the baby boomer phenomenon), many of the 75 million of us (I'm in this camp) will incur some sort of increasingly problematic eyesight. At a minimum, we'll be forced to wear reading glasses to enlarge the text on the page, but sadly some of us will suffer from drastically reduced vision. One of the best things you can do as a designer is to keep in mind that not all your viewers can easily see small fonts and images. As you go through your design, try to arrive at some sort of a happy medium so that younger viewers don't feel like they're viewing content for "old folks," but also so that older viewers don't have to work so hard to read the material. If you're crafty in your design, you can accommodate all sorts of viewers without scads of extra work.

One last note: Be consistent! If you are committed to providing limited-vision or low-vision visitors with content they can access, do so throughout your design. You can't have one scene that's supportive of limited-vision viewers and another that's not.

Designing for Hearing-Impaired and Deaf Viewers

Hearing-impaired individuals have a different Flash problem: If you provide music or sounds in your rich media, they will likely not be able to hear it. This could become a big issue if your design relies on sound media to convey the elements of your content.

The strongest and best thing you can do when thinking about accessibility for your hearing-impaired or deaf viewers is to provide descriptive text for any sound events you have going on in your content. For example, maybe you have a movie in your content that shows how to do something or that includes a person talking about a subject that pertains to your scene's content. In cases like this, your hearing-impaired viewers won't be able to hear the movie's sound, so for those viewers, you've lost the effect you trying to accomplish. Sure, some of your viewers can read lips, so maybe not all is lost, but then again, with tutorial movies you typically don't see the speaker talking—the focus is on their hands and the activity they're trying to show you.

To get around this problem, you can provide a closed-caption effect. To do this, you'll need to go through three steps:

1. Write an accurate transcript of what's being said on the screen. If there are multiple people talking, be sure to note who's doing the talking at the front of each sentence: for example, "MALE: I love you!" "FEMALE: I love you too!"

2. Create a movie clip that shows the text scrolling slowly downward so that it's readable but relatively closely timed with the speakers on the screen. This is a fairly easy task even for the Flash neophyte.

3. On the video player, add a Closed Caption button that, when clicked, simultaneously plays the movie and runs the captions.

You can also provide scene-wide support for hearing-impaired people by putting a Closed Caption button at the entry point to your content. When someone clicks the button, screen hinting becomes available, which means that at any point where you decide hearing-impaired folks would not be able to understand what's happening, you place a text box on the screen that tells them.

For example, consider Figure 1.18. When designing this scene, you might decide to record a youngster saying, "I wish Spot could come to school with me!" and then put it into your content so when viewers navigate to this scene, the clip plays. By providing a Closed Caption button, you easily send a signal to your hearing-impaired viewers that there is alternative content available for them. You can accomplish all of this by simply creating a text object such as the cartoon balloon shown in the figure, converting it into a symbol such as a movie clip, and then adjusting its alpha value to 0% upon initial entry into the scene. When a hearing-impaired viewer clicks the Closed Caption button, your AS3 code sets the cartoon balloon's alpha value to 100% and changes the text on the button to Turn CC Off (see Figure 1.19). If the hearing-impaired viewer has read the cartoon balloon and now wants to get rid of it, they simply click the button and your code reverses the preceding process.

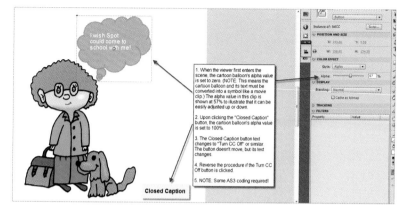

FIGURE 1.18 Little girl with doggie scene and Closed Caption button

FIGURE 1.19 Text on Closed Caption button changed

What's cool about this process is that you're not limited to the type of text box and associated text you put up: You have quite robust design freedom to match the emotion and intent of your scene.

You don't need to or may not always want to go through this process, however. Using Flash's ability to turn just about anything into a button, you can also create hot spots that when hovered over put up some text. You've seen this technique used in various computer programs. If you hover over an area very long, some text pops up to provide you with a description of what you're look-ing at or more detailed information. When the user hovers over a region that has been turned into a button, you can programmatically pop up some text that goes away as soon as they leave the area.

To accommodate this, you need an outline of the graphic you which to turn into a button. Figure 1.20 shows the little girl with her doggie as well as the doggie's outline converted into a button symbol and ready to move into place. I've already made a tan cartoon balloon with the text "Me too!" I then set the outline in the appropriate place over the doggie on the stage, and turned its alpha value down to zero.

FIGURE 1.20 Doggie button outline being moved into place

ART ASSETS NEED TO BE TURNED INTO SYMBOLS

It's important to note that most of the time when you create art assets, once you're done with them they will have to be converted to a graphic, button, or movie clip symbol so you can use them more extensively in Flash. Not all art assets need this treatment—if an asset is going to be a stand-alone element with no interaction, then it is fine to leave it as is. However, if your intent is to somehow manipulate the asset later on, it needs to be converted into a symbol. More on symbols in Chapter 6.

Designing for People with Physical Limitations

Viewers who have lost most or all of the use of their hands and fingers may not have the ability to manipulate a keyboard and mouse very easily. In fact, some users may be limited to just a couple of keys—perhaps the arrow keys, for example. The important element for users like this is a tab order assigned to the relevant objects in the scene and commensurate AS3 code that provides objects with shortcut keys. The tab order is a numbering system applied to active objects on the stage in such a way that when the Tab key is pressed, the navigation flows from one object to the next.

Providing accessibility for these users is handled via two steps:

1. Click each object in the Flash scene and then, using the Accessibility panel, give a tab order to the object (see Figure 1.21) in the Tab Index field. The tab order should fit the natural sequence in which a user traverses the scene.

FIGURE 1.21 The Flash Accessibility panel honed in on a single Button object: setting tab order

2. You should provide a shortcut in the Accessibility panel so that the screen reader reads the shortcut. Note that this does not mean it's actually usable as a shortcut in the movie. You must provide AS3 code that enables a shortcut to work.

Users who lack the use of their digits will likely not have a screen reader, so it's up to you to somehow flag that the shortcut keys are out there for them to use.

Designing for People with Cognitive Limitations

Users with cognitive limitations may not be able to keep up with rapid-fire screen movements and animations. The trick here is to craft animations that are not so slow the average user will walk away from your content but not so fast that slower users will become frustrated.

The Flash frame rate is a measurement of how rapidly each of the frames plays in a second. The default is 24 frames per second (fps), but it can be ratcheted up or down for slower or faster motion. One idea you might consider as a designer developing rich media content for a variety of users is to provide some sort of "slower-motion" button or slider that slows down rapidly playing content to a lower frame rate. This, of course, will require AS3 coding to make it happen, but it's worth considering if you believe your site will likely have a lot of viewers with cognitive disabilities. It's important to note that once the frame rate is lowered, it applies to the entire scene, so *everything* slows down. If you consider programmatically changing frame rates, you need to make sure you put them back to the original frame rate once the activity is done.

You should also note that slowing down frame rates when there is a film on the timeline (with or without narration) could be problematic.

Designing for People with Photosensitive Epilepsy

Those who have this disorder could be sent into an epileptic seizure with the right combination of jittering screen movements, flashing lights, and rapid movement through time and space in your scenes. Unless your goal is to design a rich media environment with lots of optical illusions—easily accomplished in Flash—it's best to stay away from the jittery stuff anyway. If you do happen to need animations that could affect those with photosensitive epilepsy, it's wise to put some sort of disclaimer on the front of your work so they're aware of it going in.

Understanding Project Management 101

Certification
Objective

To successfully navigate your customer's job from initial request to completed deliverable, you need to have a solid understanding of basic project management concepts. Knowing and following these principles will greatly assist you in formulating your work into a project plan, which makes it much easier for you to follow the train of activities and tasks it will take for you to complete the job.

Identifying a Project

The first thing you must understand about project management is that not everything is considered a project. For example, work that's ongoing, such as a help desk operation or a fast-food assembly line, does not qualify as a project. The sidebar "How Do You Know You Have a Project?" provides a definition to help you decide whether you are or are not looking at a project.

HOW DO YOU KNOW YOU HAVE A PROJECT?

The working definition of a project is the development of any unique product or service that has a definite beginning and ending date. The key word here is *unique*. If you're doing a process over and over (finalizing each month's accounting records, for example), the activity does not constitute a project. It's also important to realize that projects start and conclude and both dates are known in advance.

Creating the Project Plan

For the most part, you don't need to be heavily concerned with reams of paper for your project, although bigger projects certainly do have a multiplicity of documents associated with them. There are a handful of documents you should use as you develop your project. These documents are included in the project plan and will be reviewed and signed off by your customer.

In a nutshell, the project plan simply says what you're going to do and how you're going to do it. The project plan is a result of some fairly extensive requirements-gathering on your part to determine exactly what your customer wants you to do. It can be one document or several, depending on how elaborate you want to (or should) make things. A caution here: Don't go overboard with project documentation! This might be a huge turn-off to your client. Provide enough documentation so your client is convinced you know what you're doing but not so much they'll be overloaded with your verbosity.

Requirements document   The requirements document is essentially an agreed-upon listing of what you heard your customer say they wanted done, and if there was any information on how you should go about it, how they wanted it done as well. For example, if your customer says, "Look, we really need this site to be widely accessible because we have a huge audience," then it's your responsibility to figure out how accessible it should be and how wide the audience is. Requirements-gathering is an important task that may not fall under the umbrella of billable hours, but it will definitely help you more succinctly formulate your project plan.

As you compile your project plan, it's wise to separate what I call your "need-to-haves" from your "nice-to-haves." As the project unfolds, you'll find that your customer will want you to add some nice-to-haves that you and they really hadn't talked about before, some of which might actually require a good bit of time to accomplish. Project managers (PMs) call this *scope creep*. When you show your customer the project plan and its associated need-to-haves and they come back at you with a nice-to-have, you have the ability to say, "This wasn't initially agreed upon. Maybe we can catch this in version 2." Above all, what you're trying to avoid is scope creep. Don't kid yourself: Your customer and even your project team will introduce scope creep if you're not closely guarding the project!

Project budget   Another document you'll include in your project plan is the project budget. You have to be relatively detailed here, providing line by line information as to what you said you'd do and what it will cost. You'll need to be sure to include billable hours for items such as storyboards; they take no little bit of time and you shouldn't be donating your time for them. Any outsourced work such as printing, graphic artists, and so on should also be included. It's unprofessional to provide a project budget with a single line item and a single dollar figure. Customers need to know you know what you're talking about with regard to costs.

Work breakdown structure   A third element of the project plan is the work breakdown structure (WBS). The concept behind a WBS is that you break the work down into discrete manageable chunks, each of which is called a work package. Work packages are then broken down into the tasks required to make up the completed work. For example, suppose you have an animation you need to supply that includes several characters, some IK, a background scene or two, a couple of voiceovers, and some music—in other words, some fairly intricate, extensive work. The compilation of this work represents a work package, and each of the tasks beneath it represents a subsection of the work required to build the work package.

Deliverables   What are deliverables? These are the components you will be giving to your customer as the project progresses. Of course the ultimate deliverable is the Flash file or web site files, but what are some others? Various drawings and sketches, a comprehensive layout design (called "comps" in the industry), storyboards, the site's map, various prototypes and other elements that you created for the customer. Did you shoot a special photo? That's a deliverable, as is a song you created, movie you shot: these are all customer deliverables.

You don't need special software for any of these activities; word processing and spreadsheet software will do. But it does help to use a product like Microsoft Project because the software has been designed for this kind of work. Using Microsoft Project, you can manage a database of the staff members you have doing the work, the project schedule, and associated tasks. Project keeps a Gantt chart for you—a stairstep-style chart that shows when tasks begin and end and the connectedness between them.

Creating the Project Schedule

PMs who have taken and passed the Project Management Institute (PMI, see www.pmi.org) Project Management Professional (PMP)® exam don't call the WBS the project schedule or vice versa, but for most of your purposes, they are one and the same, especially if you're using Microsoft Project. You should be aware of a couple of fundamental ideas behind the project schedule:

▶ Each work package is on a primary line.

▶ Each task that belongs to a work package is on an indented line.

▶ Each task has a task duration: a beginning date and an ending date (or time, in the case of a task that takes a few hours).

▶ Each task may have a predecessor and a successor task. A task that has a predecessor requires that the predecessor be done before it can start. A task with a successor means that there is a task waiting on it to be completed. For example, you cannot finish your characters until they've been drawn and colored in.

▶ The shortest line from start to finish between adjoining predecessor and successor tasks is called the *critical path*. This is your shortest actual project duration.

▶ Some tasks can be completed without either a predecessor or a successor. It's important for you to be aware of those kinds of tasks because they can happen simultaneously alongside the other work you're doing. For example, someone can be working on the background layer while others are working on the characters.

▶ The project schedule has names tied to it: who's doing what task. Some tasks will have more than one name tied to them; others only a single name.

As important as the project schedule is, there's a balance to it. It's important that you allow the correct amount of time for each task to start and finish and not go over or under by too much. Remember that you're committing to your customer that you will finish the project by a certain date and within a certain budget.

Figure 1.22 shows an example work schedule of an animation activity using Microsoft Project 2010.

FIGURE 1.22 Animation project shown in Microsoft Project 2010

Properly Closing Out the Project

You should have a formal sign-off process at the conclusion of the project. Here's the minimum you should do:

▶ You and your team have exhaustively tested the product, and any testers your customer designates have also gone through a testing cycle to make sure any bugs have been worked out.

▶ Project closure may include such steps as end-user training and development of technical documentation.

▶ Once the customer is satisfied that the product is complete, they need to sign off on the project closure, indicating that all the work is done. Once the customer signs off, any updates or changes represent "version 2." They are not part of the original project.

Understanding Copyright Issues When Using Others' Work

One of the big disadvantages of the Web is that it has become incredibly easy to steal someone else's work. Such is the power of free speech on the Web. But just because speech is free doesn't mean you or someone else can simply use it without permission. The key to great rich media design is to be completely original in your approach; it's also the way to attract clients and foster new business.

Understanding Text Copyright

According to the Fair Use Doctrine (i.e. US Copyright Laws), your rich media content is protected when "…it is fixed in a copy or phonorecord for the first time" (see www.copyright.gov/circs/circ01.pdf). The key to this statement are the words "for the first time." If someone else said the same thing you just wrote and they beat you to it with their copyright, the text has not been said on your site for the first time. Someone else said it first.

You cannot simply copy and paste another site's content verbatim into your rich media content. If you do this, and the site has been copyrighted, you could be asking for trouble; an infringement suit could be brought against you in a court of law. Moreover, it's stealing someone else's work, regardless of whether it has been copyrighted or not. Simply put, it is plagiarism. The better approach is to either obtain permission from the site owner to copy some of their work or, better yet, gain a more robust understanding of the underlying concepts the author (and other authors) are talking about with regard to the subject and write your own text in your own words. This way you can copyright the material for yourself.

When creating a website or other rich media source a viewer will be watching, I typically affix the copyright symbol (©) and write alongside it the year the content was posted, as well as the statement "All rights reserved" and my name: © 2011 All rights reserved. William Heldman. This is a "poor person's" copyright; it does indeed protect you as the owner of the content but may not be as helpful as if you were to obtain a formal copyright registration. Formally registering your copyright creates a public record of your copyright claim, allows you to file a formal infringement suit in a US court, provides prima facie (at first sight) evidence of the validity of your copyright, allows you to collect attorney's fees when you pursue and win an infringement suit, and allows you to pursue registration with the US Customs Service to prevent foreign impingement of your copyright.

Filing for a formal copyright involves a cost and a wait time. In many cases, it may simply not be worth it. But in any case this will most likely be a decision for your client. If you understand copyright law, you are equipped to advise your client on best approaches. See www.copyright.gov for more information. You should be aware that once you've sought and received a copyright for a work, any other works that arise out of that work are called 'derivative works'. For example, you copyright a web site that includes videos, animations and maybe even some music your team wrote and recorded. These elements are derivatives of the copyrighted material on the site.

In many cases you may *cite* another person's material provided you correctly cite it in your content. If the content you want to cite has a stated policy that you must contact the owner for permission before doing so, you'd better seek said permission. You also need to be aware that copyrighted material and other inventions such as designs, songs, or videos may be someone's intellectual property, and could even be patented.

Understanding Music Copyright

The same is true with music. You cannot simply grab an MP3 of your favorite band's song and include it with your rich media content without first garnering permission. You are violating the band's copyright and could be sued.

Today's software music synthesizers and music digitizing programs make it easy for you to create your own music (or hire someone to create it for you) that brings originality to your work anyway. This may be a better way to go than risking a lawsuit by including someone else's MP3.

There is some music that's in the public domain and free for you to use. Simply Google "public domain music" to find it. You might consider this option when thinking about including music in your rich media content.

Understanding Video Copyright

YouTube and frame-grabbing software tools have made it easy to quickly grab video content. However, this content may well be protected by copyright, just like its text and music cousins. If you're building content that will run on a website, many video providers such as YouTube offer a way to embed their video in your site royalty free. With a little creativity, you can come up with unusual and interesting ways to display video content.

Understanding Animation Copyright

With so many Flash sites in the world these days, you may be tempted to try duplicating someone else's animation efforts. But animations also qualify as copyrighted work, and you could easily get yourself into trouble if your animation looks quite like another's. The trick is to think about the ideas the other animator used in crafting their animation and then come up with your own animation that may be somewhat similar in style but completely different in the way it's presented, or vice versa. The point is to not simply copy someone else's work. When you create your own work, you are thus far less likely to suffer from copyright infringement accusations.

Understanding Trademarks

A trademark is some kind of word, sign, symbol, artwork, or other type of indicator used by individuals or corporations to help others easily recognize their products or services. Note that the font or style used to create a trademark is included with the trademark.

Writers fall into the trap of using trademarks all the time, and their editors typically coach them out of it, to keep them out of legal trouble. For example, when we sneeze, you and I often ask someone if they would hand us a Kleenex. But that term is a trademark—even though it has entered the normal vocabulary as an indicator of a tissue you use to blow your nose. It's no big deal to substitute the word *tissue* to avoid any problems down the road.

In the end, look at it this way: A rich media content designer's bread and butter is the content they have crafted and are selling to others. If you simply (and scurrilously) rip off their efforts and have the audacity to call it your own, not only are you stealing, but you are potentially taking bread out of their mouths. You deserve a lawsuit!

THE ESSENTIALS AND BEYOND

Rich media is the compilation of story, media, and text brought together to make a compelling argument or statement. Because of the ubiquity of the Flash Player in web browsers and Flash content on websites, Flash is the ideal choice for you to get your rich media story out.

ADDITIONAL EXERCISE

1. Start Flash and create a new ActionScript 3.0 document.

2. Using the Flash drawing tools, draw a rectangle. The color of the rectangle does not matter at this point.

3. From the main Flash menu, select Window ➢ Other Panels ➢ Accessibility.

4. Fill in a name and description for this movie.

5. Close Flash without saving.

(Continues)

THE ESSENTIALS AND BEYOND *(Continued)*

ANSWER FOR ADDITIONAL EXERCISE

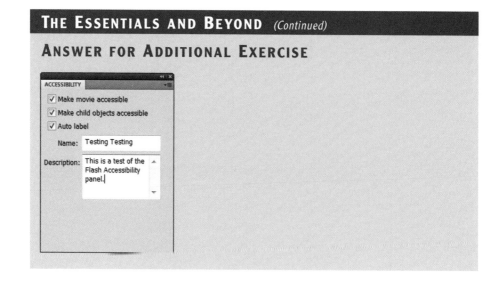

CHAPTER 2

Getting Acquainted with Flash

The Flash user interface (UI) may seem busy and confusing to you at first. But once you begin working with Flash, you'll find Adobe has done a great job of placing the tools you'll use most often right at your fingertips so you can work more quickly and efficiently.

▶ **Opening Flash for the first time**

▶ **Using Flash panels**

▶ **Understanding Flash workspaces**

▶ **Understanding Flash file types**

Opening Flash for the First Time

All graphics shown in this chapter were taken from a Mac computer, but there is very little difference between Mac and Windows in Flash.

By default, every time you launch Flash, the Welcome screen appears first (see Figure 2.1), requiring you to select what type of document you want to work with. In most cases you'll make the selection at the top of the middle column: ActionScript 3.0 under Create New. Note the other file types and templates you can select from. Templates bring with them the basic

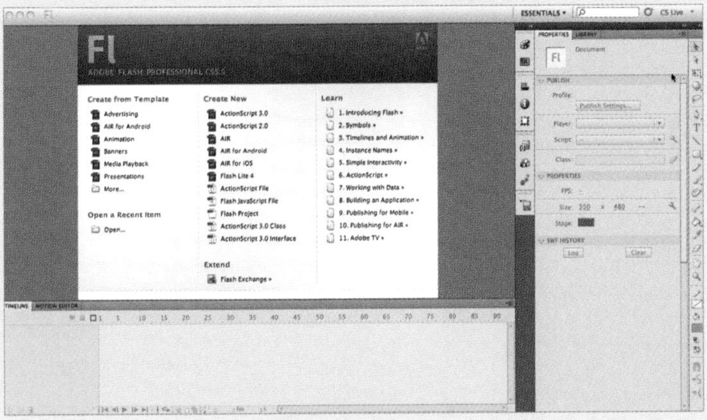

FIGURE 2.1 The Flash Welcome screen

beginning objects needed for certain media types. The other file types allow you to create Flash files for Android or iOS, or files associated with programming such as JavaScript or ActionScript 3.0 classes.

Even though the selection says ActionScript 3.0, in reality you're telling Flash you want to create a new Flash document, regardless of whether it will have any ActionScript code in it. (Most Flash documents require at least *some* AS3 code.) After this selection, you will be presented with an empty document, as shown in Figure 2.2. This is the default Flash working environment, one in which you will soon feel quite comfortable.

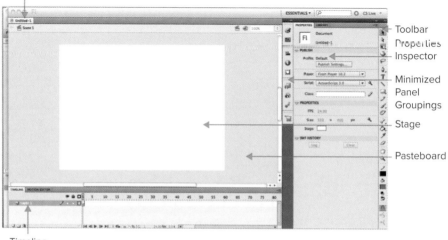

FIGURE 2.2 The normal Flash document screen

The canvas you'll work on is called the *stage*, and the gray area around it the *pasteboard*. The way to think of these elements is to imagine a piece of paper that you've taped down to the top of your desk. The area around your desk but not on the paper would be the pasteboard. Things that you don't want on the stage can be stored on the pasteboard, invisible to viewers and brought on (using movie clips) as required.

Certification
Objective
At the very right side of the screen, you'll see the *toolbar*, containing the drawing, text, manipulation, and formatting tools you'll need. Some of the tool-bar buttons have a small triangle in their bottom-right corner, which indicates that there are additional options. For example, when you click the arrow for the Rectangle tool (ninth down from top), you'll see options for the Oval, Rectangle Primitive, Oval Primitive, and PolyStar tools (see Figure 2.3). Clicking one of

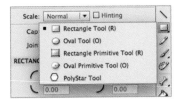

FIGURE 2.3 Multiple selections under one toolbar button

these buttons activates the current selection. Clicking it a second time brings up the entire range of selections for you to choose from.

To the left of the toolbar is *panel grouping* that contains two panels: Properties and Library (see Figure 2.2), each of which has its name on a tab. When Flash first comes up, the Property inspector panel is active, displaying the properties for the current object, which is the stage when you first start up a Flash document. Because the properties change based upon the current object, we call it the Property inspector. That is, you are inspecting the properties for the object you are currently working with. In Figure 2.2 you'll see there are two tabs in the panel grouping: Properties and Library. Because the Property inspector panel shows the properties for the stage or the currently selected object, the contents of the panel will change accordingly. The Library is a place where you will keep assets that are used in your Flash document, such as movie clips, buttons, graphics, sounds, videos, pictures, and other content. By default there isn't anything in the Library when you open a new Flash document.

To the left of the Property inspector is a vertical bar that consists of several panel groupings, all of which are minimized so that only their icons show. Think of this bar as a panel grouping of panel groupings. Clicking an icon on this bar opens a panel grouping that contains groups of panels that have something in common: Color and Swatches or Align, Info, and Transform, for example.

On the bottom of the screen is the timeline, where the machinery of animations happens. By utilizing motion changes over time, you will be able to create innovative and clever animations that tell your story.

Finally, note that the default document name is Untitled-1 (or Untitled-*x*, depending on how many untitled documents you've opened). You'll usually want to save and rename this document right away so that it's safely stored on your hard drive, is placed in a folder that you create and recognize as the holder of a specific body of work, and has a meaningful name. As you work on your document with unsaved changes, Flash puts an asterisk (*) to the right of the filename. It's important for you to perform frequent file saves so that you don't lose hours of work!

Certification Objective

Using Flash Panels

When working with Flash, you'll notice that certain tools are grouped together into what are called *panels*. For example, the Color panel, shown in Figure 2.4, has the tools in it you'll need to adjust colors in Flash. You can see all the available panels and select the ones you need by clicking Window in the main menu bar.

FIGURE 2.4 The Color panel

In addition, panels are often grouped together into *panel groups*. Figure 2.5 shows both the Color and Swatches panels together in a panel group. You simply click a panel name's tab to make it active.

Panel Name Tabs

FIGURE 2.5 The Color and Swatches panel group

You can undock panels from panel groups and move them by clicking the panel's name tab and dragging the panel elsewhere. You can redock a panel into a different panel group or leave it standing alone by itself. As you're docking a panel elsewhere, Flash will display a blue line that alerts you of the panel group into which you're docking. Flash will remember where you placed the panel the next time you open the program. Panels can be easily hidden by clicking the double-headed arrow at the top left of the panel window. When the arrows are pointing to the right this means you can hide the panel by clicking the button. When they are facing left it means you can unhide the panel.

Once you've worked with Flash awhile and you've redocked some panels, you may find that you like the current set of dockings and want to keep them permanently. Flash allows you to create a *custom workspace* for this purpose (more on this topic in a few paragraphs). For now you should keep the panels where they are and think about customizing your workspace later. If you do happen to move a panel and can't figure out how to put it back, you can simply click the workspace drop-down and then click Reset 'Essentials' (see Figure 2.6).

FIGURE 2.6 Resetting the Essentials workspace

Frequently Used Panels

The panels you'll use most often are shown automatically when you create a new Flash document, but others are represented by an icon on the minimized panel groupings area, to the immediate left of the Property inspector. When you click a button in this area, either a single panel or a panel group will open. For example, the Color and Swatches panels are grouped together in a panel group, but both have icons on the minimized panel groupings area. In Figure 2.7, I've hovered over the Color panel, and the tooltip that pops up shows me its name; you can see the panel group popped out, with the Color panel active and the Swatches panel inactive next to it. This idea repeats for the Align, Info, and Transform panels in the middle section as well as the Code Snippets, Components, and Motion Presets panels in the third section. When you click any of the buttons in a given section, the panel group pops up and shows the other panels in the section alongside. The Project panel sits all by itself on the bottom section with no other panels in its panel group.

FIGURE 2.7 The Color and Swatches panel grouping

There are two additional clickable elements you should know about that show up in every panel: the minimize button and the context menu (see Figure 2.8). When you click the minimize button, you simply cause the panel group (or panel) to reduce to icon size. This can be handy if you have a lot of panels out on the work surface and you only periodically need to use them.

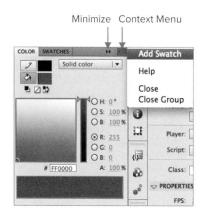

FIGURE 2.8 Other panel elements

The context menu changes based upon the panel that's currently open and pro-vides you with some alternative options for the panel. For example, in Figure 2.8 the context menu is open for the Swatches panel; You can see that the only options you have are to add swatches, close the panel, or close the group.

Other Handy Panels

There are some other panels not on the opening screen that you should be aware of because you'll use them relatively frequently. You access these panels by clicking the Window main menu option.

Actions The Actions panel (see Figure 2.9) is used for writing ActionScript 3.0 code within Flash. The upper-left pane contains AS3 classes and methods you can use in your code. The lower-left pane shows the frames that have code on them. There is a menu at the top of the Actions panel that comes in handy when in the throes of writing AS3 code.

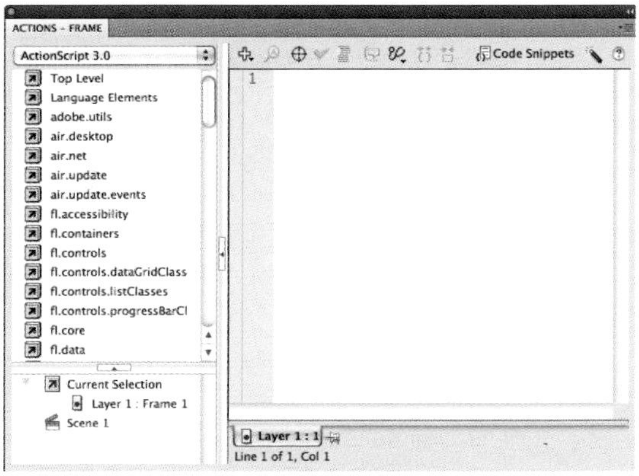

FIGURE 2.9 The Actions panel

The Actions panel is one that you'll keep open but minimize frequently once you've written the code you need.

Output This panel, a plain innocuous piece of white space typically sandwiched between the Timeline and Motion Editor panels at the bottom of the screen (hit F2 to activate it if it's not visible) is used when Flash wants to tell you something, such as compiler error output or other messages, or when you program Flash to tell you something by using the Trace() method in ActionScript.

Accessibility In Chapter 1, "Before Jumping into Flash: Rich Media Design Principles and Practice," you learned about the importance of providing accessibility in your Flash content. Depending on your requirements, the Accessibility panel may be one you frequently have open.

Debug Console Though you probably won't visit this panel for a while, the Debug Console panel found under Window ➤ Debug Panels ➤ Debug Console is useful for debugging your AS3 code (e.g., finding and fixing problems).

Flash has so many tools that you may feel more comfortable working with two monitors. Click and drag various panels to the second monitor and your work surface becomes much cleaner.

Buttons   Clicking Window ➤ Common Libraries ➤ Buttons from the main menu at the top of the Flash screen brings up an extremely useful panel that contains folders that in turn contain lots of prebuilt buttons you can easily add to your Flash content (see Figure 2.10). Please note that the button design is added as a graphic, but the button is in no way functional until you turn it into a button symbol, give it an instance name, and write AS3 code (or pop in a code snippet) to make it function as a button.

FIGURE 2.10 The Buttons panel

Sounds   When you click Window ➤ Common Libraries and select Sounds instead of Buttons, you'll be presented with a really cool library of prerecorded sounds (see Figure 2.11). It was only after a year of using Flash that I discovered this library and kicked myself because we had been recording the very sounds that are included with the library. You can hear each sound by right-clicking it and selecting Play from the ensuing context menu.

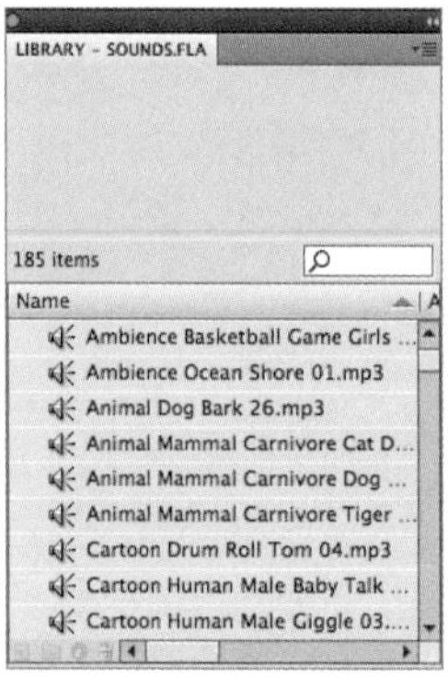

FIGURE 2.11 The Sounds panel

Motion Presets   The Motion Presets panel is found in the panel group bar to the left of the Property Inspector, or you can access it by clicking Window ➤

Motion Presets from the main menu (see Figure 2.12). Motion presets are precreated animations that you can apply to any objects you have in your Flash content, as long as you first convert the finished object to a symbol. For example, you could create a basketball using the normal Flash tools, turn the finished creation into a movie clip symbol, and then apply a motion preset (see Figure 2.13) such as bounce-in-3D.

FIGURE 2.12 The Motion Presets panel

FIGURE 2.13 An applied motion preset

Most of the time there's just no need to knock yourself out trying to create a custom animation when a motion preset will do. They're a huge time saver.

Understanding Flash Workspaces

The Flash screen has so many panels and ways of resizing and re-docking various windows that you can come up with a variety of ways to change the look and feel of your working world. Adobe has canned several of these configurations—called a *workspace*—so you can instantly change from one way of viewing your work to a different one.

The workspace drop-down is situated just above the Property Inspector (see Figure 2.14). Clicking it, you'll see that there are seven workspaces provided for you, plus the ability for you to create your own custom workspace should you wish to work a different way.

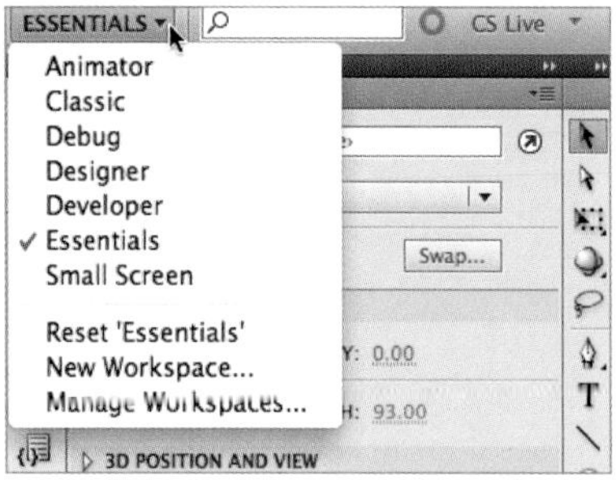

FIGURE 2.14 The workspace drop-down

Unless you set it otherwise, the primary workspace that comes up when you start Flash is called Essentials. There are dramatic differences in the way the workspaces are laid out. For example, the Animator workspace (Figure 2.15) is quite different than Essentials, and the Designer workspace is completely different than either Essentials or Animator (see Figure 2.16).

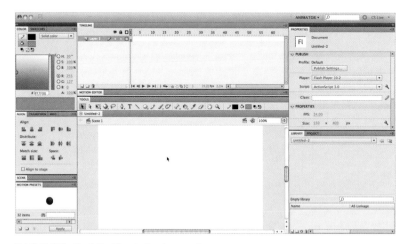

FIGURE 2.15 The Animator workspace

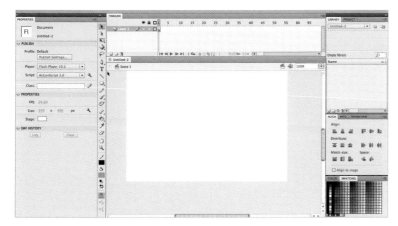

FIGURE 2.16 The Designer workspace

If you have your Flash workspace just the way you like it and you want to save your arrangement, just select Workspaces ➤ New Workspace, and give it a name. The next time you start Flash, your custom workspace will load instead of Essentials. Using the workspace drop-down, selecting Manage Workspaces allows you to delete any custom workspaces or rename them.

WORKING WITH THE TIMELINE, KEYFRAMES, AND LAYERS

The heart of Flash is in its ability to create animations, and the heart of animations is found in the timeline. It's quite important that you thoroughly understand the concept of changing content over time as well as the mechanism that makes this happen: keyframes. Another important timeline feature with which you should be intimately familiar is layers. This is such a big and important topic that I have dedicated an entire chapter to it, Chapter 4, "Getting Started with the Timeline."

Understanding Flash File Types

Certification
Objective

It's important that you understand the basic file types Flash creates when you are doing your work. There are numerous file types Flash is capable of generating, but there are only a handful you'll be interested in at first. There is a complete listing of all the file types Flash can generate at the following location:

```
http://help.adobe.com/en_US/flash/cs/using/WSd60f23110762d6b883b18f10c
b1fe1af6-7f12a.html
```

FLA

When you select File ➤ Save As, Flash will save your file with the filename extension `.fla`. This is the file type of the actual working document you'll be using when you create your Flash rich media content.

An FLA file's initial size may be minimal, but you should be aware that this file can become *really* large, especially if you're using sound or video with your content.

It's important to note that in Flash 6, even though you continue to use the `.fla` extension for your Flash file, in reality it now works like a compressed file that contains all of the various files that make up your project. You can even replace the `.fla` extension with `.zip`, giving you the ability to view all of the various files inside the `.fla`.

SWF

While you work with the FLA file creating your content, the final output is rendered as a SWF file (pronounced "swiff file"). The filename extension for the SWF file is `.swf`. (SWF stands for *ShockWave Flash* and was named that by the company that originally created Flash, Macromedia, which was acquired by Adobe Systems in 2005.)

The SWF file is created when you play your Flash movie by pressing Ctrl ➤ Enter on the keyboard from within Flash or by selecting Control ➤ Test Movie ➤ Test from the main Flash menu. The SWF file is created by default in the same folder as your FLA file.

The SWF file is the file you'll put up on a website or pass around so that people can see your work. Anyone who has the Flash Player or the Adobe Media Player installed can run the SWF file.

It's important to note what version of Flash Player you're going to require for your movie. Some features in Flash Professional CS5 or greater require Flash Player 10 and beyond to play a movie. For example, the new Text Layout Framework (TLF) text components found in Flash CS5 and beyond require Flash Player 10 or higher to work. This may be a problem for you if you expect a very broad audience for your content. Users who are using a browser with an older version of Flash Player installed may be prompted that they need an updated version to run your movie, or they may not be prompted at all and not be able to play your movie. It is up to you to make decisions about what Flash Player support you'll provide in your content. Flash Player determinations are made in the Flash Publish Settings, a topic we'll talk about in Chapter 13. Refer to www.adobe.com/products/player_census/flashplayer/version_penetration .html to see which Flash Player version is currently the most ubiquitous.

HTML

When you get ready to publish your content, you choose File ➤ Publish from the main Flash menu. In addition to the SWF, Flash creates an HTML file (filename extenstion .html) for you that can be used on your website, using the HTML settings you previously set in Publish Settings Dialog Box. The HTML file is fully editable, so make a backup before you edit.

XFL and XMP   There is one more advanced file type, and accompanying file-encoding feature you should be aware of: The XFL file format enables content developers to represent the Flash file in an XML-style open folder format. The eXtensible Metadata Platform (XMP) is used to include data regarding the file: called metadata. Check help.adobe.com using keywords XFL and XML for more information about these two file types.

WATCH THOSE FILE SIZES!

Flash brings you the ability to import various working files for use in your project including graphics and audio and video files. When coupled with your own art and animations, you can imagine that the size of your Flash movie will be very large. Keep an eye on the property inspector after you've tested a movie and you will notice the current movie's file size. There are a variety of techniques for managing file size, including:

▶ Calling your graphics and videos from outside the .swf

▶ Limiting shape tweens (you'll learn about tweens in Chapter 8)

▶ Compressing images by right-clicking them in the library and selecting Properties

▶ Compressing sounds: use MP3 for large sound files, ADPCM for small ones (see Chapter 11)

▶ Vectorizing bitmaps by using Modify ➤ Bitmap ➤ Trace Bitmap from the Flash main menu

▶ Breaking apart bitmaps

▶ Choosing *not* to break apart text.

The point is this: Keep an eye on the file size and optimize where possible. Other tips: Use symbols instead of on the main timeline art, break apart bitmaps, store assets in the library for reuse, and optimize images prior to import.

THE ESSENTIALS AND BEYOND

As you progress into animations, you'll soon realize that Flash's ability to create animations makes it an incredibly powerful website and rich media design tool; it's easy to learn and use yet brings a diverse array of new tools to designers. Once you're able to create animations, regardless of their simplicity or complexity, you've automatically expanded the toolset you can use to show your viewers what you're talking about and give your viewers a story rather than rote detail and facts.

ADDITIONAL EXERCISE

▶ Start Flash and select Create New ActionScript 3.0 Document.

▶ Rename Layer 1 to Box.

▶ Select the Rectangle tool from the toolbar (disregard color selection for now) and draw a rectangle of any size on the stage.

▶ Click frame 24.

▶ Press F5 to extend the box from frame 1 to frame 24.

▶ Create a new layer and call it Circle.

▶ Lock the Box layer, and click the Circle layer name to make sure you're working in it.

▶ Click frame 25.

▶ Right-click and select Insert Blank Keyframe from the context menu.

▶ Select the Oval from the toolbar (it's another selection in the Rectangle tool button) and draw an oval of any size on the stage, again disregarding any color selection for now.

▶ Click frame 48.

▶ Press F5 to extend the oval frames from frame 25 to frame 48.

▶ Hit Control + Enter (Command + Return on the Mac) to play your movie.

▶ You should see 1 second of your box, then 1 second of your oval.

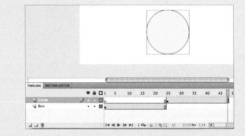

ANSWER TO ADDITIONAL EXERCISE

See the file on this book's website called BoxCircle.fla. The website is at the following location: www.sybex.com/go/flashessentials.

CHAPTER 3

Drawing Shapes in Flash

Flash comes with a variety of drawing tools that enable you to create a wide range of artwork for your rich media content.

▶ **Drawing standard shapes**

▶ **Understanding merge vs. object drawing**

▶ **Drawing primitive shapes**

▶ **Drawing polygonal or star shapes with the PolyStar tool**

▶ **Making artsy shapes with the Deco tool**

▶ **Drawing other shapes**

▶ **Working with color in Flash**

Drawing Standard Shapes

Rectangles and ovals are two of the standard Flash shapes you can use to create basic artwork, or you can combine them to form more intricate drawings.

On the Flash Tools panel clicking the arrow on the basic shapes tool button displays a drop-down with five possible selections (see Figure 3.1). The first item listed (and the default tool if you click the button once and not twice) is the *Rectangle tool*. (Remember that any buttons with a tiny black triangle in their lower right-hand corner indicate there are multiple choices in that particular button group.) The second standard shape is the *Oval tool*. Having selected a shape tool other than the Rectangle tool, the new tool becomes the current button selection until another tool is selected. In other words, you want to work with the Oval tool, so you select it. Now the Oval tool is the tool that shows up on the face of the shapes button and does not change until you select a different tool.

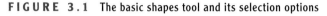

Certification
Objective

FIGURE 3.1   The basic shapes tool and its selection options

> You can also select
> the Rectangle tool
> by pressing the
> *hotkey* R on your
> keyboard, and you
> can select the Oval
> tool by pressing the
> hotkey O.

If this is the first time you've used the Tools panel, you'll be in Merge Drawing mode, depicted by the button near the bottom of the Tools panel being "off" ⬜ . The other mode is Object Drawing mode, depicted by the same icon being "on" ⬛ . It's important to pay attention to the drawing modes (covered in detail in the section "Understanding Merge vs. Object Drawing").

Let's begin your Flash drawing experience by drawing a couple of basic shapes:

1. Click the Rectangle tool button or press R on the keyboard to activate the tool.

> Flash also has the
> ability to import
> Illustrator and
> Photoshop draw-
> ings natively, which
> means for your more
> complex artwork, you
> can use Illustrator to
> create your assets and
> then simply import
> them into Flash when
> you're done.

2. Make sure you are currently in Merge Drawing mode by checking the Tools panel button shown before this exercise. If you're in Merge Drawing mode, the button will *not* have a dark-gray square around it. If this button is clicked, there will be a dark-gray square surrounding the button, which means you are in Object Drawing mode.

3. Now you need to select the *fill color*, or inside color, for the object. The fill color is denoted by a tipping paint bucket in the Property Inspector (see Figure 3.2). When you click the icon, you will open the Color Picker (Figure 3.3), which allows you to select the fill color you want for your shape. You can enter the hexadecimal value of a color if you know it. Set the transparency for the color (0 = fully transparent, 100 = fully opaque), or completely turn off the fill color.

> Make sure to check
> whether you are in
> Merge or Object
> Drawing mode every
> time you intend to
> create a drawing
> object.

Stroke color

Fill color

FIGURE 3.2   The fill color properties

Current color's hex value

Transparency (alpha) value

Turn fill or stroke off

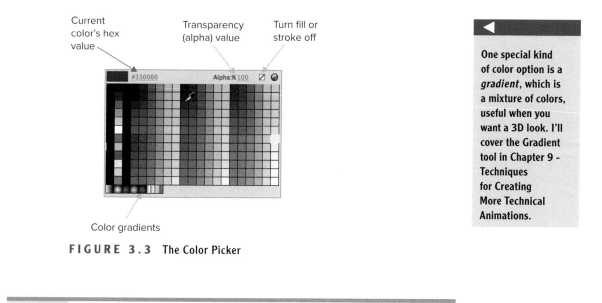

Color gradients

FIGURE 3.3 The Color Picker

One special kind of color option is a *gradient*, which is a mixture of colors, useful when you want a 3D look. I'll cover the Gradient tool in Chapter 9 – Techniques for Creating More Technical Animations.

COPYING AN EXACT COLOR

Once the Color Picker is open and you're in the process of selecting a color, you don't have to select it off of the color list, you can sample your color from any object on the stage. The cursor turns into an eyedropper (shown here). Any color you click within an object becomes the new fill color. This is tremendously useful for capturing colors such as skin tones in photographs and similar uses.

4. The other selection you make in the Property Inspector is the *stroke*, which is the outline around the shape you're drawing. When you are drawing objects, you must decide whether to have a stroke on an object because it is not required. Your decision will depend on what kind of drawing you're trying to create. For the purpose of this exercise, select a stroke color for your rectangle.

5. In the Property Inspector, just below the fill and stroke Color Pickers you'll see a slider button that allows you to change the size of the stroke. You can either click in the number area or move the slider to change the stroke size. Change the stroke size to 10.

6. Click and drag to draw a rectangle on the stage (see Figure 3.4).

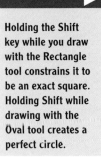

Holding the Shift key while you draw with the Rectangle tool constrains it to be an exact square. Holding Shift while drawing with the Oval tool creates a perfect circle.

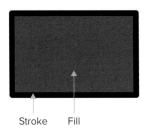

Stroke   Fill

FIGURE 3.4 A rectangle object on the stage. This object has both a fill and stroke

As long as the Rectangle tool stays selected, you can continue to draw various rectangles. For this exercise, draw several on the stage.

7. Change to the Selection tool ![selection tool icon] using the keyboard's V key.

8. Click the outer edge of one of your rectangles, noting that just one side of the stroke is selected. Whenever a drawing object is selected like this, it's easy to spot the active selection because it changes from a smooth color to a granulated view in which the individual pixels of the object are highlighted. Change the stroke color on one side.

9. With the new stroke color still active, click and drag the side away, noting that the rest of the rectangle object elements—both fill and stroke—stay where they're at.

10. Press Ctrl+Z (Command+Z on the Mac) to undo the move.

11. Click the fill area, making it active. Change the fill color using the Color Picker.

12. Double-click the fill area, noting that *both* the fill and the stroke become selected.

13. Hold down the Shift key and then double-click another rectangle. Flash selects both objects' fill and stroke.

14. Click anywhere on the stage or pasteboard to deactivate the rectangles. This is how you will ensure no objects are currently active when you're getting ready to perform another activity.

15. Making sure you're close to a rectangle but somewhere outside it, click and hold the mouse to draw a *marquee* (which always describes a rectangle or a square) around the rectangle. Both the fill and stroke become active.

16. Press the Q key on your keyboard to activate the Free Transform tool, allowing you to perform complex sizing, skewing, and rotation operations on the object (see Figure 3.5). You can also adjust the object's registration point.

Both the fill and the stroke must be selected when in Merge Drawing mode should you desire to move the object; otherwise, you'll move just the fill, leaving the stroke behind.

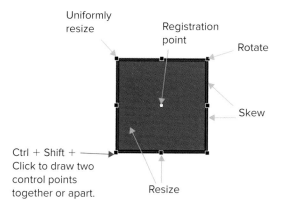

FIGURE 3.5 An object selected with the Free Transform tool

17. With the Free Transform tool still enabled, point your mouse close to a black box at one of the corners of the object (each black box is called a *control point*). The mouse cursor turns to a circular arrow, meaning you can now rotate the object. Rotate the object once or twice using different corners to observe the behavior.

18. Point your mouse directly over one of the corner control points. Now a double-headed mouse cursor appears, meaning you can enlarge or reduce the object's size. If you hold down the Shift key, you can constrain the object's proportions while resizing. Practice resizing the rectangle object.

You can press Ctrl+Z (Command+Z on the Mac) to undo your previous step.

19. Clicking the control point boxes in the middle of the lines allows you to click and drag to resize the width or height of the object. Holding

down the Shift key retains the object's proportions. Practice resizing your rectangle object a couple of times.

20. Holding down both the Ctrl and Shift keys (Command and Shift keys on the Mac), point to one of the corner point boxes. The mouse cursor changes to a white arrow with a tiny double-headed black arrow beside it. This means you can click and drag the corner control point in toward its neighbor or away from its neighbor to make a triangular or trapezoid shape.

21. With the Free Transform tool still enabled, point to any of the connective bars around the object. The mouse cursor changes to a double-headed arrow with one tip of the arrow missing on each side (see Figure 3.6). Now when you click and drag, you can *skew* the object, moving one side out of alignment with its opposite neighbor. This is useful for perspective drawing work and creating uneven trapezoidal shapes. Practice skewing a couple of times, repeatedly using Ctrl+Z to undo your work.

FIGURE 3.6 Using the Free Transform tool to skew an object—note the skew mouse cursor upper right-hand section of rectangle

22. Note the registration point in the center of the object. When the Free Transform tool is active, you can move the registration point, which alters the object's pivot point. Click the registration point of the object and then drag it to a corner.

23. Attempt to rotate the object, noting that the object now rotates around the new registration point (see Figure 3.7).

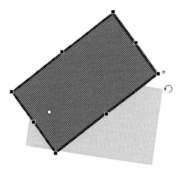

FIGURE 3.7 Rotating an object with the registration point in a different place

24. Press Ctrl+Z twice to undo the registration point changes.

25. Repeat all of these steps with the Oval tool, drawing several circles with different fill and stroke colors.

26. Deactivate all the objects by clicking somewhere in the stage or pasteboard.

27. Click the Subselection tool (hotkey A) , which allows you to select specific points on an object so you can alter them, thus sculpting the object into more complex shapes. Note that when you're using the Subselection tool, the control points look a little different, as does the cursor.

28. When you point to a control point, the cursor changes from a white arrow with a white square to a white arrow with a black square. This means you can click and drag the motion path to obtain a unique shape (see Figure 3.8).

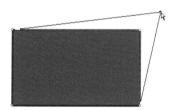

FIGURE 3.8 Modifying a rectangle with the Subselection tool

29. Practice altering the rectangle using the Subselection tool points. How does this compare with using Ctrl+Shift to resize a rectangle or square using Free Transform tool control points, as shown in Figure 3.6.

30. With the Subselection tool selected, marquee one of the circles you drew on the stage. Note that there are many more control points that make up a circle versus the number used for a rectangle.

31. Click in the stage or pasteboard to deactivate all objects.

32. Press V to activate the Selection tool.

33. Marquee just one-quarter to one-third of any one of your rectangles or circles. When you let go of the mouse button, note that just the area of the rectangle or circle you marqueed becomes active.

The Oval tool works essentially the same way as the Rectangle tool except when you click the stroke of an oval, the entire stroke becomes active.

34. Press the Delete key. The section you marqueed is deleted. When objects are in Merge Drawing mode, this is how you can delete parts of them for shaping purposes.

35. Click the stage or pasteboard to deactivate all objects.

36. Press the V key to activate the Selection tool.

37. Point to a side of one of your rectangle objects. Note that as you get close to the edge of the stroke, the mouse cursor changes to a black arrow with an arc underneath it. This means you can drag up or down to create an arc in the shape.

38. With the special cursor displayed, click the stroke of one of your rectangle objects and drag up to create an arc.

39. From the main menu, choose File ➤ Save As. Browse to the folder in which you'd like to save your work and then name this practice file. Note that the filename extension is .fla, meaning it is a working Flash document.

We will go through an exercise later in this chapter to work with the other drawing tools: Rectangle Primitive, Oval Primitive, and Star. But for now, it's important that you understand the difference between Merge and Object Drawing modes because there are significant differences in the way objects behave when they are created using one or the other.

Understanding Merge vs. Object Drawing

The key to drawing in Flash is to think about the basic shapes that make up an object and then build the object using basic Flash shapes and modifying them to fit. This is where an understanding of the difference between Merge and Object Drawing modes comes into play.

Creating Objects in Merge Drawing Mode

When you're using Flash's basic shapes to draw assets, it's quite important to understand whether you're in Merge or Object Drawing mode. We'll touch on Merge Drawing first:

1. Draw a marquee around all of the objects on the stage and then press the Delete key to erase them.

2. Make sure the shape button is still active from the previous exercises. If it is not, click the shape button or press the R key (rectangle) or O key (oval) to draw a shape.

3. You will know you're in Merge Drawing mode when you see that the Merge/Object Drawing button is *off*, in other words, without a dark gray background. When this button is on, the background is darkened and you are in Object Drawing mode. Make sure you're currently in Merge Drawing mode.

    The Merge/Object Drawing button does not show up until you click a shape button in the Tools panel.

4. This time, when you create a rectangle or circle, make sure there is no stroke selected. Create a basic drawing object.

5. Click the stage or pasteboard to deactivate the new object.

6. If you drew an oval, now select the Rectangle tool and draw a new rectangle on the stage, or vice versa if you first drew a rectangle.

7. If the second object is not active, you can double-click it to make it so. Move the second object over on top of but not completely obstructing the first.

8. If you drop the second object onto the first, the second object stays active until you click away from it (see Figure 3.9, left side). If you drop one shape onto another while in Merge Drawing mode and then move the shape away, you'll see that you've eaten a piece out of the underlying shape (see Figure 3.9, right side). Shapes that are made up of the same color and that have no strokes will merge together, which is a great way to create complex objects from basic shapes.

When you're in Merge Drawing mode, objects that you draw and place on one another will merge to form a more complex shape.

F I G U R E   3 . 9   Using basic shapes in Merge Drawing mode to eat away portions of underlying shapes

When you use the Free Transform and Subselection tools while in Merge Drawing mode to sculpt a shape and then merge it with other shapes, you can create some very intricate drawings. You are not limited to how many shapes you merge, nor their color. Designers who are comfortable boiling down complex things into their basic shapes will immediately be successful using the Flash drawing tools to create whatever they want.

Another useful technique with Merge Drawing is to draw a marquee by clicking and dragging around a part of the shape and then pressing Delete to erase the part you've marqueed, as you learned in steps 32 and 33 of the previous section, "Drawing Standard Shapes."

Suppose, for example, you want to create an equilateral triangle. Here's how:

1. Draw a perfect square by holding down the Shift key while you draw a rectangle.

2. Use the Free Transform tool to rotate the square 90 degrees.

3. Marquee the bottom half of the square and you have your triangle (see Figure 3.10).

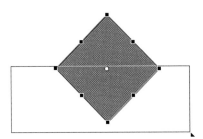

FIGURE 3.10 Using Free Transform and marquee to create an equilateral triangle

Finally, once you have all of your shapes drawn into the object you're looking for and assembled them the way you want them, most times you will want to marquee the final product and turn it into a graphic object (more on this in Chapter 6, "Working with Flash Symbols").

Creating Objects in Object Drawing Mode

When the Object Drawing button is clicked (in other words, its background is dark gray), you don't have to worry about one object eating away another. Objects created using Object Drawing mode have a square around them (which is not visible when the movie plays) and can be moved anywhere you desire. Figure 3.11 shows several objects drawn on the stage using Object Drawing mode.

The square around an object may trick you into thinking you've somehow selected a stroke when you're drawing a rectangle. No worries—you're just in Object Drawing mode. The same movement and resizing tools apply.

FIGURE 3.11 Objects drawn using Object Drawing mode (note the black square around the oval)

Let's work a little bit with drawing shapes using Object Drawing mode:

1. Click the stage or pasteboard to deactivate all objects.

2. Press the V key to activate the Selection tool.

3. Draw a marquee around all objects.

4. Press Delete to erase all objects on the stage.

5. Press the R key to activate the Rectangle tool.

6. Check the bottom of the Tools panel to make sure you're in Object Drawing mode.

7. Select a fill and stroke color.

8. Draw a rectangle.

9. Repeat steps 5 through 8, this time pressing the O key to draw an oval instead of a rectangle.

10. Press the V key to activate the Selection tool. The oval you just drew should be the active object, provided you did not click away from it after drawing it.

11. Move the oval onto the top of the rectangle.

12. Note that the oval keeps its square boundary as you move it onto the rectangle.

13. Move the oval away from the rectangle, noting that no alterations have occurred on the rectangle.

Drawing Primitive Shapes

The Rectangle Primitive and Oval Primitive tools work essentially the same way as the standard shapes. The difference is that when you create a shape using Rectangle or Oval primitives, you can alter that shape after you've drawn it on the stage. Also, you don't have the choice of Merge or Object Drawing mode—all primitive shapes are drawn using primitive-drawing mode. Follow these steps to learn how to add corner radii to Rectangle shapes and to draw a Rectangle Primitive:

1. Click the stage or pasteboard to deactivate all objects.

2. Press the V key to activate the Selection tool.

3. Draw a marquee around all objects.

4. Press Delete to erase all objects on the stage.

5. Click the black arrow in the bottom-right corner of the basic shapes Tools panel button to expose the list of available tools.

6. Select the Rectangle tool from the menu.

7. Assure that you're in Object Drawing mode.

8. Select a fill and stroke for the rectangle you're about to draw.

9. In the Rectangle Options section, there are four rectangle corner radius settings. By default, if you change one corner radius, the others automatically change. To allow different corner radii numbers at each rectangle corner, you can click the chain link icon immediately below the radii boxes to disable radii locking. For the purpose of this exercise, however, leave the radii locked. Enter 25 to tell Flash you want to draw a rectangle with four even corners.

10. Draw a rectangle on the stage.

11. Press the V key to activate the Selection tool.

12. Click the stage or pasteboard to deactivate your new rectangle.

13. Click the rectangle again. Note that you cannot adjust the corner radii settings.

14. Click the shape drop-down and select the Rectangle Primitive tool from the menu.

15. Select a fill and stroke color.

16. In the Rectangle Options field, enter 25 to tell Flash you want to draw a rectangle with four even corners.

17. Press the V key to activate the Selection tool.

18. Click the stage or pasteboard to deactivate your new rectangle primitive.

19. Click the rectangle primitive again. Note that you can adjust the corner radii settings with a Rectangle Primitive.

20. Click the shape drop-down and select the Oval tool from the menu.

21. Select a fill and stroke color.

22. Click in the inner radius box and set an inner radius of 50.

23. Draw your oval, noting that you're now creating a doughnut (its technical name is *torus*).

24. Repeat steps 17 and 18.

25. Click the oval again, noting that you cannot change the inner radius.

26. Repeat steps 20 through 25, this time selecting an oval primitive shape.

27. Note that you can indeed change an oval primitive's inner radius after the object has been drawn.

In either case—standard shape or primitive—you can always click the object after the fact using the Selection tool and then change its fill and/or stroke color.

The point is that once you've selected a shape to draw—regardless of whether you've selected standard or primitive—be sure to look at the shape's options in the Property Inspector *before* you begin drawing. You cannot always go back, select the object, and modify its attributes. Setting them in the Property Inspector before drawing is a smart way to work.

When you draw either a normal or a primitive shape, you have the ability to *break apart* the object into the individual elements making up the shape by which it was formulated:

1. With the primitive oval object you drew in the previous steps still selected, select Modify ➤ Break Apart from the main menu

or right-click the object and select Break Apart or press Ctrl+B (Command+B on the Mac) to break it apart. The object is now broken into its individual pixels, allowing you to modify them as you want.

2. Press the V key to switch to the Selection tool.

3. Draw a marquee over the object in such a way that you take up one-quarter of the object with the marquee (see Figure 3.12).

FIGURE 3.12 Oval drawn using primitive-drawing mode, broken apart, getting ready to delete a pie shape from it

4. Press the Delete key to remove the section.

5. Draw a rectangle primitive using any stroke and fill color and other settings you like.

6. Draw an oval primitive using any stroke and fill color and other settings you like.

7. Press V to change to the Selection tool.

8. Move the new oval on top of the rectangle.

9. Note that the oval remains on top of the rectangle, obscuring it.

10. Right-click the oval and select Arrange ➤ Send To Back from the context menu or select Modify ➤ Arrange ➤ Send To Back from the main menu. The oval moves to the back while the rectangle comes to the front.

Summing Up Basic Drawing

In summary, the basic drawing technique works this way:

1. Visualize the drawing you want to create as a series of rectangles, ovals, shapes and lines.

2. Use Merge Drawing techniques to carve out curves and other features you need.

3. Use Object Drawing to put objects on the stage that you do not want to merge with other shapes.

4. Use Primitive shapes for more shapes you think you may want to modify later.

5. Use the technique of breaking apart and drawing a marquee around the parts of the shape you want to delete.

6. Instead of drawing a marquee around objects, you can optionally use the Lasso tool (hotkey L) to select unusual or complex parts of a shape you want to delete. The Lasso tool allows you to perform more complex marquee operations around objects.

Drawing Polygonal or Star Shapes with the PolyStar Tool

The PolyStar tool is useful for creating geometries with more than four sides and for creating stars. You can find it within the same grouping as the shape and primitive shape tools. Follow these steps:

Certification
Objective

1. From the basic shapes button drop-down, select the PolyStar tool .

2. Select a fill and stroke color.

3. Click and drag the shape, noting that the default shape is a pentagon.

4. Click the options button, and the Polystar tool dialog box opens (see Figure 3.13).

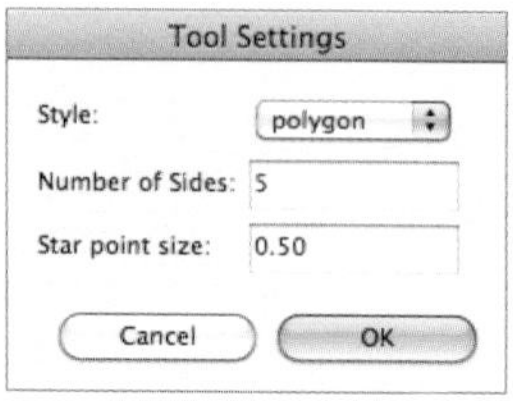

FIGURE 3.13 The PolyStar tool's options box

5. In the Style drop-down, select star.
6. Leave the number of sides at 5.
7. Leave the star point size at 0.5.
8. Click and drag a star on the stage.
9. Select the Subselection tool (hotkey A) and then click the star you just created.
10. Click and drag any corner of the star to resize it.
11. Click the Free Transform tool (hotkey Q) and readjust the star's size.
12. Press the V key to activate the Selection tool and move the star anywhere you like on the stage.
13. Move the star onto the pasteboard. Note that objects on the pasteboard do not show up when you play the movie with Ctrl+Enter (Command+Enter on the Mac).

Making Artsy Shapes with the Deco Tool

Certification Objective

One of the coolest tools in Flash is the Deco tool 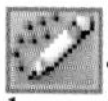. It provides you with elaborate, colorful shapes that you can paint on the stage, as you see in the following exercise:

1. Make sure the Selection tool is active by pressing V on the keyboard.
2. Drag a marquee to encase all current objects on the stage.
3. Press the Delete key to delete all current objects.

4. Press U on the keyboard to select the Deco tool.

5. Click the drop-down in the Drawing Effect section to reveal the various effects available with the Deco tool (see Figure 3.14). Note that there are many different customization options available, depending on the drawing effect you choose. You can be quite elaborate when using this tool.

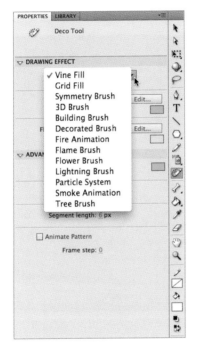

FIGURE 3.14 Fill effects available with the Deco tool

6. Select Vine Fill.

7. Click anywhere on the stage. Flash begins to draw the Vine Fill; click when you want it to stop.

8. Press Ctrl+Z to undo the Vine Fill operation.

9. With the Deco tool selected, select the Fire animation drawing effect.

10. Click and drag on the stage to paint with some Fire (see Figure 3.15).

The fill operation will continue until you click again to stop it. You can rapidly fill up the stage with a fill if you're not aware of this. If you add too much you can seriously increase the size of your final file and thus the CPU time needed to put it on the screen. Go easy!

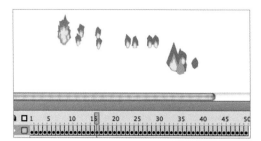
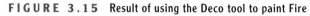

FIGURE 3.15   Result of using the Deco tool to paint Fire

Observe that Flash creates many new frames to accommodate the fire animation. This will have implications when you want to create other layers with other assets on them. I'll discuss this in more detail in Chapter 4, "Getting Started with the Timeline," and Chapter 7, "Developing Simple Flash Animations," when I start talking about placing art assets on different layers and frames.

11. Click again to stop.

12. Press the Enter key to watch Flash play the fire animation. Flash stops playing the animation when it hits the last frame. If you play the movie with Ctrl+Enter (Command+Enter on the Mac), the fire animation will play repeatedly until you close the movie. In Chapter 7 and Chapter 13, "Working with ActionScript," you'll learn more about how to use ActionScript to stop frames from playing over and over in a movie.

Drawing Other Shapes

Certification
Objective

Flash includes several other tools you'll want to know about to round out your drawing capabilities:

3D tools   The 3D Rotation and 3D Translation tools (hotkeys W and G, respectively) can be used to apply 3D-like effects to 2D images:

1. Press Ctrl+Z to undo the Fire animation from the previous exercise.

2. Press R to select the Rectangle tool.

3. Select a fill and stroke color.

4. Note that the corner radii setting from any previous Rectangle work you have done is still there. You can set the setting back to 0 if you desire.

5. Draw a rectangle on the stage.

6. Right-click the rectangle and select Convert To Symbol from the context menu. The Convert To Symbol dialog appears (see Figure 3.16).

Convert to Symbol

Name: Symbol 1   OK

Type: Graphic ▼   Registration: ▪□□ Cancel
                                  □□□
                                  □□□

Folder: Library root

Advanced ▶

FIGURE 3.16 The Convert To Symbol dialog

7. From the Type drop-down, select Movie Clip.

8. In the Name box, type **mc3D** (more on this naming convention in Chapter 6).

9. Click OK. The Convert To Symbol dialog disappears.

10. Note that the rectangle looks a little different than it did before. This is because Flash has converted the rectangle to something called a *symbol*. The symbol's type is *movie clip*. More on this in Chapter 6.

11. Click the 3D Rotation tool. The rectangle now has three rings of different colors around it. The red circle rotates the object in the x-axis, the green circle in the y-axis, and the blue in the z-axis. An easy way to remember this order is red, green, blue = RGB = XYZ.

12. Click and drag the blue circle to rotate the object on the z-axis (see Figure 3.17).

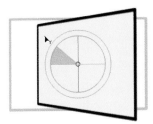

FIGURE 3.17 Using the 3D rotation tool to rotate a movie clip on the z-axis

13. Press the G key to switch to the 3D Translation tool.

▶

**When you see the
word *translate* used
with graphics pro-
grams, think "move."**

14. The rectangle now has two arrows on it. The convention used for the colors is the same as with the rotation tool (for example, RGB = XYZ).

15. Click one of the arrows and drag it to move the rectangle.

The Pen tool   You can find four tools lurking under the Pen tool button on the Tools panel [✎]. The Pen tool (hotkey P) is used just as its name implies—to draw shapes as though you have a pen in your hand. If you own a digital tablet, you'll find that the Pen tool works just fine with the device.

More interesting are the Add Anchor Point, Delete Anchor Point, and Convert Anchor Point (hotkeys =, -, and C, respectively) tools. Recall that the Subselection tool allows you to manipulate extra points you add to your drawing. How do those extra points get there? Selecting the Add Anchor Point tool, you simply click the area of the shape where you want to add an anchor point and there it is, ready to be manipulated with the Subselection tool. It does not matter whether the shape has a stroke; you can add points on either the stroke or the fill, although they're added on the edge of a shape, not anywhere inside it. You can use Delete Anchor Point to remove an anchor, as shown in this exercise:

1. Delete all objects from the stage.

2. Press the R key to activate the Rectangle tool. (It doesn't matter if Merge or Object Drawing mode is selected.)

3. Select a fill and stroke color.

4. Draw a rectangle on the stage.

5. Press the equal sign (=) on the keyboard, activating the Add Anchor Point tool [✎⁺].

6. Click anywhere on the stroke of the rectangle. Flash adds an anchor point.

7. Press A to enable the Subselection tool.

8. Click and drag any of the anchor points in or out to modify the rectangle's shape.

9. Press the minus sign key (−) to activate the Delete Anchor Point tool.

10. Click one of the anchor points you added previously. If you delete an anchor point that you used to alter the shape of the object, the object returns to its original state at that position.

11. Press the C key to activate the Convert Anchor Point tool .

12. Click and drag on an anchor point you added previously. Flash provides *Bézier curves* at the anchor point and the ability to create a curved surface at that location (see Figure 3.18).

F I G U R E 3 . 1 8 The Convert Anchor Point tool adds Bézier curves for curve drawing

WHAT'S A BEZ-EE-EH?

In digital tools such as Flash, Bézier (pronounced "bez-ee-eh") curves provide a handle that allows you to change the height of a curve's slope on either side and also allows you to enlarge the curve or skew the curve to the right or left. If you click either end of the line representing the Bézier curve, just that section of the curve will raise or lower. If you click and drag in the middle, you can raise or lower both sides of the curve uniformly, and then you can skew the curve to one side or the other. At first you may find Bézier curves tricky to work with, but once you get the hang of them, you'll be impressed with the depth of creativity you can bring to an object with them.

Text tool I will go into more detail about the Text tool (hotkey T) in Chapter 5, "Adding Flash Text and Fonts to Your Creations."

Line tool The Line tool (hotkey N) does exactly as its name implies. Select the Line tool; assign a stroke color, width, and line style; and then begin clicking and dragging. When you let up on the mouse, Flash draws the line for you. The Line tool stays active, and you're ready to draw the next line, as shown in the following exercise:

Using Ctrl+A is a quick way of quickly selecting all objects.

1. Press Ctrl+A to select all objects on the stage and then delete them.

2. Press the N key to select the Line tool.

3. Draw a series of lines that connect together, like a square for example. Zoom the screen size if needed so you can make sure the lines connect.

4. Flash recognizes that the shape is completely enclosed.

5. Press K to select the Paint Bucket tool.

6. Select a fill color from the Color Picker.

7. Click inside the square to fill it with the color you selected (see Figure 3.19).

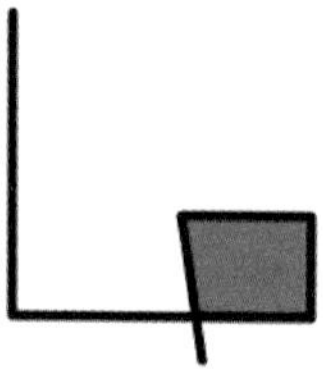

FIGURE 3.19   Filling a shape created by the Line tool

Using the above technique, you can create an unusual shape not easily sculpted with the basic shape tools and fill it with a color of your choice.

Pencil tool   Use the Pencil tool to draw lines and shapes. When you activate the Pencil tool, a shape tool becomes available in bottom of the tool bar. Use it to control the smoothness of the lines created with the Pencil tool.

Paint Bucket and Ink Bottle tools   I covered the Paint Bucket tool earlier. The Ink Bottle tool  resides within the same tool grouping as the Paint Bucket tool. Using the S hotkey, you can use the Ink Bottle tool to change the color of a stroke:

1. Using the Selection tool, select one segment of the line you drew in the previous exercise.

2. Press S to activate the Ink Bottle tool.

3. Pick a new stroke color.

4. The stroke you selected is changed to the new color.

Simply select the tool, pick a color, and then click a stroke in which you want to change the color. If you experiment with this, you'll be surprised which strokes Flash considers to be contiguous line segments. Figure 3.20 shows the line drawing I created earlier and then modified with the Ink Bottle tool and a new stroke color. Even though the line that's half green and half black was a continuous black line when I first drew it, you can tell that Flash considers the four lines used to create the square filled with red to now be combined into a separate line segment. Further, if I click the four lines making up the square, Flash considers them to be one contiguous line and fills them all in with the new color.

FIGURE 3.20 Using the Ink Bottle tool to modify a stroke color

Bone and Bind tools   The Bone tool (hotkey M) ![icon] is used to put various drawn segments together to animate them. The Bind tool (hotkey M) ![icon] is used to modify segments already connected together using the Bone tool. We'll talk about the Bone tool in more detail in Chapter 10, "Creating Characters with Inverse Kinematics (IK)."

Eyedropper tool   The 16th tool down from the top (hotkey I) ![icon] is used to sample the color of an object (whether vector drawn or photo image) to use as a fill color.

Eraser tool   The Eraser tool (hotkey E) ![icon] is used to erase drawings you've put on the stage. In some cases the bottom half of the Tools panel changes based upon the tool that has been selected up above: this is the case with the Eraser tool. Follow the steps below to learn more about using the Eraser tool.

1. Press E to activate the Eraser tool.

2. Note that as soon as the Eraser tool is selected, the bottom half of the Tools panel has three new entries on it that directly pertain to eraser operations (see Figure 3.21).

3. Click the Erase Mode button (third from bottom of the Tools panel) and make sure it is set to Erase Lines.

4. Select a fairly large eraser size.

5. Click and drag across part of the lines you created to erase them.

6. Click the Erase Mode button and set it to Erase Fills.

7. Click anywhere in the fill you created with the Paint Bucket tool.

8. Observe how much of the fill is removed with this setting.

9. Without altering the other eraser settings, click the Faucet tool button (second from bottom).

10. Click the fill again, this time noting that it is completely erased.

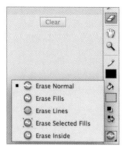

FIGURE 3.21   Setting Eraser tool options in the bottom half of the Tools panel

Hand tool   The Hand tool (hotkey H) is used to move the stage one way or another—called *panning*:

1. Click the Hand tool to activate it.

2. The mouse cursor changes to a hand shape.

3. Click and hold on the stage, moving the mouse left, right, up, and down to see how the Hand tool allows panning.

Zoom tool   The Zoom tool (hotkey Z) is used to enlarge or reduce the stage:

1. Press Z to activate the Zoom tool.

2. The mouse cursor changes to a magnifying glass with a plus sign.

3. Click an object you'd like to enlarge.

4. Flash zooms into the area and enlarges it for you.

5. Repeat the zoom maneuver.

6. Flash enlarges the view yet again.

7. Hold down the Alt key (Option key on the Mac). The mouse cursor changes to a magnifying glass with a minus sign.

8. Click the scene. Flash zooms out of the scene with each click of the Zoom tool.

Working with Color in Flash

There are some test questions that revolve around using the Color and Swatches panels in Flash, and there are also design issues that revolve around your selection of colors.

Using kuler

Adobe Systems Inc. has a website dedicated to color swatches. The site's name is kuler (lowercase), and it can be accessed at `http://kuler.adobe.com/#`. Think of kuler as a social site where registrants are able to upload color swatches that have worked for them in projects.

Because many people have a problem with color matching when it comes to design decisions, kuler is a fantastic place to go if you're looking for color matches. Follow these steps:

1. Open your favorite web browser and navigate to the kuler site.

2. Click the Register link and create a kuler account for yourself. If you already have an Adobe account, your logon will work on this site as well. You do need to have a valid account to be able to download color swatches.

3. In the search box, type a keyword for a color swatch you'd like to look for. For example, typing "Halloween" returns a variety of color swatches.

4. As you browse through the list of swatches your keyword returned, select one by clicking on its name.

5. Click the color swatch, noting that it takes up the full screen.

6. Click the swatch again to return it back to normal.

7. To the right of the swatch's name you'll see a series of three buttons . Click the middle button, "Download this theme as an Adobe Swatch Exchange file."

8. When presented with the Explorer box prompting you for the location where you will save your file, create a new folder called kuler Swatches and save the file inside this folder, using the same name as the original file.

9. In Flash, click the Swatches panel button ▦.

10. In the upper-right corner of the Swatches panel is a drop-down that, when clicked, brings up a context menu of options you can choose (see Figure 3.22). Choose Add Colors.

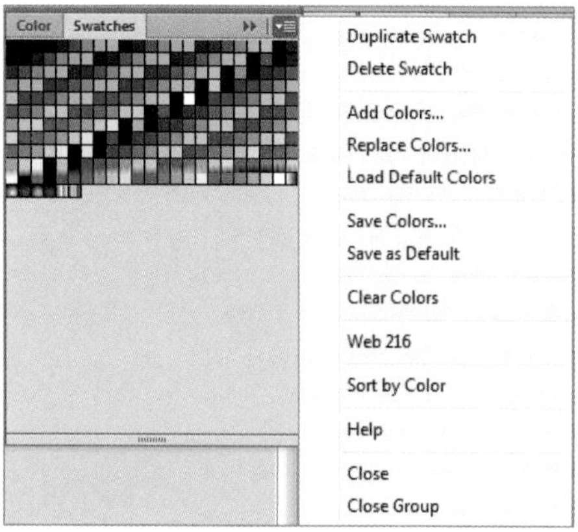

FIGURE 3.22 Swatches context menu

11. Navigate to the folder where you downloaded your kuler swatch.

12. In the All Formats drop-down, select All Files. Your kuler swatch will appear.

13. Select your kuler swatch, noting that all of the colors associated with the swatch appear in your swatches list (see Figure 3.23).

FIGURE 3.23 Choosing file formats when loading a new swatch into the Swatches panel

Saving a Color Set

Suppose you have a set of colors you've accumulated that you'd like to save in the Swatches panels so you can use them again in a future project. Using the same Swatches drop-down mentioned earlier, you can choose Select Colors and then save the current color set to your computer for future use, giving it a meaningful name. You load saved color sets the same way that you loaded your kuler file.

Working with Color Gradients

A color gradient is a representation of several colors that fade from one color into another. Gradients are useful for bringing more of a 3D-like feel to art assets on the screen. There are two types of gradients: Linear (in a line) and Radial (in a circle). Let's use an exercise to create one of each:

1. Open a new ActionScript 3.0 document.

2. Click the Color panel button  .

3. In the color type drop-down (see Figure 3.24), select Linear Gradient.

FIGURE 3.24 Selecting a Linear gradient in the color type drop-down

4. A new black and white Linear gradient appears (see Figure 3.25).

FIGURE 3.25 A new black and white linear gradient

5. On the bottom line of the gradient, somewhere in the middle of the line, left-click with your mouse. A new gradient point appears.

6. Change this point's color to red by keying (r: 255, g: 0, b: 0) in the RGB boxes, or type #FF0000 in the hex box.

7. Exit the color panel.

8. Select the rectangle tool with R or the oval tool with O. Note that your new gradient color is automatically the active color.

9. Draw a rectangle or oval on the stage.

10. Within the free transform tools there is a tool called the Gradient Transform tool (hotkey F). Activate this tool.

11. Click the rectangle or oval you just drew. Several gradient tool options are now active (see Figure 3.26).

FIGURE 3.26 A gradient with the Gradient Transform tool active

12. Move the white dot in the center to the right or left. Note that the spread of the gradient colors changes.

13. Click the circle icon in the Gradient Transform tool and rotate the gradient a quarter of a turn upward. Note that the gradient color blends shift to show an upward turn.

14. Click the box with an arrow icon and slide it to the right. Note that the gradient color blend spreads out farther. There is more distance between each of the primary colors in the gradient and more calculation of color change between them.

15. Repeat these steps, this time creating a radial gradient instead.

A NEW WAY OF ASSIGNING COLORS

HSB is another way of thinking about object colors. "H" stands for hue, "S" saturation, and "B" blend. "H" is the color you want, "S" is the amount of that color you want, and "B" is the blend of white and black you'll add to the color to create derivations of that color. This coloring technique is quickly becoming the new standard and I recommend you learn more about it as you move forward. I recommend that you Google "HSLA" for more information.

You can have multiple color points in a gradient. Click a color point to activate it so you can change its color. The triangle at the top of the color point will change from white to black, and you'll see its current color in the color spectrum box above the gradient. You can also slide a color point from side to side to make minor adjustments to the color spread. Click and drag a color point off of the gradient to remove it.

Use gradients as a way of showing light shining on a material in an object or the shadowing on an object. For example, suppose you want to have some shiny aluminum material on an object in your rich media content. Use a silver gradient, rotating the gradient in such a way that the lightest part of it points to an (imaginary) light source.

THE ESSENTIALS AND BEYOND

Adobe has crammed a lot of functionality into the Tools panel, overloading many of the buttons with several choices. Some buttons you'll use routinely; others you will probably seldom visit. By using the tools at your disposal, coupling them with great color choices—especially color gradients—and using elements such as the Bone and 3D tools, you have tremendous drawing capabilities. In this exercise, you'll create a star-filled background.

(Continues)

THE ESSENTIALS AND BEYOND *(Continued)*

ADDITIONAL EXERCISE

▶ Start Flash and create a new ActionScript 3.0 document.

▶ Change the stage color to a dark nighttime sky color.

▶ Maximize the stage size using an extremely large number (1000–1500% or greater).

▶ Create one relatively small star using the PolyStar tool—adjusting the points to your liking.

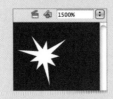

▶ Draw a marquee around the object, right-click the object, and select Convert To Symbol to turn the object into a graphic, giving it any name you like.

▶ Using the Spray Brush tool, in the Symbol section of the Spray Brush's properties, select the star graphic you just created.

▶ Make any spacing and size adjustments you desire.

▶ With the Spray Brush selected, spray to cover your background with stars.

ANSWER FOR ADDITIONAL EXERCISE

CHAPTER 4

Getting Started with the Timeline

The primary reason you want to use Flash is for its animation capabilities. The ability to create a compelling narrative using the elements of story, art, music, and video rendered over time is quite powerful, and Flash is a one-stop environment for doing this work. Given this, the timeline, the tool you use to move objects over time, may be the singularly most important feature of Flash.

▶ **Becoming acquainted with the timeline**

▶ **Working with different frame types**

▶ **Copying and deleting frames**

▶ **Working with layers**

▶ **Aligning objects with snapping**

Becoming Acquainted with the Timeline

Certification Objective

When working in the Essentials workspace, you'll find the timeline below the stage, taking up a good deal of screen real estate. (The Motion Editor, a tool you'll use to modify animations, shares the panel grouping.)

Figure 4.1 shows the timeline and all of the options available in this panel. The timeline consists of two basic parts: frames and layers. Each frame represents one instance of the frame rate—in other words, the number of frames per second in which the movie will play. For example, if the frame rate is 24 frames per second (fps), each frame is 1/24 of a second long. Thus, a 4-second movie would require 96 frames. Each layer represents one discrete unit of your overall animation. Generally speaking, it is good to separate things that move individually onto separate layers. Static content also belongs on its own layer. For example, suppose you want to have a scene in which a UFO or UFOs arrive in a pristine nighttime desert scene. One of the UFOs discovers a cow and abducts it. The nighttime scene represents one layer, each of the UFOs another, and the cow another. Different elements of your scene can come onto the stage at different times, and each element will probably require a different layer. You'll be working on the cow abduction scene starting in this chapter.

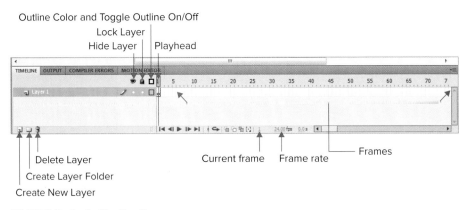

FIGURE 4.1 The timeline

As you can see in Figure 4.1 the Timeline is a busy little interface all its own. Some of the buttons you'll use every time you work with Flash, others not so much. Your artwork will, for animation purposes, reside on different layers. If you're a Photoshop user you'll immediately get the connotation. Creating new layers is easy to do with the Create New Layer button. Likewise, deleting a layer is done with the Delete Layer button. Careful! You may delete a layer with some artwork on it—artwork you did not intend to delete. If this happens just hit Ctrl-Z (Command-Z on the Mac) to undo the deletion. You can also create folders for layers that belong together.

Hiding layers is an excellent way to get some of your artwork out of the way so you can pay attention to some detail work on a given layer. Locking a layer or layers prevents you from putting artwork on the wrong layer. Shifting a layer to outline mode by hitting the Toggle Outline On/Off button takes away the detail of a layer or layers' artwork, but keeps the outline intact so you can pay attention to placement detail on the current layer in which you're working. Each layer has its own outline color (denoted in the outline box on each layer). Click the Toggle Outline On/Off button for a given layer and that layer's artwork is changed into outline mode. Click the Toggle Outline On/Off button at the top of all layers and all layers will be shown in outline mode. (Clicking the Hide or Lock button at the top of the layers accomplishes applies the activity to all layers as well.)

The playhead, a large red rectangle with a red line beneath it, highlights the current frame. Once you have several frames with content on them, you can drag the playhead back and forth, a process called *scrubbing* the playhead. Performing several playhead scrubs during an animation session helps you spot small issues and fix them in advance before they become a big problem.

Flash tells you what frame you're currently on alongside the current frame rate. Also, every fifth frame is a different color than the rest.

To the left of the current frame number is a section that includes some advanced frame management tools we won't be touching on in this chapter, such as onion skinning and working simultaneously with multiple frames. We will cover working with multiple frames and onion skinning in Chapter 7, "Developing Simple Flash Animations." Finally, to the left of that section is a set of standard playback buttons that allow you to cycle through animations.

Note that when you start a new Flash document, frame 1 has a black-outlined circle in it, denoting a blank keyframe, ready for you to add your artwork. A term often used in the industry to denote your art is *assets*. Figure 4.1 shows the playhead sitting on frame 1.

As you work through the various exercises in this and ensuing chapters, you'll have a chance to work with all of the buttons outlined in Figure 4.1.

Adding Different Frame Types to Your Animation

There are three basic frame types you'll be using a great deal: keyframes, blank keyframes, and regular frames. A keyframe is a frame that contains at least one asset. The asset could be static or moving. Blank keyframes are frames that are ready to have an asset placed on them. Frames are just an extension of a keyframe that has an asset on it. Suppose, for example, you have a beautiful background scene you've created on layer 1. Above it you have several layers with various animations on them—animations that play over multiple frames' worth of time. For the viewer to see the background while these animations are playing, you must extend the background frame out to the point where the animations stop. Since there's nothing moving on the background frame—it contains static content—all you really need to do is have Flash show the frame in succeeding frames. There's no need for a keyframe, just a frame extension. You'll get a chance to work with keyframes and animations in the next few pages.

Follow these steps to work with the different frame types:

1. Select the Rectangle tool by pressing R on your keyboard.

2. Select a stroke and fill for your rectangle.

3. Take a look at frame 1, layer 1, noting the black circle with white fill in the middle of the frame block. This means the frame has a blank keyframe.

4. Draw a rectangle on the stage.

5. Note that the black outlined circle now has a black fill, indicating that the frame has an asset on it.

 N O T E   *Keyframes* **contain some kind of asset—whether art, video, audio, or text.**

Now that you have drawn some assets on frame 1, what now? One thing you may frequently want to do is duplicate the assets on the very next frame and then make some minor changes to the assets to denote some kind of movement.

6. Click frame 2.

7. Select Insert ➤ Timeline ➤ Keyframe from the main Flash menu or right-click the new frame, and then click Insert Keyframe or press the F6 key.

8. Note that Flash makes an exact copy of the asset on the stage in frame 1 and pastes it in exactly the same location on frame 2.

9. Note that frame 2 now shows a black circle, indicating that a keyframe has been created.

10. Click frame 24.

11. Right-click the frame and then choose Insert Keyframe from the context menu.

12. Note that Flash grays out frames 3 through 23, indicating that the rectangle will be continuously displayed from frame 2 to frame 24 (see Figure 4.2).

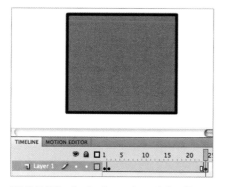

FIGURE 4.2 Extension of timeline between frames 2 and 24

When you insert a new keyframe, this action copies *all* of the assets on the previous frame to the new keyframe.

13. Make sure you're still working in frame 24.

14. Press O to activate the Oval tool.

15. Pick a fill and stroke color for the oval.

16. Draw an oval on the stage.

17. Click frame 25. Note that there are currently no art assets on the stage.

18. Right-click the frame, and select Insert Keyframe from the context menu.

19. Flash now copies both the rectangle and oval to the new keyframe on frame 25 (see Figure 4.3).

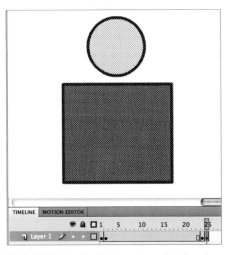

FIGURE 4.3 Flash copies all old *and* new artwork to the next frame when a new keyframe is created.

▶

You will create blank keyframes when you want new assets on the frame and do not want to carry forward assets from the previous keyframe.

Maybe you don't want any of the current frame's assets on the next frame; you want to start with a new, empty keyframe.

20. Click frame 26. Note there are no art assets currently on the frame.

21. Right-click the frame.

22. Select Insert ➤ Timeline ➤ Blank Keyframe from the Flash main menu or right-click the new frame and click Insert Blank Keyframe, or you can press the F7 key.

23. Flash inserts a blank keyframe. Note a black outline circle with a white fill, indicating a blank keyframe.

24. Draw a new oval on this frame, this time changing the fill and stroke colors.

25. Draw a new rectangle on this frame, changing its fill and stroke colors as well.

26. Click frame 48.

27. Select Insert ➤ Timeline ➤ Frame or right-click the new frame then click Insert Frame, or you can press the F5 key (see Figure 4.4).

Note that Flash puts a white rectangle with a black stroke on the ending frame and colors the frames gray in between.

Note that no artwork is copied from frame to frame. Flash simply shows the artwork on the preceding keyframe for the length of time represented by the distance from the keyframe to the ending frame. For example, in the previous steps, the animation extends from frame 26 to frame 48: 22 frames. Since the frame rate is 24 fps, the artwork on frame 26 will display for 22/24 of a second.

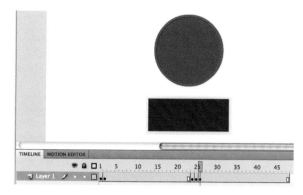

FIGURE 4.4 Inserting a frame shows a frame duration between frame 26 and frame 48.

This process is called *extending frames*. For example, in the nighttime sky background you created in the exercise in Chapter 3, you could opt to extend the frames as far as you like by simply selecting the frame to which you want to extend and then pressing F5. This is a very common thing to do: Many designers create a static background layer that includes all of the assets that will not be moving throughout the animation and then extend the frame out the appropriate length to accommodate the duration of the proposed new animation.

Suppose you find your animation will need to go a little longer than the current background's length?

28. In your current Flash document, click frame 72.

29. Right-click the frame, and select Insert Frame from the context menu.

Flash simply extends the frame, moving the end frame from frame 48 to frame 72.

30. Press the Enter key. Flash automatically scrubs the playhead for you.

31. Press Ctrl+Enter (Command+Enter on the Mac) to play the movie in Flash Player.

Note that once you have played an animation, Flash creates a SWF file with the same name and in the same folder as your FLA file. Every time you replay the movie, Flash updates the SWF file. As a reminder, the SWF file is portable—you can take it to any computer and play it as long as the Flash Player is installed.

Copying and Deleting Frames

From time to time you may want to copy a group of frames and paste them elsewhere. One of the major reasons this happens is when you go through all the work of animating an object on the stage and then realize it would be better if you turned the whole thing into a movie clip.

Since movie clips have their own timeline, often designers and animators will create their animation on a movie clip and then drag an instance of the movie clip to the stage. The primary reason this is useful is that it keeps stage clutter and stage timeline confusion to a minimum. Also, it just makes good sense to isolate animated objects from one another in separate movie clips because you're able to edit them independently. Additionally, accurate placement of movie clip animations on the stage is easier. In this exercise you'll move the animation you created earlier to its own movie clip.

1. Using your work from the previous exercise, highlight an entire row of frames you just created by clicking and dragging across the frame selection you want or clicking the first frame and Shift+clicking the last.

2. Right-click and select Cut Frames from the context menu.

3. The frames disappear. Don't worry: They are in the paste buffer, invisible to you right now but available to paste once you create a new movie clip.

4. Press the F8 key or click Insert ➤ New Symbol from the main Flash menu. You can also right-click any frame and select Insert Symbol from the context menu.

5. Create a new movie clip symbol, giving it any name you like. No need to worry about the other settings in the Create New Symbol dialog right now.

6. Flash creates a blank movie clip and puts you into movie clip editing mode. You can tell you're editing the movie clip because its name

appears in the upper-left corner of the stage, adjacent to the stage's name, Scene 1 (see Figure 4.5). Notice the gear icon associated with movie clips.

FIGURE 4.5
Currently editing
movie clip test;
note the stage's
name, Scene 1.

7. Note that the playhead is parked at frame 1, layer 1.

8. Press Ctrl+Shift+V (Command+Shift+V on the Mac); on both PC and Mac this is called the "paste in place" hotkey. You can also right-click and select Paste Frames from the context menu or, from the Flash main menu, click Edit ➤ Timeline ➤ Paste Frames. Flash will copy the frames into the new place, leaving the stage empty.

You can also copy the frames using this technique and, instead of cutting, use the paste in place hotkey or right-click and select Edit ➤ Paste Frames from the context menu.

Now that the animation is in a movie clip instead of on the stage, you have to bring it out of the library, placing it on the stage to use it.

9. Click the Scene 1 button to return to the stage.

10. If the Library tab in the Property Inspector is not clicked, click it to reveal the contents of the library. Note that your new movie clip is now in the library.

11. Note that frame 1 of the stage has a blank keyframe on it and that the frames are extended out to frame 72.

12. Click frame 2 and then Shift+click frame 72 to highlight all frames between 2 and 72.

13. Right-click and select Remove Frames from the context menu. This gets rid of all the frames with the exception of frame 1. Even if you had included frame 1 in the removal, Flash would continue to display a blank keyframe at frame 1.

14. Click your movie clip library member and drag it out onto the stage (see Figure 4.6).

Drag from here . . .
to here . . .

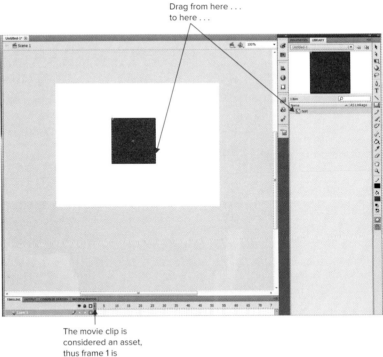

The movie clip is
considered an asset,
thus frame 1 is
shown as a keyframe
with assets on it.

FIGURE 4.6 Dragging a movie clip to the stage

15. If you wish, you can use the Free Transform tool to resize, rotate, or even skew the movie clip.

16. Press Ctrl+Enter to play the movie.

17. Save your work to a new file if you so desire. We won't be reusing this work; no need to save changes if you won't be going back to review them later.

Not a very interesting movie clip, but here's the important takeaway: Frame 1 of the stage uses only one frame but still plays the animation action. This technique will be useful for you when you create more complex animations that consist of various movie clips.

Frame Names

When you click an individual frame in the Property Inspector you'll notice a section called Label. This allows you to assign a meaningful name to the frame. There are three different kinds of frame labels you can attach to a frame:

1. Frame Label: You use a frame label to assign a meaningful name to a frame that you will later access in AS3. For example, suppose you want your program to move back to frame 2 upon completion. You could us the AS3 function gotoAndStop(2), but if you assigned a meaningful name, such as "Start" for example, the code would suddenly become more friendly because the AS3 function would now say gotoAndStop(Start). Frame labels are useful for naming frames that will be used in AS3.

2. Frame Comment: Exactly as their name stipulates, frame comments are used to provide a comment for a specific frame.

3. Frame Anchor: Think of a frame anchor as a bookmark, similar to the way an anchor element (<a>) works in HTML and you'll have the sense of what a frame anchor does. Frame anchors do not require any ActionScript, and allow you to provide navigability to users as they traverse your Flash-based site. You put your anchor into a URL destination in any given frame after that. One thing to remember: When you get ready to publish your Flash document, you must select the Flash with Named Anchors template from within the HTML settings of the document. We'll touch on publishing in Chapter 13.

Organizing Your Work with Layers

Layers are used to segment various components of your rich media. Some designers and developers use very few layers in their work; others use vast quantities. You want to find a middle ground when using layers. It's not wise to put all of your assets on one layer, nor is it prudent to put every single thing on a separate layer. You will most likely find when you first begin using Flash that you don't use layers enough—you'll have situations in which you realize you need a separate layer for several pieces of artwork you've placed on a frame and you wind up cutting the assets from the original layer and pasting them into the new one. No worries! Flash provides the ability for you to adjust and correct. However, if you get into the habit of asking yourself whether a new asset belongs on the current layer or a new one, you'll be ahead of the game.

Every horizontal line of frames in the timeline represents one layer. As new layers are created, Flash adds a new row of frames. To the left of the frames in Figure 4.1 you can see the layer name Layer 1. To the right of the layer name are some buttons you can click to control the layer's visibility, lock the layer, and turn assets on the layer from full color into outline mode. The color of the square is the same as the color of the outline.

Creating a UFO Scene

Take a look at the UFO scene in Figure 4.7. Note that there are three layers in this scene: Background, Mountains and UFO.

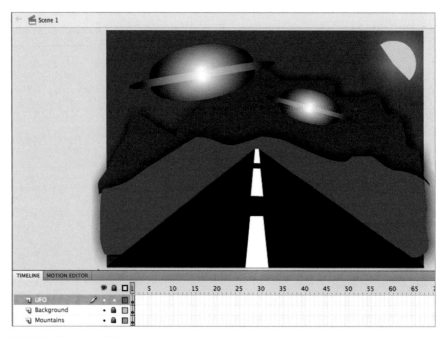

FIGURE 4.7 UFO scene: three layers

Let's use this exercise to re-create this scene:

1. Start a new ActionScript 3.0 document.

2. Click the Properties tab to show the document properties.

3. Click the stage Color Picker. This brings up the Document Properties window, which allows you to set the background color.

4. Set the stage color to a nice dark-blue nighttime-sky color such as hex #000066.

5. Double-click the layer name Layer 1 and change it to Background.

6. Click the Create New Layer button (see Figure 4.1). A new layer appears above the Background layer.

7. Name the new layer Mountains.

8. Repeat steps 6 and 7, this time naming the new layer UFO.

   You need to get into the habit of locking layers you do not want to work with right now so you don't accidentally place assets on the wrong layer.

9. Simultaneously lock the Background and Mountains layers by holding down the Alt key (Option key on the Mac) and clicking the UFO layer's padlock button. Flash locks all other layers, leaving the UFO layer unlocked.

10. Press the O key to activate the Oval tool.

11. Make sure Merge Drawing mode is active (the default with a new Flash document).

12. Select the silver gradient color from the fill Color Picker. Pre-built gradients show up in the bottom part of the Color Picker (see Figure 4.8).

13. Make sure the stroke color is turned off (see Figure 4.8).

Click this button
when setting the
stroke color.

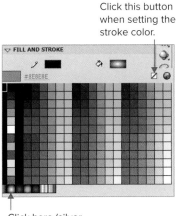

Click here (silver
gradient for fill
color).

FIGURE 4.8 Where to click in the Color Picker for gradient colors or to turn off any colors

14. Draw a skinny, fairly short oval on the stage. This will become the middle section of the UFO.

15. Press V to activate the Selection tool.

16. Marquee the bottom half of the oval and press the Delete key. This activity leaves only the top half of the oval.

17. Marquee the top one-third of the remaining oval and press Delete again. This leaves a skinny angular middle section for the UFO (see Figure 4.9).

FIGURE 4.9 Result of two cuts into the silver oval

18. With the same settings, draw another oval somewhere else on the stage. The new oval should be fatter and narrower than the first. This oval will be cut in two to make the top and bottom halves of the UFO.

19. Press V to activate the Selection tool.

20. Marquee the bottom half of the new oval. Be careful not to hit other buttons so that this half stays active because it will need to be that way in the next step.

21. Press Q to activate the Free Transform tool.

22. Move the bottom half of the oval so that it's touching the bottom half of the mid-section you created earlier. Note that the mouse cursor of the Free Transform tool shows a black arrow with a plus sign (+) in it when you are able to move the object.

23. Marquee the remaining half of the oval. The Free Transform tool should still be active.

24. Move the top half into place on the UFO (see Figure 4.10).

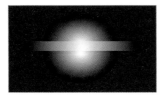

FIGURE 4.10 Building the UFO with a circle cut into two parts

25. Draw a marquee around all three objects.

26. Press Ctrl+G (Command+G on the Mac) to group all the objects.

27. Press the F8 key to bring up the Convert To Symbol dialog.

28. In the Type drop-down, select Graphic (see Figure 4.11).

FIGURE 4.11 Changing to a graphic symbol in the Convert To Symbol dialog

29. In the name box, type **grUFO**. We'll touch on symbol naming conventions in Chapter 6. Flash creates a graphic symbol and stores it in the library.

30. Making sure grUFO is selected, rotate, size, and move the UFO to your liking, keeping it somewhere in the upper third of the stage.

31. Press Ctrl+D (Command+D on the Mac) to duplicate the UFO.

32. Rotate, size, and move the second UFO somewhere else on the stage, making it a little smaller, with a different angle than the first (Figure 4.12).

FIGURE 4.12 Two UFOs on the stage

33. Click the Toggle Outline On/Off button. Note that Flash takes away all of the color, leaving only an outline to represent the UFOs on the screen.

34. Click the Toggle Outline On/Off button again to reshow the colors in the UFOs.

The outline feature is useful when you have a lot of busy artwork on the stage and you're tying to make sense out of what's where. Additionally, artwork can sometimes be distracting—putting some objects in outline mode allows you to concentrate on placing other objects in the scene in the correct location.

Hanging the Moon

Now it's time to put the moon on the stage:

1. Alt+click the Background layer. This activity unlocks the Background layer and locks all the others.

2. Click the Background layer to make it active.

   If you lock all other layers but do not move to the layer you want to work on, Flash sees that you're on a locked layer. As soon as you try to put art content on the stage, Flash alerts you that you're attempting to do so on a locked layer and offers to unlock it for you. This can happen frequently when you're a beginner, so it's a good idea to check to make sure you're on the layer you kept unlocked so it's active and ready for work.

3. The Oval tool should still be active in the basic shapes area but you can press O on the keyboard just to make sure.

4. Select a white or eggshell fill color for the moon, with no stroke.

5. In the Oval Options section, change the ending angle to 182.5. We want a waxing half moon, but if you draw an exact half oval, the moon will look too mechanical.

6. Draw the oval on the stage.

7. Press Q to switch to the Free Transform tool.

8. Rotate, size, and move the moon into the upper-right corner of the stage. Keep in mind that the moon is in the background so it should be smaller than the UFOs, which you want to appear as closer to the viewer.

9. With the moon still active, press F8 to bring up the Convert To Symbol dialog.

10. In the Type drop-down, select Movie Clip.

11. In the Name field, type **mcMoon**.

12. Click OK. Flash creates a movie clip out of the moon, places it in the library, and shows it on the stage. You can tell the moon is a movie clip this way: Looking in the Property Inspector, you see "instance of mcMoon."

13. Note in the Property Inspector that for the moon movie clip there is a new section called Filters near the bottom of the screen. Click the triangle to open up the Filters selection (see Figure 4.13).

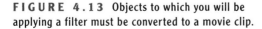

Copy To Clipboard button

Filter Presets button

New Filter button

FIGURE 4.13 Objects to which you will be applying a filter must be converted to a movie clip.

14. With the moon still active, click the New Filter button.

15. Select Glow as the filter type. Flash creates a glow filter and applies it to the moon.

16. In the properties section for the filter, change the color to white by clicking the Color Picker.

17. In the Blur X setting, click and drag the number to the right to about 50. Note that Flash simultaneously adjusts the Blur Y setting because the two are locked by default.

If the moon was going to change over time—for example, you wanted to show the path of the moon as time elapses—putting it on the Background layer wouldn't be the best option. It would be better to create a movie clip and use tweens and an elliptical motion path to set the moon's motion. We'll touch on this topic in Chapter 8.

Organizing Your Layers: Using Layer Folders

When you have a lot of layers in a scene, the timeline can become cluttered. Layer folders are useful because they allow you to group into a folder layers that have a commonality; the layer folders can then be expanded and contracted as needed. We will have three sets of hills/mountains in our scene. It may make sense to have each on its own separate layer, nested within a layer folder. Follow these steps to create layer folders:

1. Deactivate all objects on the stage by clicking anywhere on the stage or in the pasteboard.

2. In the timeline, click the middle button to create a new layer folder.

3. Rename the new layer folder Mountains/Hills.

4. Click the Lock Layer button (padlock icon) to lock the Background and UFO layers.

5. Drag the Mountains layer so it's immediately under the new Mountains/Hills layer folder. When you let go, the Mountains layer should show up indented, to show it's now a part of the Mountains/ Hills folder.

6. Click the New Layer button. Because your last activity was inside the layer folder, Flash assumes you want to create a new layer inside this folder.

7. Name the new layer Hills.

8. Repeat steps 6 and 7, this time naming the new layer Foothills (see Figure 4.14).

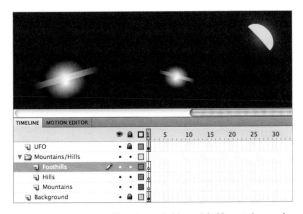

FIGURE 4.14 New layer folder with Mountains and Hills layers underneath it

Note that the Hide Layer, Lock Layer, and Toggle Outline On/Off radio buttons are still available for all art layers, but now that two of the layers are inside a layer folder, simply clicking the layer folder's Hide Layer, Lock Layer and Toggle Outline On/Off buttons applies the same to all the layers that are inside it.

Because the Mountains layer is underneath the Hills and Foothills layers, it will appear to be in the back in terms of the display order.

9. Lock all layers except the Mountains layer by Alt+clicking the padlock button on the Mountains layer.

10. Click the Mountains layer to make sure it's the active layer.

11. Press B to activate the Brush tool.

12. Change the color of the brush by clicking the Fill Color button near the bottom of the toolbar. Select a color that's lighter than the nighttime sky but still relatively dark.

13. Using the brush, draw a set of mountains across the stage, down the right side, across the bottom, and up the left side, connecting to your original starting point. *Do not* let go of the mouse until you have completed the loop.

14. Press K to activate the Paint Bucket tool. The fill color should remain the same as the color you picked for the brush.

15. Click inside the loop you just created. Flash fills the loop in.

16. Press V to activate the Selection tool.

17. Click the mountain scene you just created to activate it.

18. Right-click and select Convert To Symbol from the context menu.

19. Make sure the type is still set to Movie Clip.

20. Key in the name **mcMountains**, and then click OK. Flash turns your Mountains artwork into a movie clip, storing it in the library and displaying it on the stage.

21. Add a new Drop Shadow filter.

22. Drag the Blur X slider to about 45.

23. Repeat steps 9 through 22, this time on the Hills layer, making sure the hills are a little lighter in color than the mountains.

24. Repeat steps 9 through 22, this time on the Foothills layer, making sure the foothills are a little lighter in color than the hills.

   Your UFO scene is now complete (see Figure 4.15). For a reference point, see the file UFO.fla on this book's website at www.sybex.com/go/flashessentials.

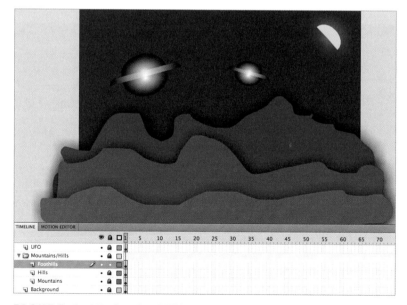

FIGURE 4.15 Completed UFO scene

COLOR OUTSIDE THE BOX

There is a design decision here: Most of the time, it's wise to keep your drawing of things outside the stage (such as the mountains) to a minimum because these elements add to the overall file size. In other words, restrict your drawings to the stage. However, I have seen drawings that go over the bounds of the stage to be quite effective when the FLA file is made to go full screen (e.g., user clicks the maximize button when the movie is playing, or you write some AS3 code to force the movie to play in full screen). The latter technique places the drawing on a planar surface, as though the artist intended the stage to be in the center of the canvas. As a beginner to Flash, it's probably best that you restrict your assets to the limits of the stage for the time being.

LAYER UPON LAYER

Remember that as you build new layers over a layer, the art assets in the layers above will display first and you will not necessarily be able to see the assets on the lower layer. I say "not necessarily" because if an object on a higher layer has an alpha (transparency) value lower than 100 applied to it, you may well be able to see at least some of the detail on the lower layer. The concept of the precedence of one layer over another is going to require that you think about which objects should be placed on which layers. Generally speaking, background layers are always on the bottom. However, backgrounds can consist of many things. In the case of the UFO scene, for example, the background could comprise the road, mountains, fences, cattle, street lights, telephone poles, and all sorts of other accoutrements you see fit to put into your scene—some things that *will not be moving*, others that will. The primary question is this: Which elements do you want to *always* be visible and which elements are okay to hide should an animation on an upper layer move over them? Note that in animations, an element may be in motion, in which case, objects that are on a layer beneath it will be visible only part of the time.

Working with Special Layer Types

There are two specialized layer types you should be aware of: guide and mask.

Guide layer A guide layer is used to simply guide the placement of objects in your scene. Right-click a layer and select Guide from the context menu to change a layer to a Guide layer. Flash assigns a different icon to the layer. When the movie plays (i.e., is converted to a SWF file), it will not show the guide layer; the user will never see the guide layer. In this exercise you'll create a guide layer.

> Most people create a topmost Actions layer, reserved for any AS3 code they write. If you're not planning on writing any AS3 code, you do not need this layer.

1. Start Flash and create a new ActionScript 3.0 document.

2. From the Flash main menu, click View ➤ Rulers. To unview Rulers simply reverse the process.

3. From the Flash main menu, click Modify ➤ Document. Using the Ruler Units drop-down, make sure the ruler units are in inches (decimal) (see Figure 4.16).

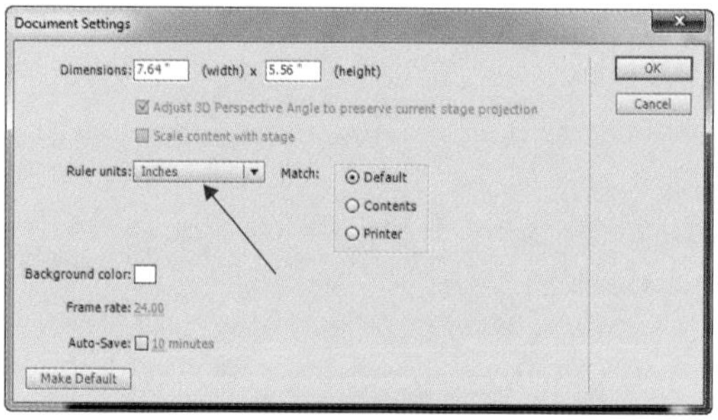

FIGURE 4.16 Document Settings window

4. Make sure the guides are enabled by clicking View ➤ Guides.

5. Click View ➤ Guides ➤ Edit Guides, change the guide color to black, and then click OK.

6. Right-click the layer and select Guide from the context menu.

7. Rename the guide layer Guide.

8. Click on the horizontal ruler and drag out a guide to the 1 inch mark on the vertical ruler.

9. Click on the vertical ruler and drag out a guide to the 1 inch mark on the horizontal ruler.

10. Create a new layer called Box.

11. Lock the Guide layer by clickling View ➤ Guides ➤ Lock Guides from the main Flash menu. Unlock the same way.

12. In the Box layer, draw a rectangle with its upper-left corner abutting the southeast corner of the guides.

13. Note that the Property Inspector shows you the exact x and y location of your object. You can click either coordinate to key in exact values (see Figure 4.17).

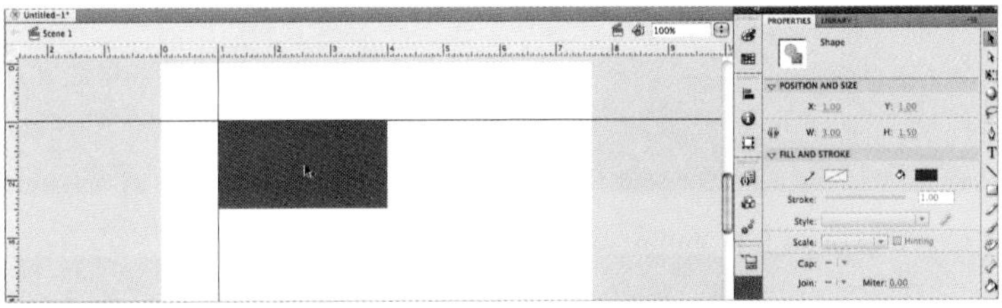

FIGURE 4.17 Adjusting an object's location using the x- and y-axes

14. Play the movie with Ctrl+Enter (Command+Enter on the Mac), noting that the guide layer does not display when the movie plays.

There are other guide properties you can adjust while in the Guide Properties dialog. In particular, the snapping mechanism by which objects on the stage will align themselves. By default, objects will snap to the guides placed out on the stage, but you can adjust this through the Guide Properties.

Mask layer   Have you been to a theater event in which there's a spotlight in use? In cases like that, you can see the activity where the spotlight is pointing and not very much anywhere else on the stage. The mask layer works basically the same way. You simply right-click the layer you want to make into a mask, select Mask from the context menu, then drag layers participating in the mask underneath the mask layer. Flash gives mask layers a different icon.

Certification Objective

A mask layer is used almost exclusively in animations and shows only a part of the layers beneath as the animation progresses. Similar to the way a layer folder has layers underneath it, a mask layer has other layers that are participating in the mask grouped beneath it. Not all layers in the animation need to be grouped beneath the mask layer. In this exercise you'll create a mask layer.

1. Start Flash and create a new ActionScript 3.0 document.

2. Change the stage color to a darker color.

3. Name the first layer Mask.

4. Draw a gray oval about 1/3 to 1/4 the size of the stage in the bottom-right corner of the stage. Note that the color of the oval does not matter.

5. Right-click the Mask layer and select Mask from the context menu.

6. Create a new layer, name it Box, and drag it beneath the Mask layer, noting that it indents itself.

7. Draw a rectangle of another color in the upper-left corner of the stage, a little smaller than the oval. Make sure the box does not touch the oval! (See Figure 4.18.)

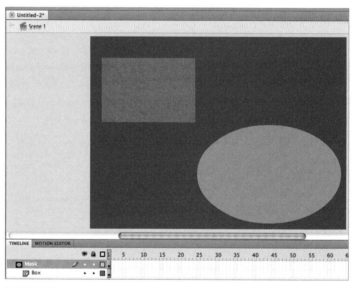

FIGURE 4.18 The oval is the mask, the rectangle the object to be masked.

8. In the Mask layer, click frame 24 and then press the F5 key to create a new frame, or right-click and select Insert Frame from the context menu. The rectangle disappears.

9. In the Box layer, click frame 24 and then press the F6 key to create a new keyframe, or right-click and select Insert Keyframe. The rectangle shows up highlighted and ready for movement.

10. Move the rectangle so it is inside the oval. See Figure 4.19.

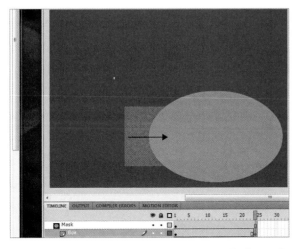

FIGURE 4.19 Moving the rectangle inside the mask

11. Press Ctrl+Enter (Command+Enter on the Mac) to play the movie. Note that the rectangle appears once a second, only when it's within the oval you created on the Mask layer.

12. Click the eye icon on the Mask layer and then replay the movie, noting that hiding the Mask layer from view does not alter the movie. Try clicking and unclicking the Lock Layer button on the masked layer to see how the mask will work.

Actions layer If your animations are going to have ActionScript code in them, you'll need a layer named Actions *at the top* of all of the other layers. If you don't have an actions layer and you select a snippet of code from the Snippets panel, Flash will create an actions layer for you.

If you know you're going to be writing ActionScript code in your content, simply create a new layer, make sure it's at the top of the layers, and rename it Actions. More on this in Chapter 13, "Working with ActionScript."

Aligning Objects with Snapping

If you've worked with computer programs for any length of time, you've probably experienced the *snapping* feature. The computer program knows about a series of exact coordinates called *snap points*, and when a drawing object is placed on the work surface (in this case the Flash stage or symbol) and moved, it aligns itself into the most adjacent snap point.

You can view and change Flash's default snap settings by choosing View ≻ Snapping from the main menu. You can also edit snapping by clicking View ≻ Snapping ≻ Edit Snapping from the main menu. The Edit Snapping dialog box opens (Figure 4.20).

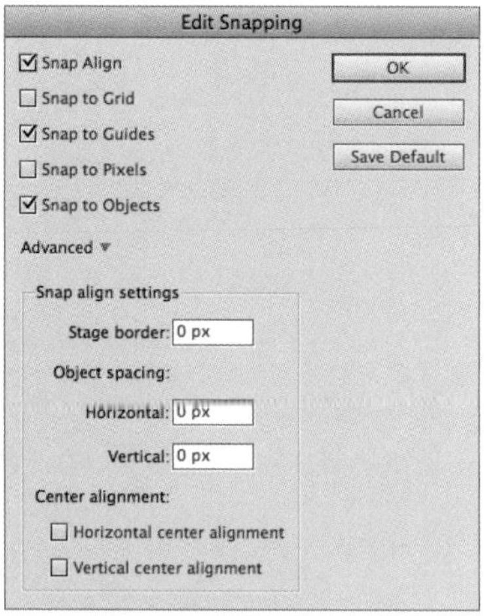

Edit Snapping

☑ Snap Align
☐ Snap to Grid
☑ Snap to Guides
☐ Snap to Pixels
☑ Snap to Objects

OK
Cancel
Save Default

Advanced ▼

Snap align settings
  Stage border: 0 px
  Object spacing:
    Horizontal: 0 px
    Vertical: 0 px
  Center alignment:
    ☐ Horizontal center alignment
    ☐ Vertical center alignment

FIGURE 4.20 The Edit Snapping dialog with the Advanced button clicked

Generally speaking, it's probably a good idea to leave the snap settings right where they are. However, if you do change some snap settings and would like to put things back to normal, don't forget to just click the Workspaces drop-down and select Reset Essentials. The default snap settings will be put back into place.

THE ESSENTIALS AND BEYOND

You must be sure you thoroughly understand the concept of the timeline as it pertains to movements over time, separating your assets on different layers, and the notion of keyframes. Once we begin talking about tweens, you'll discover that there are other keyframes you can use for more complicated operations. For now though, the majority of your efforts should be focused on working with the basic frames, keyframes, and layers.

▶ Using the technique we talked about earlier to make a star part of a custom Deco tool, use the tool to spray-paint your sky with stars.

▶ Allow the Deco tool to randomize the size.

▶ Also put a few stray stars on the screen without benefit of the Deco tool—larger than the ones the Deco tool sprays, but not so large as to overwhelm the scene.

ANSWER TO ADDITIONAL EXERCISE

▶ Reference UFOScene.fla to see an example of what your outcome may look like.

CHAPTER 5

Adding Flash Text and Fonts to Your Creations

Flash brings you a wealth of ways to introduce text into your content. When you want to add text to your creation, you'll use the Text tool (hotkey T), which will create a space for text called a text field. There are three basic kinds of text fields, based upon the kind of work you'd like to do: input, dynamic, and static.

With the input type, you allow viewers to input text into your content. For example, you can use the input text type to create an online form that requires users to key in their contact information.

You use dynamic text when you want to present a text field in which the text changes based upon certain events but is *not* changeable by the viewer. For example, when the user clicks a button, you want a certain text field's caption to change. Finally, you use the static type for text that doesn't need any interaction, such as the title of a website.

Easy enough, right? But, as with all things technical, there have been some improvements in the way Flash handles text fields. In fact, there is now an old text system called *Classic Text* and a newer one called the *Text Layout Framework* (TLF). Although the names of the text fields are a little bit different, the behavior is the same. We will discuss both in this chapter because there are varying reasons you would choose one over the other.

▶ **Understanding when to choose Classic vs. TLF**

▶ **Picking the best font**

▶ **Using Classic text**

▶ **Using the Text Layout Framework**

Understanding When You Can Use TLF Text Fields

Before we get started talking about Classic versus TLF, you need to understand the three rich media delivery components that will directly affect your text decisions.

Flash Player

An example of a major version is Flash Player 10, and an example of a minor version is Flash Player 10.2.

Viewers use Flash player to see your rich media content, whether on the desktop or in a web browser, and there are currently 10 major versions and several minor versions of Flash Player.

The most popular browsers today (with the exception of Apple's iPhone and iPad) all allow Flash Player to consume Flash content in a website and accommodate Flash Player updates as provided by Adobe. But that does not guarantee that all of your viewers will have the latest and greatest Flash Player version installed, nor is it necessarily certain your viewers are using one of the most popular browsers: Internet Explorer, Firefox, Opera, Chrome, or Safari. There are lots of one-off browsers a viewer might be using.

The version of Flash Player you want to target will have an impact on the text field selection you make: Classic or TLF. TLF text fields cannot be viewed using anything less than Flash Player 10.0.

Try this exercise to discover your own browser's Flash Player version:

1. Navigate to the We Choose The Moon website at www.wechoosethemoon .org (or any other site you suspect might be using Flash).

2. Right-click anywhere in the site to reveal the current Flash Player version for the browser you're using (see Figure 5.1).

Browser's current Flash Player version

Zoom In
Zoom Out
Show All

Quality ▶

Print...

Settings...
Global Settings...
About Adobe Flash Player 10.3.183.7...

FIGURE 5.1 Discovering a browser's Flash Player version

If you have a version of Flash Player earlier than 10.0, you won't be able to test your TLF content. It's wise for you to upgrade to the latest and greatest Flash Player or stick with Classic Text.

ActionScript

ActionScript is an evolving powerful language. Many applications have been written using ActionScript for Flash, or its desktop cousin, Adobe Integrated Runtime (AIR). The current version of ActionScript is 3.0, called AS3.

That said, there is a lot of AS2 code out there, along with older Flash Players and older browsers.

You cannot create TLF text fields and code with anything less than AS3. In other words, if you plan on writing AS2 code or you want to include TLF in a project that currently uses AS2 code, you will not be able to do so until you upgrade the project to AS3.

How can you determine what you're going to use in your new project? If you don't change anything, by default your Flash project is set for AS3 and Flash Player 10.2. Here's how to find out what Flash is currently set for:

1. From the Flash main menu, click File ➤ Publish Settings.

2. The default publish settings display (see Figure 5.2).

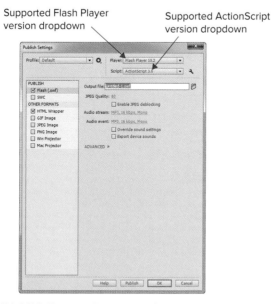

FIGURE 5.2 The Publish Settings dialog

You have lots more publish settings to be aware of; we'll touch on them in more detail in Chapter 13.

Flash Builder

Besides being able to write ActionScript 3 (AS3) code in Flash, you can use an integrated development environment (IDE) called Flash Builder from Adobe. It allows professional software developers to write AS3 code for more complex applications. The version of Flash Builder you are using will also dictate whether you use Classic or TLF.

You cannot create TLF text fields using anything less than Flash Builder 4.0.

Picking the Best Font

Certification Objective

Fonts are software files installed on computers. They can vary (sometimes widely) depending on the computer's operating system and whether a person has downloaded special fonts (either intentionally or as a part of some software they purchased).

Choosing Serif or Sans Serif

In the English language, there are two basic font categories: *serif* and *sans serif*. Serifs are the decorations at the edges of letters. The word *sans* is a French word that means "without." So a font that doesn't have serifs is denoted as sans serif. To see the difference, follow these steps:

1. Open up a new ActionScript 3.0 Flash document.

2. Press T to activate the Text tool.

3. At the top of the Property inspector for the Text tool, click the text engine drop-down and select Classic Text.

4. In the Family drop-down, select Times New Roman (TNR).

5. In the size box, key in a font size 42, or drag the numbers to the right till you hit 42.

6. Select a font color from the Color Picker.

7. Click the stage and type the capital letter *R*.

8. Repeat steps 4 through 7, this time selecting Arial (see Figure 5.3).

Serif   Sans serif

FIGURE 5.3 Serif vs. sans-serif fonts

TNR looks nice on the page, prints cleanly, and is a widely installed and utilized font on Windows, Mac, and Linux machines. There are other similar serif fonts, such as Garamond.

Arial is an equally widely used sans-serif font. There are similar sans-serif fonts, such as Helvetica.

With the evolution of HTML standards, various *families* of fonts have been designated. Web developers often create web pages that denote a serif or sans-serif font family rather than pointing to a specific font. This way, if someone doesn't have the font TNR installed on their computer but does have Garamond, the computer can substitute the font and the viewer will see the page essentially as intended.

The problem is this limits the designer to categories of fonts that can be rendered by the browser. But there are so many great fonts being designed by typographers that would look great with your designs! Why limit yourself? What if there was a way to tell Flash about the fonts you want to use so that the viewer doesn't have to have it installed on their computer to view it? Well, fortunately, there is: by embedding your fonts.

FLASH VS. HTML5, CSS3 AND JAVASCRIPT

This is a good time to briefly mention HTML5, CSS3 and Javascript—the powerful troika that is currently in the process of revolutionizing web development. Steven Jobs, former chairman and CEO of Apple, decided to forbid iPads from being able to run Flash-enabled content. Why? Because he claimed HTML5, the newest HTML standard, has the same basic kinds of abilities built into it (in concert with CSS3 and Javascript), and he was right. Thus, the argument is that there is no need for Flash because one can simply develop HTML5/CSS3/Javascript pages to do the same work. Here's the problem: The HTML5 and CSS3 standards are very new and it will be years before they are fully introduced and enabled across the world's web servers and websites are rewritten. Most of the major browsers have introduced HTML5 compliance in their newest releases, and Adobe's web development product, Dreamweaver, ships HTML5 ready, but cross-browser compliance

(Continues)

FLASH VS. HTML5, CSS3 AND JAVASCRIPT *(Continued)*

is dicey at best at this juncture and requires plenty of workarounds. Flash may not be going away any time soon for several reasons:

▶ Flash is hugely prevalent in websites all over the globe, so rewriting those sites could be a lengthy, arduous process. Production time is always a concern in web development.

▶ There is a battle of proprietary formats and lack of agreed-upon standards in video and audio, particularly between Google and Apple.

▶ Flash plays outside the browser (such as in kiosks and mobile apps).

▶ Games built in Flash have more security than those built in HTML5; the latter are easily hacked because the HTML 5 source is accessible.

▶ Videos bundled in Flash may be more pirate-proof than those bundled in HTML5 sites.

▶ The new Web Open Font Format (WOFF—see http://en .wikipedia.org/wiki/Web_Open_Font_Format) has not yet been universally embraced (or even fleshed out for that matter), leaving Flash to be the only interface to date that natively allows for font embedding (see below).

For more information on HTML5, see www.html5rocks.com.

For more information on Adobe Lab's efforts to bring about a tool for HTML5 development (called AdobeEdge), see http://tinyurl.com/3rvgzm2.

Embedding Your Font

These days, regardless of whether you choose Classic or TLF, you have the ability to *embed* the font(s) you select for your work so that Flash Player is able to display the fonts you intended to display and not make any substitutions regardless of whether the viewer has a particular font installed on their computer or not. You can embed specific font families or choose to embed only certain portions of a font family—for example, maybe you want to exclude the special characters associated with a given font family because you know you won't be using special characters in your work. Note that various font families have lots and lots of segments called *character ranges* that consist of *glyphs*, that is, symbols. So Times

New Roman may not necessarily be just an English font. There may be character ranges that represent the TNR typography in different languages and for special characters such as various currency symbols, punctuation, and so on. You will use this exercise to learn how to embed fonts.

1. Using the Flash document you just created, click Text ➤ Font Embedding from the Flash main menu to bring up the Font Embedding dialog (see Figure 5.4). Clicking the plus-sign button on the left side of the Font Embedding dialog actually embeds the font in the file. The newly embedded font will also show up in the library.

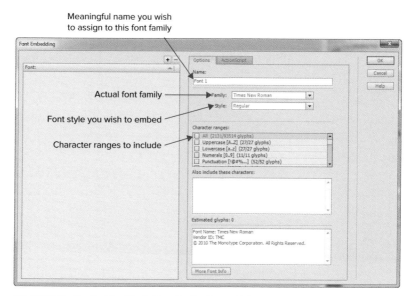

FIGURE 5.4 The Flash Font Embedding dialog

2. Because you drew a TNR text field first, the Font Embedding dialog shows it first.

3. In the Name box, type **Times New Roman**.

4. The Family drop-down shows the Times family, which is okay for now.

5. The Style drop-down is set for Regular, which is also okay.

6. Let's suppose you don't plan on including any special characters or numbers in this content. Click the Uppercase and Lowercase check boxes.

7. Click OK. The TNR font family is embedded in the current Flash document.

8. Repeat steps 3 through 7 using Arial in the Name box, selecting Arial from the Family drop-down, and choosing the same character ranges as you did with TNR.

Why embed fonts? It's useful if it is likely the viewer will not have the font installed on their local computer. Maybe you purchase a special font from a typographer, or download a group of fonts from a design software company such as Adobe, or you're using non-English characters such as Japanese kanji. Odds are fairly good the viewer will not have the font or special characters installed, thus the need to embed them.

Why would you *not* want to embed fonts? Embedding fonts makes your SWF file larger, which may not be good, especially if the file is already fairly large and the fonts you're using are common. Remember, the larger the file, the longer the viewer has to wait for it to load, which may frustrate and drive away the viewer. There's really no need to embed common fonts such as Arial or Times New Roman because they are likely installed on most English-language computers.

Starting with Creative Suite 5 (CS5), when you test your movies, Flash warns you that you may want to embed fonts, even though the font you're using is quite common.

Using Placeholder Text

It's beneficial for you to know about *Lorem Ipsum*, which is a fake Latin-like language that was invented so that designers could have non-readable text to put into text fields. The concept is this: If you're a designer working on text fields, you have two issues. First, the content may not be ready before the design. Second, if it is, reading it may take you away from the actual design's look and feel.

Lorem Ipsum allows you to take care of both situations easily. A Lorem Ipsum generator site you can use is www.lipsum.com. You simply tell the site how many paragraphs of Lorem Ipsum to generate for you, then copy and paste it into your text boxes. Once you have your layout squared away, you can go in and write the content or pass the writing work on to your content writers.

Checking Your Spelling

Nothing looks more unprofessional than unintentional spelling errors in your textual content. Follow these steps to avoid that:

1. From the Flash main, click Text ➤ Check Spelling to start spell-checking.

2. Click Text ➤ Spelling Setup to adjust the spell checker's options.

KEEP YOUR FONT CHOICES TO A MINIMUM

Keep your font choices to one or two selections. Overloading your content with multiple fonts may look cool but will ultimately drive viewers away because the content appears too busy. Also, for the same reason, avoid the desire to use fancy fonts that may be difficult to read. Finally, be aware that a black font on a red background or vice versa may be very difficult for color-blind users to read, especially if the font is small.

Using Classic Text

Even though TLF exists, there may be a lot of occasions when you opt to go with Classic text instead. TLF brings a lot more capability to the party, but in many cases it's not required.

Deciding to Use Classic Text

You should definitely use Classic Text if you're not at all certain which versions of Flash Player your viewers will be using. For example, if you are crafting a multinational site and you're afraid many of your viewers won't have the latest version of Flash Player installed, Classic Text is a good choice.

If you're not going to do anything fancy with your text fields, you're using ordinary well-known fonts, and you don't require the typography tools that TLF brings to you, Classic Text is a good option.

Inserting Classic Text Boxes

There are three kinds of Classic Text boxes you can create in Flash:

Input text   This is a text field in which the user is allowed to key in data. ActionScript is required to make them functional.

Dynamic text   With this kind of text field, you change the text using ActionScript.

Static text   These text fields just display text on the screen and do nothing else.

The Text Type option is important. When you're new to Flash and you don't know any AS3, you'll likely settle for the Static text field type. This means the text simply sits on the screen and there are no expectations of it, apart from showing readable text. Use Static for titles, labels, and other such text requirements. One good use for static text is for button labels. The following exercise will show you how.

Certification Objective

1. Press T to activate the Text tool.

2. From the text engine drop-down, make sure Classic Text is selected.

3. From the text type drop-down, make sure Static Text is selected.

4. The first things you notice in the Property inspector are several text options (see Figure 5.5).

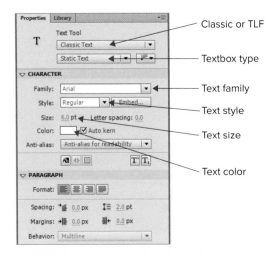

FIGURE 5.5 Text options in the Property inspector

5. Click anywhere on the stage and type in a long sentence. Notice that Flash does not bother wrapping the text; it just keeps extending it beyond the edge of the stage.

6. Click away from the text field you created in step 3 and then click and drag to create a new text field.

7. Type in a long sentence, noting that the text goes to the edge of where you finished dragging and then begins to wrap (see Figure 5.6).

8. Click away from the text fields, and then click to begin a new text field.

9. Before you begin writing some text, click the Align Center button in the Paragraph section. Flash will now center any text you type.

The Paragraph drop-down allows you to set the type of justification (paragraph alignment) you want the text to have: left, right, center, or fully justified. The default is left-justified, right-ragged-edge text. Caution: With fully justified text, Flash makes decisions about letter spacing to provide a nice smooth line of letters on each side of the paragraph and you may wind up with some funny-looking text because of the width variations. You also have the ability to set margins and line spacing in the Paragraph section.

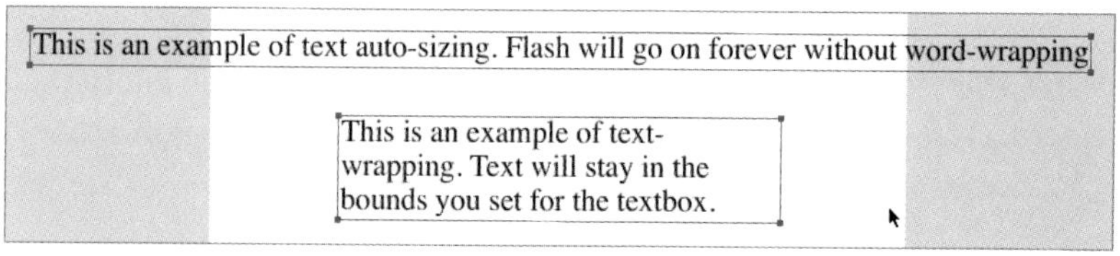

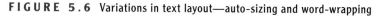

FIGURE 5.6 Variations in text layout—auto-sizing and word-wrapping

N O T E A text field you purposely size with given proportions is called a fixed-width text field. Text fields that are able to auto-resize to accommodate an increase in text are called expanding-width text fields.

Apart from the font you want to use and its size, style, and color, when you're first beginning to use Flash the advanced options probably won't make much difference to you. *Kerning*, for example, is the spacing between letters. Note that *auto-kerning* is turned on by default in Flash, so you can rely on Flash to handle the letter spacing for you.

Once you have created some text, two new items pop up in the Property inspector (see Figure 5.7):

We will deal with programmatically manipulating text fields using AS3 in Chapter 13.

Options This drop-down allows you to select text to which you'd like to link a website. You key the site's URL in the Link box and select the way in which you want the page to appear when selected.

Filters You have the ability to apply text filters to your text. More on this later on in the chapter.

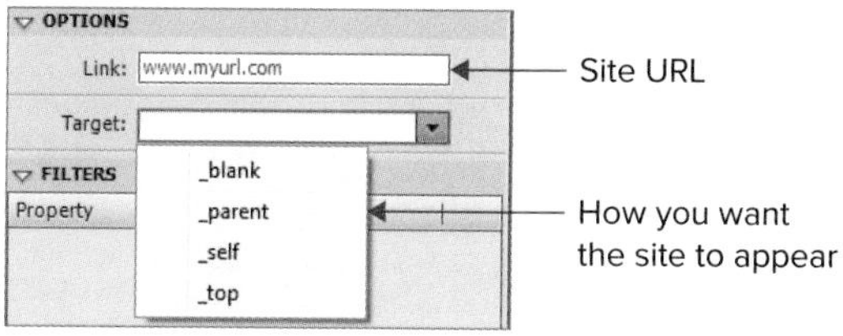

FIGURE 5.7 Additional options that show up in the Property inspector when text is created

Using Text Layout Framework

Starting with Flash Professional Creative Suite 5 (CS5), Adobe modified the product to include a new way to create text and utilize fonts. This new system is called the Text Layout Framework (TLF). The new text engine was built entirely using ActionScript 3.0 and will not work with Flash documents utilizing ActionScript 2.0. Additionally, TLF will not work when viewers are using Flash Player 9 or earlier versions. Viewers must be using Flash Player 10 or higher for TLF to work.

Deciding to Use TLF

TLF is a typography *engine*, the purpose of which is to bring more granularity to typeface and formatting characteristics. In certain ways it is somewhat similar to Classic Text, in the sense that the adjustments you make to the text are similar. However, TLF brings a lot more control to your text manipulation. Figure 5.8 shows the TLF screen.

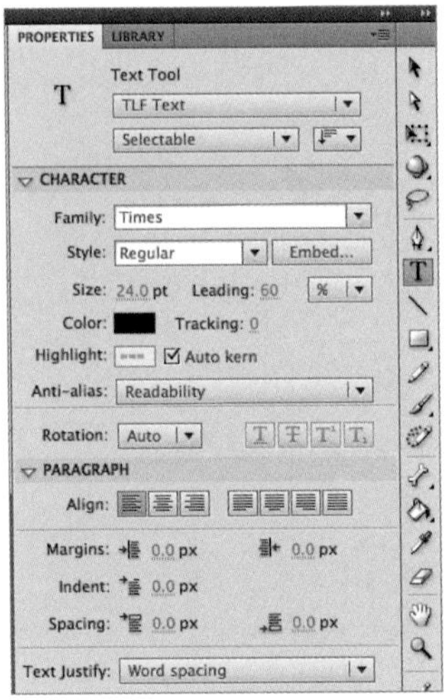

FIGURE 5.8 TLF properties screen

Recall that you switch from Classic to TLF text by simply clicking the text type drop-down at the top of the properties screen.

There are some additional features those who are new to Flash may be interested in with TLF:

Leading The typographic term *leading* (pronounced "ledding") refers to the distance between lines of text. TLF provides a leading setting, which gives designers more flexibility in how the text is vertically spaced.

Paragraph last line alignment   TLF also provides the ability to manage how the last line of each paragraph is aligned relative to the paragraph: start, center, end, or fully justified.

Text rotation   You can rotate your text using the TLF text rotation capability.

Strikethrough and Underline   With TLF, a couple of new buttons are included next to Toggle the subscript and Toggle the superscript: Strikethrough and Underline. Strikethrough is a useful thing when various people are editing the same text. An editor can use strikethrough to denote text that should be deleted and send it back to the author along with suggestions for revision. Incidentally, this is how it works in the book-writing business as well. Note that underline is not available with Classic Text.

Inserting TLF Text Boxes

Somewhat similar to Classic Text, TLF has three different text field selections:

Editable   Similar to Classic's input text type, editable allows users to key data into the text field. AS3 is required to take what the user typed and do something with it.

Selectable   Basically translating to Classic's dynamic text type, selectable means you can get at the text field with AS3 and manipulate it in code.

Read Only   Similar to Static text in the Classic version, this is the text field type you'll select when you want static text on the screen. A read only text field allows you to create an *instance name* for the box, which makes it addressable in AS3. For example, if you were to have a read only text box on the screen you wanted to use AS3 code to move it if a certain event happens. You cannot do this with a Classic static text field but you can with dynamic and input text fields.

MAKING YOUR FONTS LOOK SMOOTH

Both Classic and TLF include the ability to adjust *anti-aliasing* capabilities. What is that anyway? Sometimes vector fonts are better when they are *not* vector based, but instead raster based. For example, when a font is very tiny, it may render better as a raster-based font because the individual pixels can be adjusted to show a truer image. Anti-aliasing deals with figuring out which pixels actually make up a letter and adjusting the color of the pixels accordingly so that the letter displays more correctly. For more information on anti-aliasing, see http://en.wikipedia.org/wiki/Font_rasterization.

You will use this exercise to create a Read Only TLF text field.

1. Press T to activate the Text tool.

2. Select TLF from the engine type drop-down.

3. Select Read Only from the text type drop-down.

4. In the Paragraph section, make sure the alignment is set to Align to start (first box on left).

5. Set the font size to 24.

6. Set the font to Times New Roman.

7. Click and drag a square on the stage to begin the text field.

8. Type in a long sentence, noting that Flash does not wrap the text.

9. Click away from the current text field. The Text tool remains active.

10. Click and drag right and down to create a box about one-third the size of the stage.

11. Type in a paragraph, long enough to go just to the bottom of the box you drew.

12. Observe the two text flow boxes (see Figure 5.9).

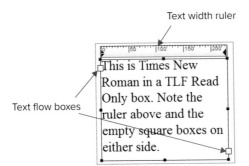

FIGURE 5.9 A TLF Read Only text field—note ruler and text flow boxes

Note that the ruler units are dictated by the settings in the Document Settings screen brought up by clicking Modify ➤ Document in the Flash main menu.

Additionally, and more important, Adobe has implemented a feature taken from its desktop publishing product InDesign: text flow boxes. The concept is straightforward and easy to implement. You've read articles in magazines or newspapers that stop at one page and start at another. This is handled in desktop publishing software by designating text fields that are chained together using *flow boxes*. This is great because you can set up your text fields to match the size restrictions of the page you are designing; you're not forced to accommodate by reducing text size or other page features.

13. Click away from the current text field, noting that the Text tool remains active.

14. Click and drag a second text field about the same size as the first.

15. In the text field you created in the previous steps, click at the end of the last sentence you wrote to begin adding more text. (This will require two clicks: one to activate the previous text field, another to get you to the end of your sentence.)

16. Type another paragraph, extending the previous one you wrote.

17. Note that you cannot read all of the text you just typed because Flash won't display anything below the lower boundary of the text field.

18. In the first text field, click the lower-right flow corner. The icon changes to show you're in text field linking mode (see Figure 5.10).

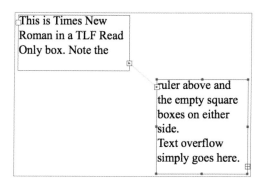

FIGURE 5.10 Linking TLF Read Only text fields (note mouse cursor change)

19. In the second text field, click the upper-left flow box.

20. The text that won't fit in the first text field shows up in the second. Selectable and Editable text fields also provide the linking feature. As with Classic Text boxes, once you've selected the type of TLF text field you want, you either single-click and begin typing or click and drag to change the size. TLF text fields automatically provide control points at the corners and in the middle of the box boundaries for changing the size of the box.

> **N O T E**   You can double-click the white box (of which two are shown in Figure 5.10) to convert it to an auto-sizing text field. If you started with an auto-sizing text field, the white box is replaced by a white circle. Double-clicking the white circle turns it into a box you must deliberately resize.

21. In one of the text fields you just linked, click one of the black square control points to resize the box. The mouse cursor changes to a double-headed vertical or horizontal arrow, depending on the direction of resize you wish to initiate. Pointing to the corner shows an angular double-headed arrow, meaning you intend to resize both horizontal and vertical measures at the same time.

22. As the box diminishes in size, some text no longer displays.

   Once you have keyed some text into a TLF text field, many more options show up in the Property Inspector. For example, you have the ability to show your text in 3D (Figure 5.11) and are given an additional z-axis. Changing the property makes the text field jump out of the page a bit, giving it the image of being farther toward or farther away from you, depending on which number you set.

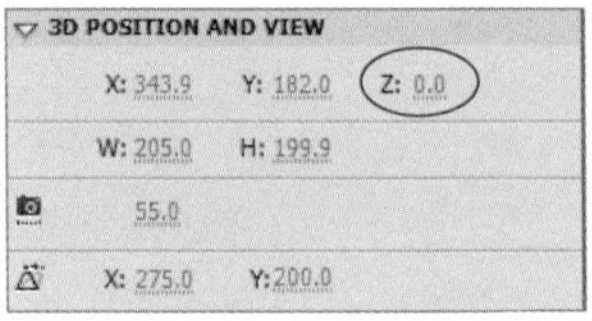

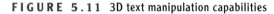

FIGURE 5.11 3D text manipulation capabilities

   You can provide a link to a website and adjust the way the new link shows up as well as use some advanced tools for managing the case of your text (uppercase, lowercase, caps to small caps, lowercase to small caps, see Figure 5.12). A neat new feature is the ability to break the text up into columns (Figure 5.13). You can manipulate the color effect of the font (Figure 5.14) and you can modify the display characteristics of the text (Figure 5.15). Some of these features are advanced; others you may find yourself using fairly regularly. It's relevant to your design expertise and experience, especially in the area of typography.

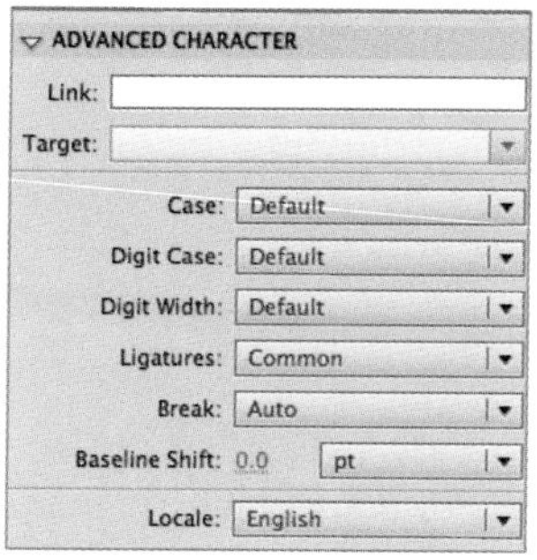

FIGURE 5.12 Managing the text's case

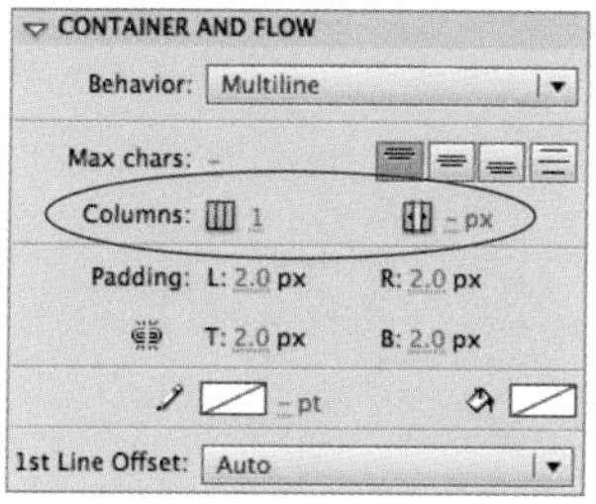

FIGURE 5.13 Column display setting

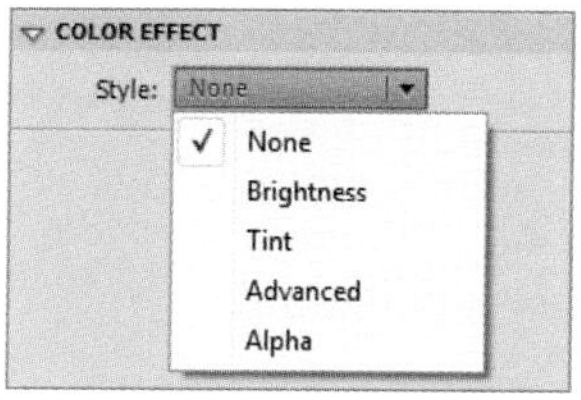

FIGURE 5.14 Color effect options for text

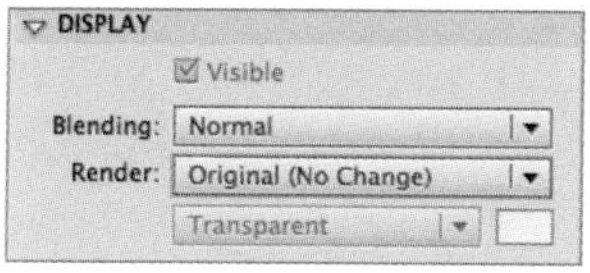

FIGURE 5.15 Changing display characteristics of text

The best thing to do is create some new read only text fields and simply start changing the text inside to see how the settings affect the text.

Finally, you can apply text filters to your text. This changes the text to add some features that pop the text off the screen a bit. Used judiciously, text filters can help you create some stunning effects.

23. Press V to activate the Selection tool.

24. Marquee around all of the active text fields.

25. Press Delete to erase them.

26. Press T to activate the Text tool.

27. Make sure TLF Read Only is still active.

28. Click and drag a smallish text field.

29. Type in some text.

30. In the Property inspector, scroll to the bottom where you'll see the Text Filters section (Figure 5.16).

31. Click the lower-left button to create a new filter: you'll see a pop-up like the one in Figure 5.16.

32. Select Drop Shadow. Your text should look similar to Figure 5.17.

33. In the filter options, change the drop shadow color from the default black to red.

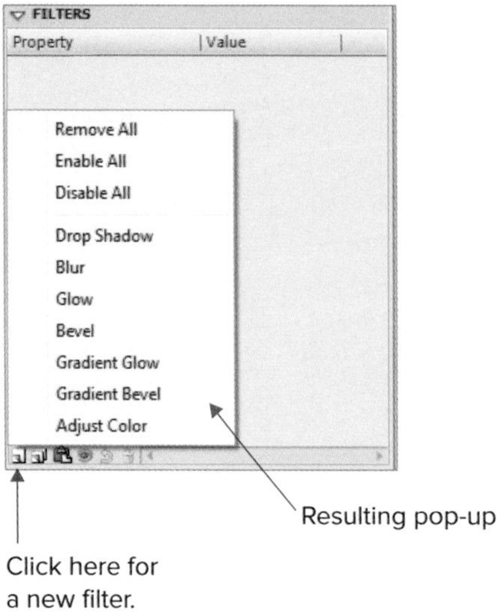

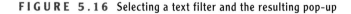

FIGURE 5.16 Selecting a text filter and the resulting pop-up

FIGURE 5.17 A Drop Shadow text filter applied to some text

You are allowed to apply more than one text filter, but go easy. You can get some pretty messy-looking text if you go overboard.

WHAT ELSE DOES TLF BRING TO THE PARTY?

In addition to the above-listed new features, the updates to text formatting via TLF are astounding: TLF allows for you to introduce multiple languages into the same (or separate) text fields, including right-to-left reading. The list of typographic controls has been greatly enlarged with TLF as well: allowing for both typographic and digit case capabilities, support for super and subscripts, advanced kerning, tracking and leading functions, a feature called "discretionary hyphens" meaning that the hyphens appear when text needs to be broken at the end of a line, graphics which can be included in line with the text, support for tabs, and the ability to programmatically style text using XML, and new anti-aliasing support for compact format font (CFF) fonts, among others.

THE ESSENTIALS AND BEYOND

This chapter was about how to put text in Flash rich media documents. You learned there are two text engines: Classic and TLF. You also learned that there three basic kinds of text fields: those for static text, those for dynamic text you intend to change in the field using AS3, and those for input text you will use to garner input from the user. You also learned about the new offerings in TLF text.

Now you should try your hand at using TLF text flow from one frame to another.

1. Visit www.lipsum.com and generate two paragraphs' worth of Lorem Ipsum content.

2. Use your mouse to highlight the Lorem Ipsum.

3. Press Ctrl+C (Command+C on the Mac) to copy the content.

4. Open a new ActionScript 3.0 document.

5. Right-click frame 2 and select Insert Blank Keyframe from the context menu.

6. Click frame 1.

7. Activate the Text tool by pressing T on the keyboard.

8. Select the text engine type TLF.

(Continues)

THE ESSENTIALS AND BEYOND *(Continued)*

9.   Set the text type to Read Only.

10. Select a font you like.

11. Select a font size of 24, color black.

12. Click and drag a square in frame 1 that takes up about one-quarter of the stage's surface.

13. Repeat step 12 for frame 2.

14. Return to frame 1 and click on its text field.

15. Press Ctrl+V (Command+V on the Mac) to paste the Lorem Ipsum in the text field. Flash copies all of the text in to the text field.

16. Press V to activate the Selection tool.

17. Click the lower-right text flow box on the text field. The mouse cursor changes to show a black arrow and a little paragraph.

18. Navigate to frame 2.

19. Click the upper-right text flow box in frame 2's text field. Flash flows as much of the Lorem Ipsum content as it can from frame 1's text field to frame 2's. Note that the lower-right text flow box has a marking in it, indicating it cannot accommodate all of the text.

> ipsum. Phasellus est sapien, convallis a auctor ac, gravida non nunc. Nulla eget odio nec elit imperdiet euismod nec vel odio. Proin purus nulla, dapibus sit amet pharetra ac, tempor sit amet turpis. Maecenas velit dolor, mattis id cursus eu, fermentum et mi. Pellentesque lorem nibh, semper at cursus sit amet, luctus ut ante. Morbi eleifend dolor vitae justo aliquam viverra. Nullam mi massa, sagittis a sodales vulputate, varius sit amet nisl. Donec blandit placerat lacinia. Etiam pulvinar elit

20. Repeat the process by inserting new frames and text fields until all of the Lorem Ipsum text is visible.

Using this technique, you can stream text from frame 1 of your scene to outlying frames—magazine style.

ANSWER TO ADDITIONAL EXERCISE

See TextFlow.fla if you need help getting started.

CHAPTER 6

Working with Flash Symbols

When you draw something on the stage and you like it, you may decide you want to store it and reuse a copy of it later, or you may decide you want to use multiple copies of it in your current document. Likewise, once you learn how to create buttons, a very efficient thing to do is create a generic button, store it, and then modify it for different purposes. Finally, one of the most powerful elements you can create in Flash is a movie clip that you store just like any other graphic element. You then just drag it onto the stage when you need it.

All of these things in Flash—graphics, buttons, and movie clips—are called *symbols*. This chapter shows you how to create symbols, the differences between them, and how to reuse them. You'll also learn about the place where you store your symbols: the library.

▶ **Creating graphic symbols**

▶ **Creating button symbols**

▶ **Creating movie clip symbols**

▶ **Understanding symbol instances**

Creating Graphic Symbols

Five elements can be converted into a graphic symbol: artwork, photo(s), main-timeline-level animations, text fields, and FLV video.

The remainder of this chapter deals with creating your own graphics. However, Flash supports the ability for you to import graphics from outside sources as well as the choice of whether to import external graphics to the stage or the library.

There are a variety of supported graphic file types Flash cam import: Adobe Illustrator (.ai) and Photoshop (.psd), AutoCAD (.dxf), bitmaps (.bmp), enhanced Windows metafile (.emf), FutureSplash player (.spl), GIFs and animated GIFs, JPEG and JPGs, PNGs, older Flash Player files (.swf), Windows metafile (.wmf) and Adobe XML graphic files (.fxg). If you have QuickTime 4 or later installed you can also import TIF or TIFF files and QuickTime images (.qtif).

The choice of whether to import to the stage or library primarily depends on whether you intend to reuse the graphic or if it's a one-time instance. For example, importing a background photo to the stage might work for you whereas importing a photo you intend to use for button decorations would be something you'd decide to import to the library and reuse as an instance (more about instances later on in this chapter).

Converting Assets to a Symbol

Certification Objective

Follow these steps to create an art asset and convert it into a graphic symbol:

1. Open a new ActionScript 3.0 document.

2. Draw a rectangle or oval on the stage using both a stroke and fill color. (It does not matter if you use Merge- or Object-Drawing mode.)

3. Press V to activate the Selection tool.

4. Draw a marquee around the object you just created.

5. You now have three choices for bringing up the Create New Symbol dialog:

   a. Right-click and select Convert To Symbol from the context menu.

   b. Select Insert ➤ New Symbol from the Flash main menu.

   c. Press the F8 key.

6. The Create New Symbol dialog appears (Figure 6.1)—virtually the same box you'll use for any of the three symbols (graphic, button, movie clip).

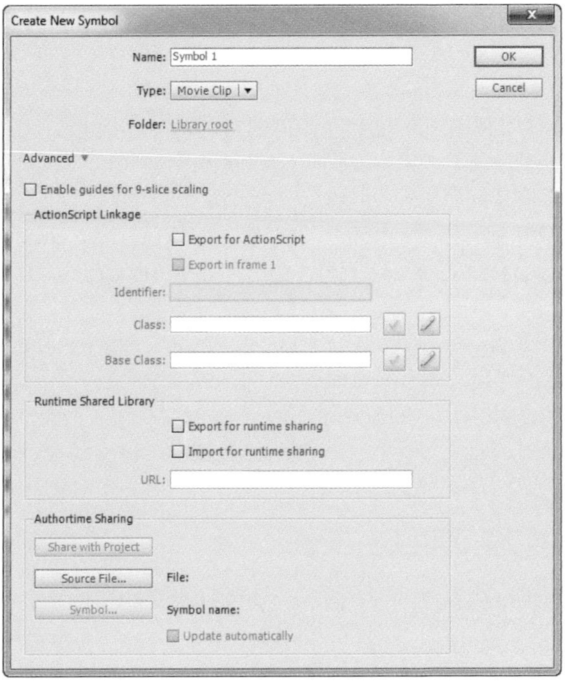

FIGURE 6.1 The Create New Symbol dialog

7. Select Graphic from the Type drop-down.

8. In the Name box, give the symbol a name such as grRectangle. (More on establishing a naming convention momentarily.)

9. Click OK.

10. Flash creates the symbol and stores it in the library.
    When you are in the Essentials workspace, the library is accessible via a tab on the top right side of your screen. It is a storage area where Flash keeps symbols and other files that are used in the document.

11. In the Property Inspector area, click the Library tab to see your new library member. If you're in a different workspace than Essentials and cannot see the Library tab, simply click in the Flash main menu Window ➤ Library.

The Advanced drop-down in the Create New Symbol dialog shown in Figure 6.1 is more for ActionScript coding purposes and not necessary to worry about at this point; however, you'll read a little bit more about it near the end of the chapter.

Artwork in Flash is usually created from various shapes put together to make up the object you wish to draw. Photographs can also be used as graphic symbols, as can animations you create on the main timeline. If you opt to turn a main timeline animation into a graphic symbol, both sounds and controls such as buttons that you may have built into the animation cannot be included in the new graphic symbol.

Grouping Assets

Once you have the shapes arranged to your liking, in most cases you should group them before creating a symbol out of them. You can always ungroup the objects if you need to make a change. Grouping them keeps everything intact and prevents you from the danger of accidentally moving a shape, distorting your artwork.

1. Continuing from the steps in the previous section, make sure the Selection tool is still active.

2. Click away from the object on the stage or the pasteboard to deactivate it.

3. Click the rectangle graphic object you just created and delete it from the stage.

4. Note the object does not disappear from the library. It is available for reuse at any time.

5. Using the Rectangle, Selection, and Free Transform tools, create a cardboard box similar to Figure 6.2. Remember that when you have the Free Transform tool activated, you can skew the sides of a rectangle to create an oblique shape and then move or rotate them into place.

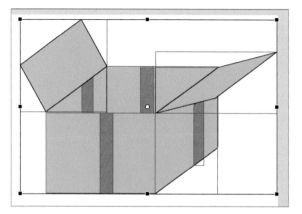

FIGURE 6.2 All of the shapes making up the cardboard box artwork, marqueed and ready for grouping

6. Once you're satisfied with your cardboard box, press V to activate the Selection tool.

7. Marquee all of the objects on the stage.

8. Press Ctrl+G (Command+G on the Mac) to group the object. Or you can click Modify ➤ Group from the Flash main menu.

9. Using the same technique you used in steps 5 through 9 in the preceding exercise, convert your cardboard box into a graphic object, giving it the name grCardboardBox.

10. Flash creates the new symbol and stores a copy of it in the library alongside the rectangle you previously created, as shown in Figure 6.3. (If you need assistance, you can open the file Box.fla on this book's website at www.sybex.com/go/flashessentials.)

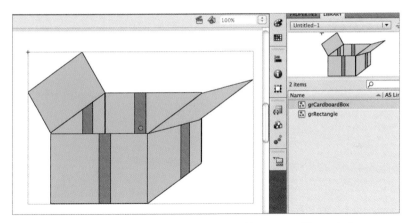

FIGURE 6.3 Cardboard box artwork turned into a graphic symbol

Once you've created your symbol, you can manipulate it just as you would shapes on the screen, resizing it, using the Free Transform tool, even setting its Color Effect options. Because it's in the library, on any frame you can simply drag the symbol out of the library, place it on the stage, and change the settings.

The Property Inspector for a graphic symbol has only a few simple controls (see Figure 6.4). You can edit the size (which you could do with the Free Transform tool as well), change the object's x- and y-coordinates, and apply a color effect such as altering the object's brightness, tint, or alpha value.

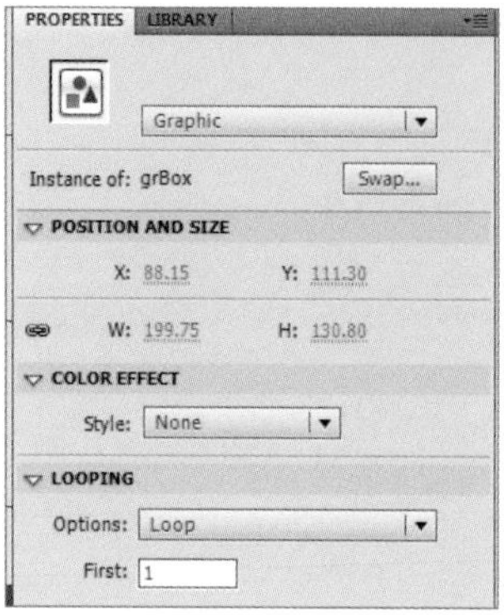

FIGURE 6.4 Graphic symbol properties

Dragging a copy of the symbol to the stage does not alter the symbol itself. Each copy you drag out of the library is called an *instance* of the object. (See the section "Understanding Symbol Instances" later in this chapter.) This is quite important because instances of a single symbol in the library take up far less disk space than if you drew several isolated pieces of artwork that looked essentially the same and then turned each of them into different symbols that you subsequently store in the library. Storing a mishmash of symbols that ultimately make up a single object may have advantages when there are different objects that can be created from their baser components, but usually it's best to just consolidate everything together into one object saved in the library.

Using the Library

Certification
Objective Like the timeline, the library is an extremely important component of Flash. In the following sections, you'll work with the library and library members.

Using the Symbols from the Library

Flash gives graphic, button, and movie clip symbols each a unique icon so you can easily recognize them in the library.

1. Press V to activate the Selection tool.

2. Click away from the cardboard box graphic, either on the stage or pasteboard, to deactivate it.

3. Click the cardboard box graphic symbol again.

4. Using the same technique you used previously to create a graphic, create a button out of the cardboard box, giving it the name btnCardboardBox.

5. Repeat steps 1 through 4, this time creating a movie clip out of the cardboard box object, giving it the name mcCardboardBox.

Your library should look similar to the one shown in Figure 6.5. The icon for button symbols looks like a hand with a finger pressing a button; movie clip symbol icons look like a gear; and graphic symbol icons show a grouping of three shapes.

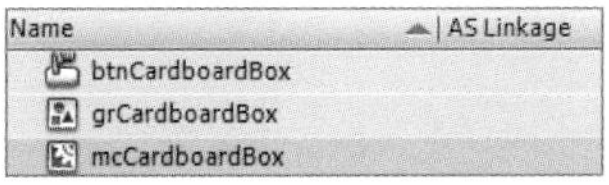

FIGURE 6.5 Library symbol icons

Implementing a Library Naming Convention

You can name your symbols anything you like (and easily rename them by double-clicking their name in the library or right-clicking them and selecting Rename). But many designers and developers like to maintain some sort of naming convention so that they can easily recognize a file by name as well as by the symbol icons automatically assigned by Flash. Also, maintaining a naming convention makes things easier when you get ready to write ActionScript code.

In Figure 6.5, you can see an example naming convention using a technique called *camel case*. When you use camel case, your filename consists of at least two words or groups of letters; the first is lowercase, and the second is shown in proper case. For example, in the case of Flash symbols, you might decide to use names beginning with *gr* for graphic symbols, *btn* for buttons, and *mc* for movie clips. Then all you need to do is add a meaningful word to the name for a particular symbol.

You don't have to use camel case, but you should consider some kind of naming convention that you consistently use to help you keep your symbols organized regardless of the project you're working on. If you're working on a team developing rich media, you should agree on what naming convention you will use.

Grouping Common Objects in the Library

Once you start filling the library up with different symbols, you'll find it time consuming and perhaps even frustrating shuffling through all of the listings. Fortunately, Flash provides the ability to create folders in the library. You can either drag existing symbols into the folder or create new symbols directly in the folder.

1. If you're not already viewing the library, click the Library tab to view the objects in your library.

2. Click the New Folder button [ICONS] to create a new folder. For example, you might make a folder called Buttons, another called Movie Clips, and one called Graphics.

3. Drag mcCardboardBox to the Movie Clips folder, grRectangle and grCardboardBox to the Graphics folder, and btnCardboardBox to the Buttons folder.

When you're done your layout should look similar to Figure 6.6.

FIGURE 6.6 Library objects grouped into folders

Depending on your work style, you might find you use graphic symbols a lot, storing them in the library and pulling them out to copy and edit for a new setting. Or, you may be the type that doesn't use them very much, opting instead to re-create artwork as needed. It's your call—there are no set standards by which you should work, and Flash easily adapts to various work habits.

Creating Button Symbols

Certification
Objective

Buttons are used when a logical decision or activity is required. For example, you might want a button that advances the viewer to the next scene in your project or one that closes a window or plays a movie.

Buttons don't have to be visible! Using transparent buttons can be quite useful in certain situations, and is perfectly permissible in Flash. One way to create an invisible button is to make the button the same color as the background; or you can hide a button in a lower layer, underneath art assets that would cover up the button. Transparent buttons can be created by simply dialing down the asset's alpha value to 0.

This is a good place to talk about the concept of a flowchart. Whereas storyboards are cartoon panels that show the basic flow of the intended artwork, flowcharts help you determine when there's a change in the *logical* flow of the content as opposed to scene change in a storyboard.

Consider a basic Flash game in which there are two decision points, each of which leads to either a good or a bad consequence. Your flowchart might look like Figure 6.7. This flowchart was created using Microsoft Word, but you could just as easily create it using Flash.

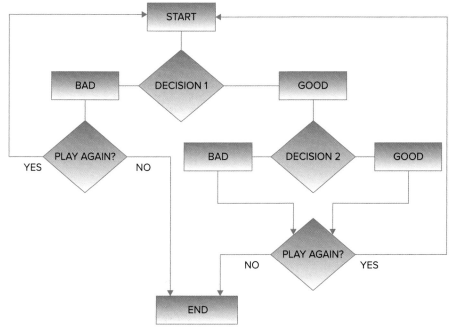

FIGURE 6.7 Sample flowchart

At the places where the Yes and No choices are located, you probably want to put some buttons that, when clicked, allow the transference of the current content to a new scene. For example, you might have one scene on frame 1, another on frame 2 and so on. When the movie plays, the viewer is first sent to frame 1, and then at decision time, the location is changed.

Buttons are animations, but they're special animations with only four frames:

Up   This is what the button looks like in its normal state, when it is not being pressed or hovered over.

Over   When you move your mouse over the button, the Over state is determined by this frame.

Down   When the viewer presses a button, the Down state frame is played.

Hit   We touched on this in Chapter 1: the Hit state is used to manipulate the area on the stage where Flash should consider the button to be pressed. The Hit state can be represented by an irregular shaped or a regular shape simply placed elsewhere on the stage.

When I use the word *scene*, I mean the view on one frame versus another. Flash has a different concept for scene, a concept we won't touch on in this book.

Manually Creating a Button

To manually create a button, do the following:

1. Using the Selection tool, marquee and delete any items currently on the stage.

2. Create a shape or shapes you'd like to have for your button. You are not limited to what kind of shape, color, or style you want to use.

3. If you've created the button out of various shapes, once you're happy with the outcome, marquee them and group them into one grouped object using Ctrl+G.

4. Now you're at a decision point: Will you need this button only one time, or do you think you'll reuse it later in a different scene?

5. If you think you'll reuse the button, save it in the library as a button object without applying any text to it.

6. If you'll be using the button only one time, create some text for it and drag it over the shape, marquee both the shape and the text, group them, and then save as a button in the library.

7. Place the button in the appropriate location on the stage.

8. You can use the Free Transform tool to resize, reshape, or rotate the button as you see fit.

You don't want to put text on the generic button shape you've created so you can apply text to new buttons as you create them and then save them in the library with a new button symbol name. Suppose, for example, you have a button with the club shape from a playing card. You want to make Begin, Next, and Exit buttons from this button shape.

1. First create the club shape using Oval and Rectangle tools as needed in merge-drawing mode. No need for a stroke color; just select a fill color (see Figure 6.8). Since merge-drawing is used, there's no need to group the objects because Flash automatically combines them into one object.

FIGURE 6.8 Club shape made using standard shape tools in merge-drawing mode

2. Click away from the object anywhere on the stage or pasteboard just to make sure nothing else is selected.

3. Press V to activate the Selection tool.

4. Right-click the club object and select Convert To Symbol from the context menu.

5. Select the movie clip type for the object, giving it the name mcGenericClub. In the area where it says Folder, click Library Root to see a drop-down of the folders in your library (see Figure 6.9). Put mcGenericClub in the MovieClips folder.

FIGURE 6.9 Saving mcGenericClub to the MovieClips folder

6. Press T to activate the Text tool.

7. Click the Property Inspector tab.

8. Set the text engine to Classic and the type to Static.

9. Select an appropriate text color, such as white, as well as a sans-serif font and a font size such as 12. (All settings can be adjusted once the text object is dragged onto the club shape.)

10. Type the word **Begin**.

11. Switch to the Selection tool and drag the text onto the club shape.

12. Click away to deactivate both objects.

13. Make sure the Selection tool is still active and then marquee both objects.

14. Right-click and select Convert To Symbol from the context menu.

15. Make this a button symbol with the name btnBeginClub, saving it in the Buttons folder.

16. Check the library, noting that two new symbols now exist: one in the Graphics folder and one in the Buttons folder.

Turning the Button into an Instance

Certification
Objective

Once a button has been created, it does nothing until you've given it an instance name and you've written some AS3 code to activate it.

Whenever you create a button, since you know it's going to require an instance name to be usable, you should assign one right away.

1. Make sure the button btnBeginClub is selected.

2. If you're currently viewing the library, click the Properties tab to switch to the Property Inspector.

3. Note at the top of the Property Inspector that there is an area where you can type in an instance name. Key in the name **btnBeginClub** (see Figure 6.10).

F I G U R E 6 . 1 0 The Instance Name field for a button

You *cannot* have more than one instance with the same name in your main timeline. Suppose you wanted to use btnBeginClub more than once. In that case, you'd have to come up with two different instance names. The name of the object in the library would stay the same, however.

Editing a Button

Certification
Objective

Regardless of whether you've assigned an instance name for the button or written AS3 code for it, you can *always* edit a button by simply double-clicking it—whether it sits on the stage or has not yet been dragged to the stage but is merely represented in the library.

1. Double-click button btnBeginClub, which brings you to the button editing screen shown in Figure 6.11.

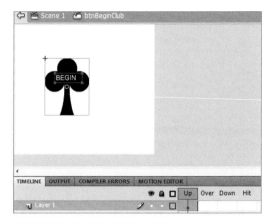

FIGURE 6.11 Button editing screen

You can see in Figure 6.11 that you're no longer on the stage—it is represented on the left side with the name Scene 1. Instead, you're editing the button symbol btnBeginClub. Additionally, in Figure 6.11 you can see the button timeline for btnBeginClub.

When you're in button-editing mode, double-clicking the button again will take you to a new editing section where you can directly edit each of the elements making up your button. Don't like the text size? In this second editing mode you can change it. When you're done, click Scene 1 to go back to the main area.

2. While still editing btnBeginClub. double-click the object.

3. You are now taken to a third level: in this case mcGenericClub. In other words, Flash is telling you that btnBeginClub is made up of the original mcGenericClub plus some text. You could make modifications to mcGenericClub at this time, but you should note that any modifications made to mcGenericClub will affect *all* other buttons made from its shape and any instances of btnBeginClub that are on the stage.

4. Click btnBeginClub to navigate back to the button with text on it.

5. In the btnBeginClub timeline, click the Over frame.

6. Right-click the Over frame and select Insert Keyframe from the context menu. Flash makes an exact copy of the image on the Up frame and places it on the Over frame.

7. Look at the Property Inspector for btnBeginClub, noting that you have a new setting called Filters (see Figure 6.12).

FIGURE 6.12 Filters options

8. In the Filters section, select Add Filter and then select Glow from the menu.

9. Change the blur color to yellow.

10. Change the Blur X and Blur Y percentage to 100.

11. Click the Inner Glow check box.

12. Click Scene 1 to exit back to the stage. Your original btnBeginClub should still be on the stage.

13. Play the movie with Ctrl+Enter (Command+Enter on the Mac).

14. Move your mouse over the button, noting that it changes to the blur color you set on the Over frame.

15. Save the changes you've made to Box.fla.

When in button-editing mode, you can simply click each of the frames, insert a new keyframe or a new blank keyframe, and modify away. Your button will reflect the changes you make when you run the movie. Recall that without an instance name and AS3, your button won't really be functional, but you can test it to see how it looks even without those functionality prerequisites.

Using a Prebuilt Button

Adobe has included some pre-built *components* you can put into your scene, one of which is a prebuilt button. When using a button component, you don't need to go through the work of creating a shape and applying text and then converting the two into a button. You simply select the Components panel, navigate to the User Interface section, and double-click the button object or drag it onto the stage.

1. From the Flash main menu, click File ➤ New to create a new ActionScript 3.0 document.

2. Open the Components panel (third panel from bottom in the panel column just left of the Property Inspector).

3. Navigate to User Interface and double-click Button. A new button shows up on the stage (see Figure 6.13).

4. Click the Library tab to note that Flash creates the button plus a Component Assets folder with support files needed for the button.

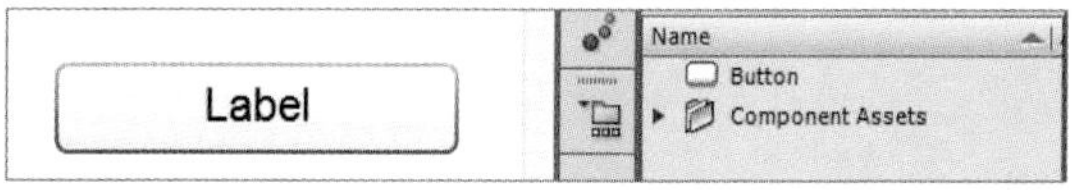

FIGURE 6.13 Creating a new button using a button in the prebuilt components panel

5. Switch back to the Property Inspector.

6. Using the Selection tool, move the object to where you'd like to place it

7. In the Component Parameters drop-down in the button's properties section, change button's label to My Button (see Figure 6.14).

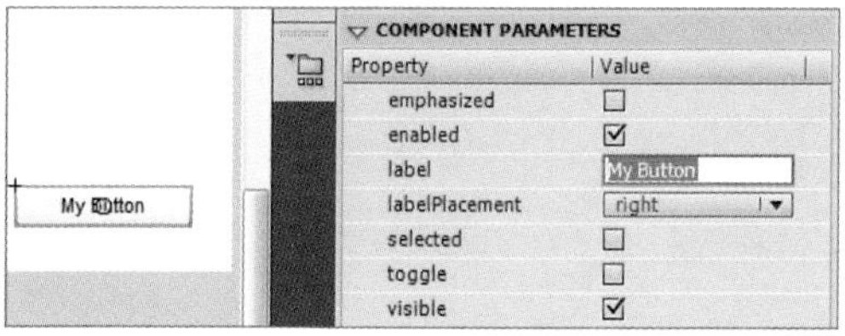

FIGURE 6.14 Creating a new button using a button from the prebuilt components panel

8. Play the movie using Ctrl+Enter (Command+Enter on the Mac) and test the button, noting that the Down frame is already set for you, thus the button darkens when you click it.

9. Close the document you used to create a prebuilt button without saving changes.

In the case of custom or pre-built buttons, the primary thing you're shooting for is consistency. Don't put a bunch of different styles of buttons on the page for viewers to click. Once you've got a pattern you like, stick with it throughout.

The advantages of a prebuilt button component are obvious: You don't have to go through all the heavy lifting to create a button. And there are more properties you can set than with a conventional button object.

The disadvantage of a prebuilt button component is that you can't control its shape, but you can control the color effect and apply a filter. The button looks professionally crafted and has more hit state options, which is great. But there may be times when you want to send a different kind of stylistic signal with your button. So there's a creative aspect you'll want to consider when coming up with your button ideas, decisions that may lead you to create custom buttons or opt for a prebuilt button component.

Creating Movie Clip Symbols

Certification Objective

Movie clips are the engines of animation. When you understand how to create a movie clip, a whole new world opens up: You have practically unlimited ways of presenting your ideas in motion.

Movie clips are made by developing frames and layers that change over time. Sounds easy, but it takes quite a bit of thought when you're architecting a movie clip. When do you want things to happen? At what point does the scene entirely change? What artistic elements appear in the movie clip and when? Will you be happy with 2D or do you require 3D motion or elements in your animation?

You can create animations directly on the stage in the main timeline or as a separate movie clip symbol. When you create a movie clip symbol for your animations, just drag them onto the stage at the point where you want them to appear.

If you've created an animation on the stage and you want to convert it into a movie clip, simply highlight all the frames in all of the layers that make up the animation, right-click the highlighted frames, and select Edit ➤ Cut Frames from the context menu. Next create a new movie clip symbol and paste the frames into place by right-clicking frame 1 of the movie clip symbol and selecting Edit ➤ Paste Frames. The frames that the animation comprises will be moved from the stage to the new movie clip symbol.

1. From the Flash main menu, create a new ActionScript 3.0 document.

2. From the Flash main menu, click Insert ➤ New Symbol.

3. In the New Symbol dialog, make sure Movie Clip is selected in the Type drop-down and give the move clip the name mcMyMovieClip.

4. Click OK. You are immediately taken away from the stage into editing mode for your new movie clip.

5. Note that the timeline looks *exactly* like the main timeline, but it is not! This timeline belongs to the movie clip.

6. Note the small cross in the middle of the stage denoting the movie clip's registration point. This is useful when you want to center objects in the movie clip.

7. Draw a large oval on the stage. You can choose a stroke or not, just remember that if you opt for a stroke and you're in merge-drawing mode, you'll need to double-click the object to select both the fill and stroke if you want to move it.

8. Click the Align panel (third from top in the vertical line of panels to the left of the Property Inspector).

9. Click the Align To Stage button.

10. Click the upper-left button in the Align panel (Figure 6.15). This button aligns the left edge of the object to the stage (in this case, the plus sign in the middle of the movie clip editing screen).

11. Click the fourth button from the right on the top row. This button aligns the object's top edge with the stage.

FIGURE 6.15 The Align panel

12. The object is now properly centered (Figure 6.16). The Align panel works with objects on the stage or in editing mode for movie clips, buttons, or graphics.

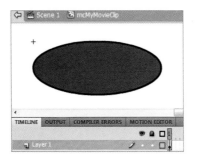

FIGURE 6.16 An oval movie clip object

13. Right-click frame 2 and select Insert Keyframe from the context menu. Flash makes a duplicate copy of the oval on frame 1.

14. Make a change to the oval in frame 2. Change its color, size, stroke color, or whatever you like. Make the change obvious enough that it will show up when the movie plays.

15. Repeat for the next five to seven frames, making alterations to each succeeding object.

16. Click Scene 1 to exit movie clip editing mode and go back to the stage.

17. Drag a copy of the movie clip from the library onto the stage.

18. Use the Align tool's Match Width and Match Height buttons to size the movie clip to the exact size of the stage.

19. Play the movie using Ctrl+Enter (Command+Enter on the Mac).

20. Note that the movie loops over and over. Once it reaches the end frame, it starts back at the beginning and plays again. ActionScript is required to make the movie stop in one loop iteration.

21. If you desire, save the file with a meaningful filename; then close the file, returning back to the file containing btnBeginClub.

Creating and Editing Symbol Instances

Certification Objective

When you drag a symbol out of the library and place it onto the stage, you've created an *instance* of that particular symbol object. It doesn't matter which frame or layer you drag a new instance to. You can have several instances sharing the stage with one another, or you can have instances in succeeding frames. You can even place instances on the same frame but on different layers. The Property Inspector will alert you that an object on the stage is an instance of a given named symbol (see Figure 6.17).

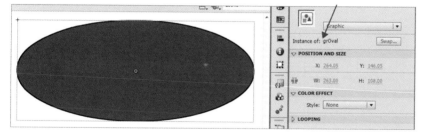

FIGURE 6.17 The Property Inspector shows you have an instance of a graphic object

Note that something as simple as a color change can be affected on an instance-by-instance basis.

1. Open the Box.fla file from this book's website at www.sybex.com/go/ flashessentials. You'll use the following steps to create, edit, and alter an instance.

2. Using the Selection tool, click btnBeginClub and delete it.

3. From the library, drag an instance of grCardboardBox out onto the stage.

4. Use the Free Transform tool to resize, rotate, or skew the object as desired.

5. Drag a second instance of grCardboardBox onto the stage and use the Free Transform tool to resize it as well.

6. With the second instance you just dragged out still active, in the Color Effect section in the Property Inspector, select Tint from the Style drop-down.

7. Alter this instance's color (see Figure 6.18).

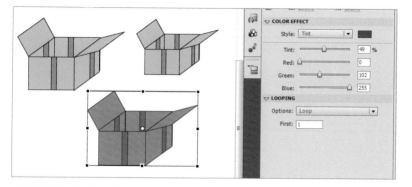

FIGURE 6.18 Altering a single instance's properties

When you drag an instance of a symbol onto the stage and double-click it to edit it or double-click the object in the library to edit it, the changes you make are made to *all* instances of the object that happen to be on the stage at any frame or layer. But when you edit one instance on the stage, such as you just did by changing its tint, you change only that object's attributes.

If you want make more complicated changes to a symbol but keep the original design intact, you should right-click it and select Convert To Symbol in the context menu to make a new symbol out of it, giving it a new name. Double-click the new symbol to make the changes you desire.

Note that you cannot assign an instance name to graphic symbols.

Understanding ActionScript Linkages

Most library settings shown in Figure 6.1 are obvious, but one may be confusing to you: ActionScript Linkage. The concept is this: *with the exception of graphic symbols*, anything on the stage or in the library that you want to manipulate using AS3 code must have a name associated with it. Nongraphic symbol items on the stage are given instance names. Button and movie clip symbols stored in the library are given *ActionScript Linkage* names.

1. Suppose that you want to make btnBeginClub useful by keying in some AS3 code for it. The first thing you need to do is drag an instance of btnBeginClub to the stage.

2. Using the Free Transform tool, resize btnBeginClub to your liking.

3. Make sure btnBeginClub is selected; then in the Property Inspector at the top of the screen, type in an instance name such as btnBeginClub (see Figure 6.19). (It's not important that the library name matches the instance name as long a this is the only instance of the object. Multiple instances each require a unique instance name.)

FIGURE 6.19 Assigning an instance name to an object on the stage

4. Switch to the library by clicking the Library tab.

5. In the library, right-click the symbol btnBeginClub and select Properties from the menu.

6. In the Symbol Properties dialog, click the Advanced link.

7. In the ActionScript Linkage section, click the Export For ActionScript box.

8. Note that Flash puts the name of the library symbol in the Class box. Type in the letters AS at the end of the name (see Figure 6.20). By putting AS at the end of the name, you avoid duplication of the name given to the object you already have on the stage.

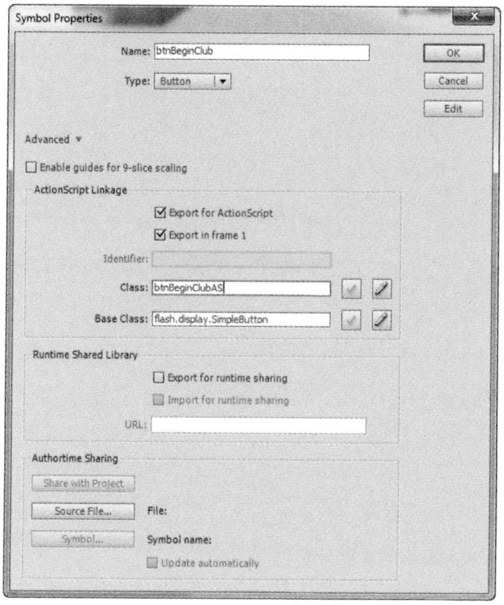

FIGURE 6.20 Linking a button with an ActionScript name. Note that the instance name btnBeginClub and the AS linkage name btnBeginClubAS are two different things. One is the name of the object in the library; the other is the name by which you will refer to that object in AS3.

9. As soon as you click OK, you're presented with the dialog shown in Figure 6.21. This is perfectly acceptable. Click OK in this dialog.
    Note that Flash now shows the new ActionScript linkage name next to the name of the object in the library.

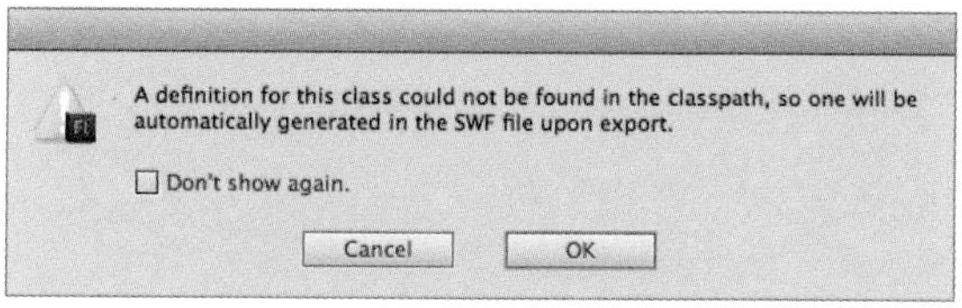

FIGURE 6.21 Symbol Properties dialog

Object, Instance, and Linkage Names

An object saved in the library could potentially have three names: The name by which you saved the object in the library, the ActionScript linkage name you gave the object in the library and the instance name you gave the object when you dragged a copy of it out on the stage. It might be helpful to think of all this naming activity this way: An object in the library doesn't need to be dragged onto the stage to exist there. You can put it on the stage using AS3 and the object's associated AS linkage name. Or else, you can drag an object to the stage and give it an instance name, thus allowing you to directly manipulate the object on the stage using AS3. Generally speaking, if you will not be programmatically adding objects in the library to the stage (or taking them off the stage), you don't need the AS linkage name, but you *do* need the instance name.

Linking a symbol in the library is an entirely different process than giving it an instance name on the stage. When a symbol has an ActionScript linkage, you can refer to it using AS3 code, programmatically putting it on the stage, resizing it, and so forth. Giving an object on the stage an instance name means you can programmatically access that symbol *instance* while it's on the stage, changing its size, shape, and color and even removing it from the stage. Thus, many symbol instances could be on the stage, and they could each have a distinct instance name, providing you with the ability to programmatically and individually manipulate each instance. You cannot assign the same instance name to different instances of a symbol, nor can you assign duplicate ActionScript linkage names to symbols in the library.

The Essentials and Beyond

In this chapter you learned about how Flash uses objects called symbols. There are three kinds: buttons, graphics, and movie clips. While you'll use all three types, the two you'll use over and over are buttons and movie clips. Think of graphics as building blocks toward buttons or movie clips. Symbols are great because they're stored in the library and available on any frame for work you want to do. They're also available in other Flash files thanks to the ability to share library contents among open files.

Buttons have a special timeline consisting of just four frames: Up, Over, Down, and Hit. You can customize buttons to look the way you want so they'll fit a given design, or you can use the buttons that Flash supplies in the Components panel. Remember that in order for a button to work, AS3 must supply the code to make it happen.

Movie clips are pieces of animation you create to take care of specific views or scenes. You create your movie clip, store it in the library, and when you're ready to use it, drop it on the stage. We've just started to touch on movie clips; there's more to come. However, the work people have done with movie clips is encyclopedic: There's simply no way a single book, especially a beginner's guide, could cover all of the amazing things folks all over the world have done with movie clips. Promise yourself that you'll perform significant movie clip research on the Web in an effort to perfect your knowledge and expertise. Just as you go to art galleries to view various artists' work, so should you make a habit of visiting various Flash-based websites to get a feel for how different designers handle the product's movie clip capabilities.

Now try your hand at a little bit more detailed custom button: one that uses more than one graphic and changes text depending on whether the button is up (i.e., not being pressed) or down (i.e., being pressed). (See `CustomButton.fla` on this book's website, `www.sybex.com/go/flashessentials`, for help.)

1. Open a new Flash ActionScript 3.0 document.

2. Name the document CustomButton.

3. Select the PolyStar tool and set its options to seven-sided star.

4. Select a fill color of red and no stroke.

5. Draw the star on the stage: Don't make it too big, but not too small either. The star should sit nicely in the lower-left corner of the stage, as though it's a button.

6. Draw a second star, this time with a yellow color.

7. Position the red star over the yellow star and rotate the red star in such a way that both star points are visible.

8. Activate the Selection tool.

9. Marquee both star objects and convert them to a graphic symbol called grStar.

10. Activate the Text tool.

11. Select the Classic Text engine and Static text type. Make the font Comic Sans, 24-point, and white.

12. Type **HELP!** in the text field.

(Continues)

THE ESSENTIALS AND BEYOND (Continued)

13. Position the text field over the grStar graphic.

14. The entire group of objects—grStar and text field—should still be active. Right-click, select Convert To Symbol, and create a button called btnStar.

15. Verify that you have grStar and btnStar in the library.

16. Double-click btnStar to enter button-editing mode.

17. In button-editing mode, click the Over frame.

18. Right-click and select Insert Keyframe from the context menu. Flash makes an exact copy of the star on the Over frame.

19. Right-click the star and select Break Apart from the context menu. Flash breaks all of the objects that were connected and makes them individual items.

20. Change the front star color to blue.

21. Change the back star points to green. (Note that if you used object-drawing mode to create the stars, you'll have to make only one change. If you used merge-drawing, however, you'll need to click the first point and Shift+click the rest to gather all the points. This is because in merge-drawing mode, Flash merges the objects together so there really is no yellow behind the blue star; there are just seven star points.)

22. Change the text to ME! instead of HELP!

23. Once your work is done, click back and forth between the Up and Over frames or scrub the playhead to make sure the button will appear correctly. The Up frame should have red and yellow stars with the word HELP! The Over frame should have blue and green stars with the word ME!

24. Click the Over frame to make sure it's currently active.

25. Right-click the Down frame and select Insert Keyframe from the context menu. Flash makes a copy of what's on the Over frame.

26. In the Down frame, change the front star's color to black and the back star's color to gray.

27. Change the wording to PLEASE! You may have to use the Selection tool to lengthen the text field to accommodate the new word. Make sure it's centered over the star.

28. Make sure the Selection tool is active.

29. Marquee all the objects on the Down frame.

30. Right-click and select Convert To Symbol from the context menu.

31. Make this object a movie clip with the name mcDarkStar.

32. Apply a glow filter with a yellow color and Blur X and Blur Y settings of 50 pixels.

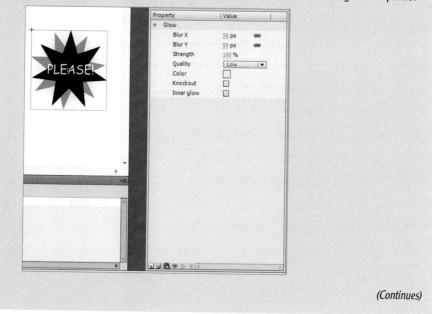

(Continues)

THE ESSENTIALS AND BEYOND (Continued)

33. Repeat steps 28 through 32 for the Over frame, calling the movie clip mcBlueStar, giving the blur a red color, and keeping the same Blur X and BlurY pixels.

34. Click Scene 1 to go back to the stage.

35. Play the movie and test the button to make sure it works. When your cursor is not close to the button, it should display the red and yellow star with the word HELP! When you hover over the button, it should turn to a blue and green star with the word ME! and you should see a red glow. When you click the button, it should turn to a black and gray star with the word PLEASE! and you should see a yellow glow.

36. Note that the button is ready but not functional because we have not yet used any AS3 to make it work. We will deal with that subject in Chapters 11, 12, and 13.

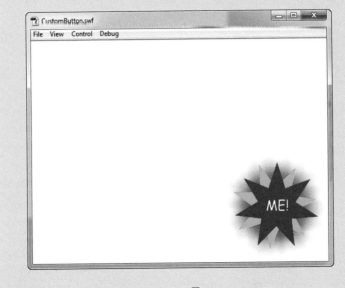

ANSWER TO ADDITIONAL EXERCISE

Refer to the file CustomButton.fla if you need additional help.

CHAPTER 7

Developing Simple Flash Animations

There are a couple of ways to create animations: frame by frame or using tweens, a technique you'll learn about in the next chapter. In this chapter, we'll start with frame-by-frame animations.

▶ **Using storyboards to describe your animation**

▶ **Creating a frame-by-frame animation**

▶ **Differentiating between a stage animation and a movie clip**

Developing Storyboards to Describe Your Animation

When you start with a new animation, generally you'll want to create a storyboard.

Storyboards are nothing more than basic cartoon panels in which you draw each of the major turning points in your scene. They frequently include labels or some descriptive text for scene elements that are complicated or in which you need to leave yourself or others some kind of reminder. You can use storyboards if you're going to work alone, but they really make sense if you're working on a team. Storyboards show the active elements of a scene, include any examples of dialogue characters might engage in, illustrate how much time has elapsed between panels, and pinpoints where the viewer's eye should be in the scene. Storyboards show transitions between scenes, sequencing of the activity in scenes, timing and navigation, and may include link information as well.

Although you can draw your storyboard panels using pencil and paper or buy storyboard software, there's really no need to do either since you have Flash, which naturally lends itself to storyboarding. You can use a layer in Flash for your storyboard panels, each of which takes up one frame, and then simply delete the panels once your artwork is finished. Don't forget you can also hide and unhide a layer. As you're working, if you want the storyboard layer out of the way, you can simply hide it and work without having to look at it.

Another advantage you have in Flash storyboarding is that you can create the background for your scenes on a layer, getting it right and then essentially leaving it alone while you flesh out the story in upper layers.

Creating a Storyboard for Cow Abduction

Certification
Objective

In Chapter 4 you created a UFO scene. Now you're going to expand it into a frame-by-frame animation called Cow Abduction (thanks to one of my students, Ginger, for his idea). You'll show a lonely desert road, move the UFOs and the moon across the scene, and include a surprise. You can use the assets from Chapter 4, but you'll start first with the storyboard.

1. In Flash, start a new ActionScript 3.0 document.

2. Name the document Cow Abduction Storyboard.
    Now you'll change the stage color or add any nuances to the scene. You'll simply use the Shape, Pen, Pencil, Eraser, and Text tools to create your storyboard. Remember, the storyboard is not the polished product: It is a rough approximation of your ideas. No need to create the Sistine Chapel at this point. For help, reference CowAbductionStoryboard.fla on this books website at www.sybex .com/go/flashessentials.

3. Using the Pencil tool, sketch a basic road moving out to a vanishing point. You can hold down the Shift key to inscribe a straight line. (We'll deal more with perspective drawing later on in the chapter.)

4. Use the Eraser tool to erase any stray lines. (Don't forget you can adjust the magnification of the document to zoom in on specific areas of work.)

5. Use the Brush tool to create mountains, hills, and foothills.

6. Use the shape tools (no fill, black stroke) to create a couple of UFOs. Remember to marquee all shapes that make up a UFO and then press Ctrl+G (Command+G on the Mac) to group them into one object.

7. Use the Brush tool to create a cactus or two.

8. Use the Text tool to write any notes about the scene.

Your first scene should look somewhat like Figure 7.1.

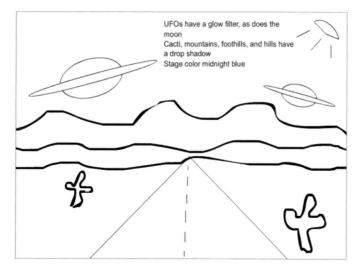

FIGURE 7.1 Starting the storyboard first panel with a vanishing point

9. Click in frame 2, right-click, and select Insert Keyframe from the context menu. Flash copies all of the art from the first frame to the second.

10. Click away from all objects.

11. Press V to activate the Selection tool.

12. Move the UFOs, rotate, and resize as needed to show they've flown from one location to another.

13. Write a note about the new scene (see Figure 7.2).

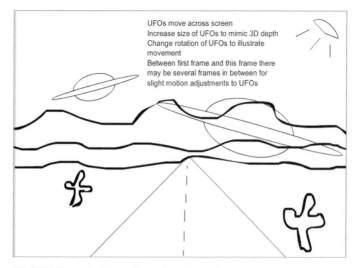

FIGURE 7.2 Second storyboard panel

Note that you don't need to include a panel in your storyboard for every frame in your animation. You'll need to use several frames, slightly adjusting the movement, rotation, and size of the UFOs to convey the motion you're looking for, which isn't the point of the storyboard.

14. Click in frame 3, right-click, and select Insert Keyframe from the context menu. Flash copies all of the art from the second frame to the third.

15. Using the various shape tools or the Brush tool, draw a cow somewhere on the pasteboard.

16. Using the Selection tool, marquee the cow to select all lines.

17. Press Ctrl+G (Command+G on the Mac) to group the elements.

18. Right-click the cow and select Insert Symbol from the context menu.

19. Make the cow a graphic symbol with the name grCow.

20. Move the cow graphic onto the stage just below the closer UFO.

21. Using the Brush or Pencil tool, make a force field image surrounding the cow (see Figure 7.3).

22. Update the notes for this panel.

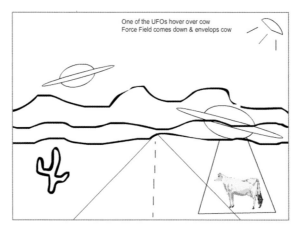

FIGURE 7.3 Third storyboard panel. Cow Image by Zero Gravity, used under Creative Commons license.

23. Click in frame 4, right-click, and select Insert Keyframe from the context menu. Flash copies all of the art from the third frame to the fourth.

24. Using the Selection tool, move the cow up to show that it's being taken into the UFO (see Figure 7.4).

25. Update the notes for this panel.

26. Be sure to save your work, but *don't close the file yet* because you'll use the cow graphic in another file.

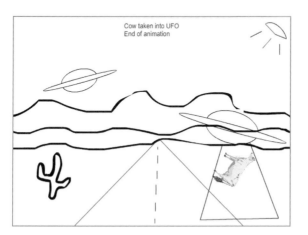

The text describing activity in your storyboard needs to be out of the way of the artwork and unobtrusive.

FIGURE 7.4 Fourth storyboard panel

Animating the Cow Abduction

Now that you have a storyboard, you can begin the actual frame-by-frame animation steps needed to create Cow Abduction.

Certification
Objective

Drawing things like a horizon and a straight road using pencil and paper requires a ruler, at minimum. But with Flash's Line tool, rulers, and guides, you can easily create your perspective views and be quite accurate at it.

1. Open the UFO file—CowAbduction.fla—included again for you here in Chapter 7.

2. From the Flash main menu, click Modify ➢ Document.

3. Set the ruler units to inches and then click OK.

4. If locked, unlock the Background layer. Make sure all other layers are locked and that the Background layer is selected.

5. Make sure the Selection tool is activated.

6. Click in the stage somewhere.

7. In the Property Inspector, change the document's size to 8" × 6".

8. From the Flash main menu, click View ➤ Rulers.

9. Drag out two vertical guides, placing one at 2" and one at 6".

10. Drag out one horizontal guide, placing it at 2".

11. Hide the Mountains/Hills folder and the UFO layer so that you can see your work on the road.

12. Click the magnification drop-down in the upper-right corner of the stage and select Fit in Window.

13. Using the Rectangle tool in Object Drawing mode with no stroke and a black fill, draw a rectangle from the bottom left and right corners of the vertical guides to meet the horizontal guide at the 2" mark. Note that Flash draws a circle around the guide points as you're drawing the rectangle. This is an indicator that you've snapped to the guides.

14. Press Q to activate the Free Transform tool. If you've somehow clicked away from your new rectangle object, click it so it's active.

15. While holding down the Shift and Ctrl keys (Command key on the Mac), point to the top-right or top-left corner of the black rectangle until you see the mouse cursor change to a white arrow with two smaller black arrows pointing at each other. Drag quickly inward and Flash will move the two corners together to form a triangle.

16. Remove the vertical guides, but leave the horizontal guide in place for use in placing the mountains, hills, and foothills later (Figure 7.5).

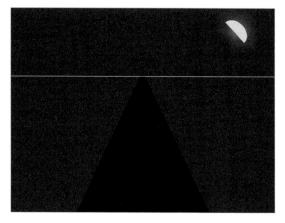

FIGURE 7.5 Starting the animation's first panel with a vanishing point

Now you'll work on the road stripes using the same principle you used for the road. Because the rulers are still visible, they will be helpful for you in performing these next steps. As the stripes become smaller, keep in mind that you'll need to enlarge the magnification so you can move a stripe into place and resize it accordingly.

17. Draw a small white rectangle in the middle of the road at the bottom of the screen. This will be your starting stripe.

18. With the Free Transform tool selected, use the Ctrl+Shift technique to squeeze the top corners of the first stripe together. Don't squeeze them together into a point at the top; leave the top points slightly apart from one another.

19. With the stripe still selected by the Free Transform tool, press Ctrl+D (Command+D on the Mac) to duplicate the stripe object.

20. Move the duplicate up above the first stripe. Flash will provide a line so that you know the two are aligned.

21. Hold down the Shift key and, clicking one of the bottom corners of the duplicate, resize the object so it's a little smaller than the lower stripe.

22. Repeat steps 19 through 21 until you have the road completely striped (see Figure 7.6).

FIGURE 7.6 Drawing the road's stripes

Now for the hills and mountains.

23. Unhide and unlock the Mountains layer underneath the Mountains/ Hills folder.

24. Make sure all the other layers are locked.

25. Press Q to activate the Free Transform tool.

26. Resize the mountains to more accurately fit the scene. Use the technique of holding down the Shift key while pointing to one of the corners to keep the initial proportions. You can also resize them horizontally and vertically.

27. Place the mountains so their base is right on the horizontal guide (see Figure 7.7).

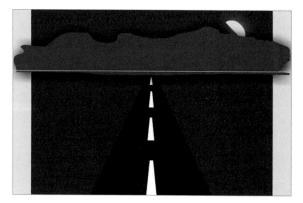

FIGURE 7.7 Moving the mountains into place

28. Repeat steps 23 through 27 for the Hills and Foothills layers.

29. When finished, drag the horizontal guide off the stage.

30. Relock all layers.

31. From the Flash main menu, click File ➣ Save As, giving this file the name Cow Abduction.

32. Hide the rulers if you desire.

33. Use this time to put permanent (i.e., nonmoving) items in the scene, such as a cactus or two, and/or some miscellaneous ground cover lines that you think would enhance it. Make sure they're on a separate layer.

   Next it's time to put the UFOs into their initial position for their flight.

34. Unhide and unlock the UFO layer.

35. Using the Free Transform tool, resize and rotate the objects to your liking.

36. Move the UFO objects into place. This is your completed starting animation scene (see Figure 7.8).

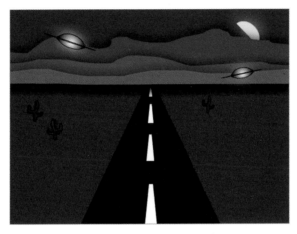

FIGURE 7.8 Moving the UFOs into place

   You can also put the cow in place, but there is something to consider when thinking about the cow. You don't want it to be completely visible until the one of the UFOs is over it ready to abduct it. What to do? The best step may be to start the cow out with a zero transparency and gradually adjust the transparency as the UFO gets close to the cow. This keeps the cow relatively out of sight until you want it to appear underneath the UFO.

37. The CowAbductionStoryboard file should still be open. For this reason, you can use objects in its library in your current file.

38. Make sure you are working in the Cow Abduction file.

39. Create a new layer called Cow. Make sure it's at the top of the layer stack, that it's the active layer, and that the other layers are locked.

40. Click the Library tab.

41. In the File drop-down, select CowAbductionStoryboard.fla, making it the active library file (see Figure 7.9). The grCow object appears.

FIGURE 7.9 Changing the file from which to view library objects

42. Drag the grCow object onto the stage. The object is copied into the Cow Abduction file's library.

43. Using the Free Transform tool, resize and adjust the cow graphic's placement as needed.

44. In the Color Effect section in the Property Inspector, click the Style drop-down, select Alpha, and drag the slider to 0%. The cow disappears from the stage.

45. Save your work.

46. Close the CowAbductionStoryboard file. Name the document CowAbductionStoryboard, select CowAbductionStoryboard.fla, making it the active library file.

As you get ready to start animating, there are a couple of things you can do to help you concentrate on the important elements in the animation. First, you can turn on highlight mode in any layer that contains objects that will not be animated (see Figure 7.10). This takes all the color away in the things you've drawn, showing only their outline. This helps get the noise of the scene out of your way. Note that even though the cow's alpha value is set to zero, it shows up in outline mode.

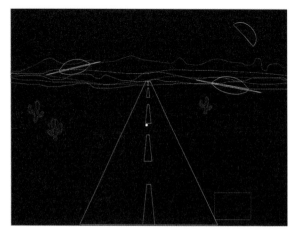

FIGURE 7.10 Scene in outline mode

The other thing you can do is to temporarily change the stage color scene back to white so you can clearly see the elements you're animating. This may or may not be productive; it depends on the colors you intend to use in your final scene. However, it's easy to switch back and forth between a white stage color and the stage color you actually intend to use in your production animation, so there's nothing lost either way.

Creating a Frame-by-Frame Animation

Now that you have your starting scene, you can create a new keyframe, copy the contents of the previous frame over to the new one, and then move the animation objects to a new location in the new frame. Note that the objects will probably need to be altered in their size and maybe their rotation as you move them across their path. You can also change an object's color or even delete it and replace it with a new object. The point is that the action changes from the previous to the current frame.

You have three steps you have to go through at each frame in the first section of this animation: move the dominant UFO, move the nondominant UFO, and slightly increase the cow's alpha value.

1. Make sure CowAbduction is the active open file.

2. Unlock the UFO and Cow layers. Make sure all other layers are locked.

3. Right-click frame 2 of the UFO layer and select Insert Keyframe from the context menu, or you can press F6. Note that the rest of the art in the scene disappears. This is because the frames for the other layers have not been extended.

4. Right-click frame 2 of the Cow layer and select Insert Keyframe from the context menu (or you can press F6). Remember that the cow's alpha value is currently zero (invisible).

5. Click and highlight frame 2 the remaining layers. Right-click and select Insert Frame from the context menu (or press F5). Flash extends the view of the artwork on frame 1 to the next frame. It's important to remember that the only copy of the artwork on the stage is currently on frame 1. When you use this technique, Flash puts a white rectangle in the ending frame. It does not matter if the layers are locked when you're extending a frame.

When a UFO object is active, you can use your arrow keys to "nudge" the object slightly in one direction rather than using your mouse. This allows for more granular changes.

6. In the UFO layer, click one of the UFOs. Move it slightly and rotate/resize it as required to show slight movement toward you or away from you.

7. Repeat the process for the second UFO.

8. In the Cow layer, frame 2, increase the alpha value to 7. The cow will begin to be slightly visible.

9. Click the top layer of frame 15 and highlight all layers below the Cow layer. Press F5 to extend the frames.

10. Repeat steps 6 through 8 for the UFO and Cow layers until you arrive at frame 15, moving the UFOs in a flight pattern. Remember that you want one of the UFOs to wind up directly over the cow. Incrementing the cow's alpha value by seven each time will result in a completely visible cow at frame 15.

ORDER OF OBJECTS IN LAYERS

Remember that an object may appear in front of another even though you don't want it to. This can happen for two reasons: One object is on a layer that's higher than another, or in the drawing order of two objects on the same layer, one is in front of another.

Both issues are easy to solve. In the first case, just drag the layer down below the one that contains the object you wish to be in front. In the second case, simply click the object you want to be in back and from the Flash main menu, click Modify ➤ Arrange ➤ Send To Back. (You can also right-click the object and click Arrange ➤ Send To Back.

A great tool you can use to view the placement of the UFOs in the animation is called *onion skin* (see Figure 7.11). The name is taken from the translucene of a onion skin layers; you can see one beneath another. When you turn on onion skin, you are shown all of the components of your animation, allowing you to alter the placement in each frame to be more precise. You click the onion skin icon to produce a slider over the top of the frames. Simply drag the slider to include or exclude frames you want to see. Figure 7.12 shows the UFO in onion skin mode with all of the frames selected.

Frames included
in onion skin

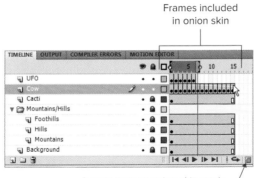

Icon to turn on onion skin mode

FIGURE 7.11 Onion skin icon and slider

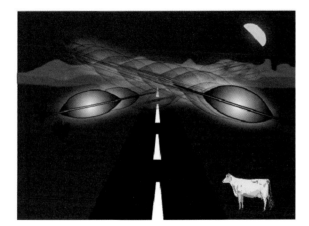

FIGURE 7.12 UFO animation shown in onion skin mode

11. Turn onion skin on.

12. Note the pattern your UFOs make. Are they in a consistent flight pattern?

13. Go back to various frames and make adjustments as required to attain a more consistent flight pattern.

14. Turn onion skin off.

Drawing the force field over the cow consists of essentially the animation process you used earlier, except that the UFO hovering over the cow will remain still while the force field is on. Additionally, you'll want to move the now visible cow up into the ship, but not for a few frames while the force field is grabbing onto the cow.

15. In the UFO layer, frame 15, use the technique you learned earlier to create an oblique rectangle. Make the rectangle green or some other eerie color.

16. Right-click the rectangle and select Convert To Symbol from the context menu.

17. Make the rectangle a movie clip with the name mcForceField.

18. Set mcForceField's alpha value to 50%.

19. Add a glow filter to mcForceField, adjusting the Blur X and Blur Y settings till you get a sufficient glow,

20. Position the rectangle under the UFO so that its narrower end is emanating from the UFO and the wider end is encompassing the cow. Adjust as necessary (see Figure 7.13).

FIGURE 7.13 Force field over cow

You want the force field to come down on the cow, so you'll need to use the frame-by-frame animation techniques you used earlier to accomplish this.

21. In all of the layers except for the UFO layer, right-click frame 25 and select Insert Frame. (Don't forget that you can click and drag in frame 25 to include contiguous layers at once.)

22. In the UFO layer, with the force field highlighted by the Free Transform tool, click the registration point—the white circle in the middle of the force field—and drag it to the top of the drawing.

23. Click the bottom middle control point. The mouse cursor changes to a two-headed arrow. Drag up to shrink the force field so that it's barely visible.

24. Repeat step 23 till you reach frame 25, each time moving the force field down a little bit until it's fully extended at frame 25.

25. Try playing the movie by pressing Ctrl+Enter (Command+Return on the Mac). The movie will loop over and over, which is normal behavior when there is no ActionScript code to stop it from doing so.

26. Close the movie.
Now you have to make the cow disappear into the ship, followed by the force field rolling up and disappearing and, finally, the UFOs flying away.

27. Extend all of the layers with the exception of the Cow layer to frame 35. When there are noncontiguous layers, you can hold down the Ctrl key (Command key on the Mac) and click each layer you want to select.

28. Press F5 to extend the frames or right-click and Select Insert Frame from the context menu. Note that the Cow layer stops at frame 25.

29. In frame 26, press F6 or right-click and select Insert Keyframe from the context menu. Flash copies the cow on frame 15 to frame 26.

30. Using the Free Transform tool, move the cow up slightly, resize it so it's slightly smaller, and, if you desire, rotate it a bit.

31. Decrease the cow's alpha value by nine.

32. Repeat steps 30 and 31 till the cow has gone up into the ship and complete disappeared.

33. Delete the cow altogether on the ending frame. Figure 7.14 shows the process about halfway through the frames.

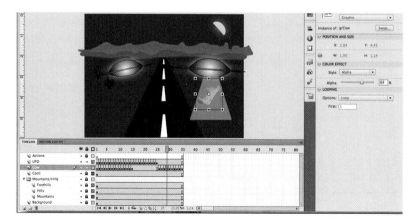

FIGURE 7.14 Cow disappearing into ship

Next, to roll up the force field, simply extend all layers with the exception of the UFO and Cow layers to frame 45. (The Cow layer does not need to be seen any longer.) Repeat steps 23 and 24 in the UFO layer, this time rolling the force field up till it's completely gone. On the end frame delete the force field altogether.

For the frames in which the ships are flying away, extend all layers with the exception of the UFO and Cow layers to frame 60. Repeat steps 6 and 7 to make the ships fly away (off screen, in this case).

Finally, you'll need a tiny little snippet of ActionScript code to make the animation stop at the end.

34. Create a new layer called Actions.

35. Move the layer to the top.

36. In frame 60, right-click and select Insert Blank Keyframe from the context menu.

37. In the new blank keyframe, right-click and select Actions. The Actions panel appears.

38. At line one of the Actions code window, type in this code: **stop();**.
Optionally, in the Actions panel, click the Code Snippets button then select Timeline Navigation and double-click Stop at this Frame to insert the required code. Another method would be to use the Script Assist tool, which can be found by clicking the magic wand button in the Actions Panel. From there click the plus sign that appears and select flash.display ➤ MovieClip ➤ Methods ➤ stop. This inserts the command to import a Flash library and then execute the code

not_set_yet.stop(). Delete the not_set_yet and the dot to leave just the stop() function call.

Play the movie to test its animation. You can go back and make adjustments on any frame until you're satisfied with the results.

Differentiating between a Stage Animation and a Movie Clip

There are an awful lot of frames on the main timeline that really don't need to be there. For example, you've extended the cactus, mountains, foothills, hills, road, and background frames clear to frame 60 when you really don't need to do so.

The only two layers that really need to have numerous frames in them are the UFO and Cow layers.

You can fix this by creating movie clips, dragging them to the stage, and putting them in the places they need to be. By using movie clips instead of making animations directly on the timeline you gain several advantages: reduced file size (if you're re-using an animation), ease of global editing, and consistency. You can also share them between projects (because they're stored in the library). And, you can add interactivity to them. In most cases, you're better off to make your animations in a movie clip, then place them on the stage when you're ready.

1. Click frame 1 in the UFO layer and Shift+click the end frame to highlight all of the frames.

2. Right-click and select Cut Frames from the context menu.

3. Press the F8 key and create a new movie clip symbol, giving it a meaningful name, like mcUFO for example.

4. Right-click frame 1 of the movie clip and select Paste Frames from the context menu. Flash not only copies the frames in, it also creates the layers with the same names you used on the main timeline.

5. Insert a new layer, name it Actions, and move it to the top.

6. Check to make sure there isn't a blank keyframe at frame 1 of the Actions layer. If so, right-click frame 1 of Actions and select Clear Keyframe from the context menu.

7. Right-click the ending frame of the Actions layer and click Insert Blank Keyframe.

8. Right-click the new blank keyframe and select Actions from the context menu.

9. In the Actions window, type **stop();**. You should end up with something similar to Figure 7.15.

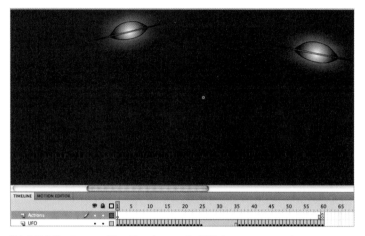

F I G U R E   7 . 1 5   Timeline frames in UFO layer converted to movie clip

10. Click Scene 1 to return to the stage.

11. Repeat the process for the Cow layer.

12. To get rid of the excess frames on the main timeline, click frame 2 in any of the layers and then Shift+click the ending frame. The entire section of frames from frame 2 to the end are highlighted in blue.

13. Right-click somewhere in the group of frames and select Remove Frames. Flash removes everything except for frame 1.

14. Repeat the process for all of the remaining layers except for the UFO and Cow layers.

15. In the UFO layer, drag mcUFO from the library to the stage and place it on the stage where it was when it was on the main timeline. You may now delete grUFO.

16. In the Cow layer, drag mcCow from the library to the stage, making sure it's in the same place it was then the frames were on the main timeline. You may now delete grCow.

17. You should end up with a one-frame movie using movie clips, similar to Figure 7.16. Play the movie to test it.

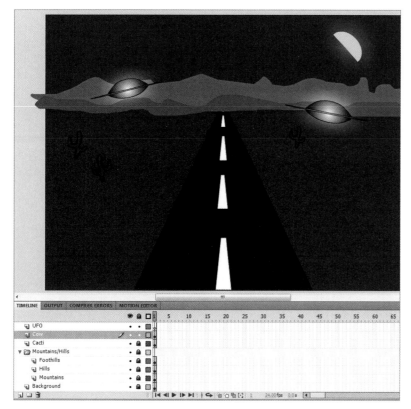

FIGURE 7.16 Finalized cow abduction scene

Simply clicking either of the UFOs in the UFO frame will alert you in the Property Inspector that you're viewing an "instance of mcUFO." This is how you know the animation's coming from an instance of a movie clip placed on the main timeline.

THE ESSENTIALS AND BEYOND

In this chapter you've learned how to create frame-by-frame animations by going through the process of moving individual assets and resizing and moving them as required to accomplish motion. You've also cut frames from the main timeline and moved them to a movie clip, which you then dragged back onto the stage.

When do you choose to use a movie clip as opposed to creating frame-by-frame animations on the main timeline? Good question, and one of individual choice—there's no right or wrong answer. That said, in most cases it makes sense to keep the main timeline as neat

(Continues)

THE ESSENTIALS AND BEYOND *(Continued)*

as possible. There's not a big change in the size of the SWF file generated, but in addition to cleaning up the main timeline, having movie clips in the library brings you one other advantage: If you want to use a movie clip in another movie, Flash provides the ability to look at another project's library and bring items from that library right into the current scene, making the movie clips truly reusable. There are some issues though. If you have movie clips doing all of your animation work and you decide to export to a QuickTime file, QuickTime will ignore all of the embedded movie clips, making your movie kind of dull. A word of advice from one of the pros: Use movie clips when you intend to use ActionScript to manage them, otherwise go with frame-by-frame animations on the timeline.

Time to create a title for the cow abduction scene.

1. Activate the Text tool.

2. Select the text engine Classic Text, text type Static Text, font Showcard Gothic (or similar UFO-ish font), font size 72, and an eerie green color.

3. Click the stage to begin typing the title.

4. Type **Cow Abduction!** in the text field.

5. Use the Selection tool and Align panel to move the title to the bottom center of the screen and center it.

ANSWER TO ADDITIONAL EXERCISE

Play the movie to see your work.

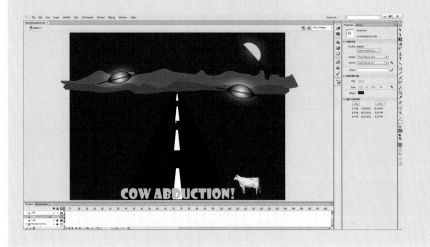

CHAPTER 8

Using Tweens

One of the key difficulties when working with animations is in showing changes over time within a given scene. There are lots of examples:

- ▶ You want to show a shape that starts out looking like one thing but morphs into another.

- ▶ You want to show movement—a bicycle, car, airplane, and so on.

- ▶ You want to illustrate a scene change: the sky changing from morning to evening, for example.

- ▶ You want to show something spinning.

In the old days of animation, each of these changes had to be drawn frame by frame, showing subtle alterations in each to convey the sense of movement and change. What a daunting, monotonous process!

Fortunately for you, Flash uses a device called *tweens* to do this work for you. There are three different kinds of tweens: shape, motion, and classic. We'll talk about each in this chapter.

- ▶ **Creating shape tweens**

- ▶ **Creating motion tweens**

- ▶ **Understanding classic tweens**

Creating Shape Tweens

Certification Objective

Suppose you want to create an animation in which one shape morphs into another over time. For example, perhaps you have need for a circle to change into a square for some reason. This is the time for a shape tween. The idea is relatively simple: You provide the way you want things to look in the first and last frames and then create a shape tween and let Flash calculate the changes over time for you. The following exercise is a simple illustration to show you how shape tweens work:

1. Open a new Flash ActionScript 3.0 document.

2. On frame 1, draw a blue circle. (It doesn't matter which drawing mode you're in: Merge Drawing or Object Drawing.)

3. In the Property Inspector for the blue circle, set both the x- and y-coordinates for the object to 200.

4. Right-click frame 10 and select Insert Blank Keyframe from the context menu. Recall that you need to insert a blank keyframe on frame 10 to have a frame in which you can draw a red square. Inserting a regular keyframe on frame 10 would copy the contents of frame 1 to frame 10—not what you want.

5. Insert a red square on frame 10.

6. Set the red square's x- and y-coordinates to 200.

7. You now have a blue circle on frame 1, a red square on frame 10, and blank frames in between (see Figure 8.1).

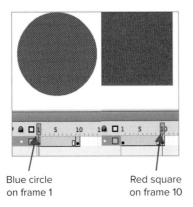

Blue circle
on frame 1

Red square
on frame 10

FIGURE 8.1 Blue circle on frame 1, red square on frame 10

8. To insert a shape tween, all you need to do is click somewhere in between the two frames (or click frame 1 or frame 10).

9. Right-click and select Create Shape Tween from the context menu (see Figure 8.2).

10. Flash calculates the changes in the shape as well as its size *and* color over time and represents the changes frame by frame.

FIGURE 8.2 Creating a shape tween

One thing you will note once you've created a shape tween is that Flash does *not* create the changes and display them as individual frames. You can tell this because Flash colors the section between the beginning and ending frames green and puts a direction arrow in as well (Figure 8.3).

FIGURE 8.3 Resulting shape tween

11. Scrub the playhead to observe the changes in your shape over time.

12. Press the Enter (Return on the Mac) key to watch the tween play.

13. Click an individual frame to see how Flash has calculated and displayed the change at that time. These are not individual frames; they are part of a whole called a shape tween.

14. To convert Flash's work to individual frames, all you need to do is highlight the frames you want to convert.

15. Right-click and select Convert To Keyframes from the context menu. In most cases, however, you won't need to do this: the shape tween will be just fine as it is.

16. If you opted to convert your shape tween to keyframes, you'll need to undo. Press Ctrl+Z (Command+Z on the Mac) to undo the conversion. Keep this file open because you'll be working with it in the next exercise.

Making Changes to a Shape Tween

Once you have that green box and arrow, you need to pay attention to it as you make changes. There are times when a change you introduce may break the tween.

1. In the same file you used in the previous exercise, click frame 10. Now highlight and delete the red box.

2. Flash puts a dotted line through the green box to alert you that you've broken the shape tween (Figure 8.4).

FIGURE 8.4 Shape tween broken due to deletion of red box

3. Press Ctrl+Z (Command+Z on the Mac) to undo the deletion.

Suppose you wanted to make a change like replacing the red box with a yellow star. Clearly you can't just delete the red box because you break the tween. Here's how to make such a change.

4. Right-click one of the frames in which the shape tween exists and select Remove Tween.

5. Click frame 10.

6. Delete the red box.

7. Insert a yellow star.

8. Right-click any frame and select Create Shape Tween (see Figure 8.5).

FIGURE 8.5 Rebuilt shape tween

Can you have multiple shapes in a shape tween? Experiment with it to see how it works.

9. In frame 1 of your current shape tween, add a red square.

10. Add a blue circle to frame 10.

11. Note that Flash calculates the changes needed for the newly introduced shapes (see Figure 8.6).

    This may not be optimal because now you have four different shapes to worry about: the deletion of any of the starting or ending keyframes will break the tween.

FIGURE 8.6 Adding shapes to a shape tween

In most cases if you have a need for multiple shape tweens it may be better for you to create them on separate layers. This would be especially true if you wanted one tween to work faster than another (i.e., the number of frames occupied by a tween is shorter than another).

12. Click Ctrl+Z (Command+Z on the Mac) twice to undo the addition of the red square and blue circle to your original tween.

13. Add a new layer.

14. Create a shape tween with a red square on frame 1 and a blue circle on frame 10. Make sure the shapes are above the shapes in the first tween on the stage.

15. Play the movie.

Note that shape tweens work just fine when created inside a movie clip and the movie clip is then dragged to the stage. This is hugely useful because you can drag the movie clip anywhere you want on the main timeline and resize or rotate as needed. You can also drag out multiple instances of the movie clip on a single frame or drag a new instance out on a new frame.

16. Click and drag to highlight all frames on layers 1 and 2.

17. Right-click and select Cut Frames from the context menu.

18. Press F8 to create a new symbol.

19. Create a movie clip called mcTweens.

20. Right-click frame 1 and select Paste Frames from the context menu.

21. Click scene 1 to exit back to the stage.

22. Delete the second layer.

23. Drag your new movie clip from the library. Resize and rotate as needed (see Figure 8.7).

24. Play the movie.

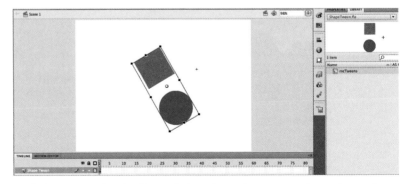

FIGURE 8.7 Movie clip consisting of two shape tweens dragged to main timeline

Adding Shape Hints

Suppose you have a couple of complex shapes to which you want to apply a shape tween. You may be surprised to find some problems once you build the tween. Let's look at what happens, as well as how to fix it.

1. Open a new Flash ActionScript 3.0 document. You can use the file ShapeHints.fla on this book's website (www.sybex.com/go/ flashessentials) as a reference.

2. On frame 1, draw a jigsaw puzzle shape using Flash shape and drawing tools.

3. On frame 10, draw a second jigsaw puzzle shape using the same techniques (see an example in Figure 8.8).

FIGURE 8.8 Blue and red jigsaw puzzle shapes

4. Create a shape tween between the two.

5. Scrub the playhead and you'll see that Flash didn't do a very good job of building the tween: Flash made its best estimate as to how the image should look at any particular stage of the animation. Depending on how complicated your jigsaw shapes are, you might find that there are scraggly parts in some places, overlapping places in others, places that jut out (see Figure 8.9).

6. Play the movie using Ctrl+Enter (Command+Enter on the Mac) and you'll see that the movie plays the same way, with all of the irregularities.

FIGURE 8.9 Flash didn't quite get the morphing right

When you have nonuniform shapes in a shape tween and you experience this kind of difficulty, *shape hints* can rescue you.

7. Scrub the playhead again, this time paying attention to the areas where Flash encounters shape tween problems.

8. On frame 1, click Modify ➤ Shape ➤ Add Shape Hint from the main Flash menu. Flash places a small red circle with a black stroke and a letter in the middle on the screen.

9. Drag the shape hint to the location where you think the shape is incorrectly morphing on its way through the tween (see Figure 8.10).

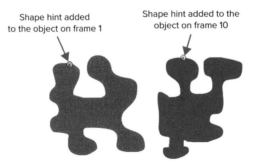

Shape hint added
to the object on frame 1

Shape hint added to the
object on frame 10

FIGURE 8.10 Shape hint at frame 1 and frame 10

10. Repeat the process on the ending frame, noting that Flash has already placed a shape hint (this time a green one) on the frame. You just have to move it to the location that corresponds to the ending of the morphing process.

11. Replaying the movie, you'll be delighted to see that Flash has corrected at least that portion of the tween.

12. If you want to consult the file for later reference, save it with the name ShapeHints.fla.

You can add 26 shape hints, which is why there's a letter in the center of them. As you add shape hints, the letter changes, making it easy to match beginning to ending locations using this system.

SHORTENING OR LENGTHENING TWEENS

If you don't like the length of time the tween is taking to complete, you can simply click the ending frame—noting that the mouse cursor changes to a small arrow with a white box—and drag it left or right to decrease or increase the duration of the tween.

Creating Motion Tweens

Motion tweens automate the motion of an object from one place to another. You'll create one in this exercise. (The completed Basketball.fla file is on this book's website if you need help.)

Certification Objective

1. Start a new ActionScript 3.0 document.

2. Using your shape tool, draw an orange oval.

3. Using the Line tool, draw two black lines across the oval.

4. Click away from the lines.

5. Activate the Selection tool with the V key.

6. When you just point to one of the lines but don't click it, you'll see that the mouse cursor changes to a smaller black arrow with a curve underneath it. This means you can alter the shape of the line into an arc.

7. Draw each of the lines inward to the other so that you come up with a drawing of a basketball (see Figure 8.11).

FIGURE 8.11 Using Flash tools to draw a basketball

8. With the Selection tool still active, marquee all of the objects on the stage (orange oval and two black lines).

9. Right-click and select Convert To Symbol from the context menu.

10. Make a graphic object with the name grBasketball.

11. Save the file as Basketball.fla.

12. Now that you have the object you want to tween in place, right-click the object and select Create Motion Tween.

13. Unlike with a shape tween, you do not need an ending frame to create a motion tween. When creating the motion tween, Flash creates a tween with as many frames in it as the default frame rate for a movie.

14. You can just drag the ending frame out or in to accommodate the length of tween you desire.

    Once you have the tween created, you have lots of choices you can make with regard to how the rest of the tween is built.

15. Right-click the end frame of the motion tween and select Insert Keyframe.

16. Note that there are a number of different keyframe types you can insert (Figure 8.12). These are not actually referred to as keyframes: They're called *property keyframes* and specifically apply to motion tweens. The point here is that you may not want to change the position of the object, for example, but instead you want to change its rotation or skew or scale (or in most cases you can simply select All).

    Select All as the type of keyframe you want to create.

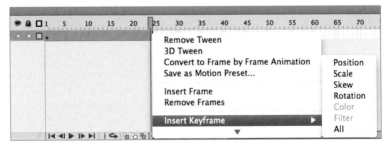

FIGURE 8.12 Motion tween property keyframe selections

17. Flash copies the basketball from frame 1 to frame 24 (provided you did not stretch or shrink the motion tween's length), putting the new basketball in the same location as the basketball image on frame 1.

18. Drag the basketball on frame 24 to the right, putting it close to the end of the right-hand part of the stage (see Figure 8.13).

FIGURE 8.13 Completed motion tween – note motion path

19. You can see that a *motion path* has been drawn by Flash in between the two.

20. You can click and drag any point along the motion path to describe an arc of movement as opposed to lateral (Figure 8.14).

FIGURE 8.14 Altered motion path

21. Press Enter (Return on the Mac) to watch Flash play the animation on the timeline.

22. Play the movie by pressing Ctrl+Enter (Command+Enter on the Mac).

You can also right-click anywhere in the tween itself and insert a new property keyframe of the type you desire. When you insert a property keyframe in a motion tween, Flash denotes it with a black diamond. You can add new keyfames at any point in the motion tween to make modifications to the tween as you see fit.

Rotating Objects

Rotating objects using a motion tween is easy to accomplish. (The completed file Sawblade.fla file has been provided for you on this book's website in case you need help.)

1. Start a new ActionScript 3.0 document and name it Sawblade.fla.

2. Using the PolyStar tool, draw a red saw blade similar to the one shown in Figure 8.15. Use the Subselection tool to modify the points of the star for the saw blade shape.

FIGURE 8.15 Saw blade drawn using PolyStar and Subselection tools

3. Right-click frame 1 and select Create Motion Tween.

4. Flash notes that the object you've drawn is not a symbol and offers to create one for you. Click OK.

5. In the Property Inspector, set the rotation to clockwise (CW) and set the saw blade to rotate just one time (see Figure 8.16).

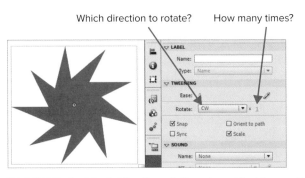

FIGURE 8.16 Setting the rotation of an object in a motion tween

6. Add a property keyframe to the end of the tween, moving the object to the right side.

7. Play the movie. Flash shows a rotating saw blade moving across the screen.

Using Parallax Scrolling

Certification
Objective

One of the animation techniques you use motion tweens to accomplish is called *parallax scrolling*. This is useful when you want to show the movement of several things that appear to be moving at different speeds. For example, suppose you want to show a car driving along from left to right, with foothills, hills, and mountains in the background. The hills move along faster than the mountains in back. (See the file ParallaxScrolling.fla on this book's website if you need assistance.)

1. Start a new ActionScript 3.0 document.

2. Using your Paintbrush tool, create a set of mountains. When you use the Paintbrush tool like this, knowing you want to fill it in with the same color as the outline, be sure to complete the loop before continuing.

3. Using your Paint Bucket tool, fill the mountains in with the same color you used with your paintbrush (see Figure 8.17).

FIGURE 8.17 Using the Paintbrush and Paint bucket Tools to create mountains

4. Create a motion tween.

5. Flash sees that you have not converted your mountain shape to a symbol and offers to do it for you. Click OK.

6. Because the mountains will move more slowly than the middle hills or foothills, drag the ending frame of the motion tween out to frame 72.

7. Insert a property keyframe of type All on frame 72 and move the mountains until they are about half offscreen to the right (see Figure 8.18).

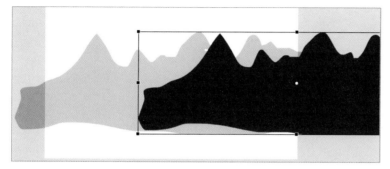

FIGURE 8.18 Setting the movement of the mountains

8. On a new layer, repeat for a middle set of hills. These hills are lower than the mountains but higher than foothills. They should be a lighter color than the mountains.

9. Create a new motion tween. Note that the new tween is assumed to be the same length as the mountains tween.

10. Decrease the number of frames to 48, insert a property keyframe, and move the middle hills offscreen to the right as well.

11. On a new layer, repeat again for the foothills.

12. Create a motion tween, decrease the number of frames to 24, and move them offscreen to the right just like the others (Figure 8.19).

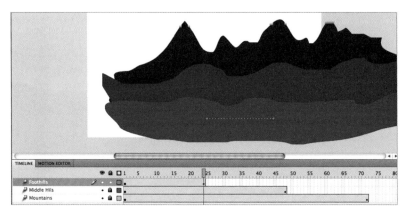

FIGURE 8.19 Re-creating motion tweens for hills and foothills, decreasing number of frames for each

13. Play the movie with Ctrl+Enter (Command+Enter on the Mac). You should see the foothills moving faster than the middle hills, which move faster than the mountains.

14. If you're not satisfied with the motion, just drag each layer's frames out or in to extend or decrease as needed to make the required adjustments.

15. Save the file as Parallax Scrolling.fla.

Once you have created a motion tween, you can use the Motion Editor to apply more granular modifications to your tween.

Applying Granular Changes with the Motion Editor

The Motion Editor panel sits right alongside the timeline in the Flash Essentials workspace, so it's easy to move to once you've created a motion tween. The Motion Editor is still prevalent, but it's inactive if no motion tweens exist in your document. (See the file `ParallaxScrolling.fla` on this book's website if you need assistance.)

Certification Objective

1. With the Parallax Scrolling document still open, change the stage resolution to Fit In Window because the Motion Editor takes up a lot of real estate while you're working in it.

2. Click one of the motion paths created when you made the motion tweens for the mountains, hills, and foothills.

3. Click the Motion Editor tab, hover your mouse cursor over its top bar until you see a double-headed arrow, then expand it so you can see more of it (Figure 8.20). Because Fit In Window is enabled, the drawing on the stage shrinks as you expand the Motion Editor window.

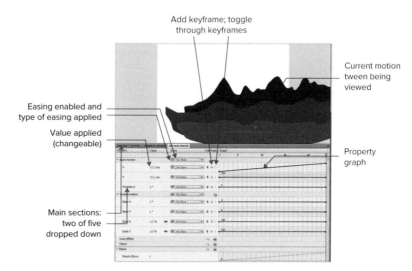

FIGURE 8.20 The Flash Motion Editor

4. Save your changes and close the file.

EXPLORING THE MOTION EDITOR

There are several sections of the Motion Editor that can be expanded or contracted by clicking the triangle next to them: Basic Motion, Transformation, and Eases. Each section has five basic columns you can work with:

Property   This is the element of the motion tween you want to affect. For example, maybe you want to make a change to the tween's Y motion. This is found in the Basic Motion section, in the Y row.

Value   Here you either key in or drag right or left to alter the value of the property you wish to change.

Ease   Easing is the speed with which a motion tween starts (ease in) or stops (ease out). You can apply eases to all of the possible motions of the tween. I'll talk more about eases later in this chapter.

Keyframe   Use this column to add a property keyframe if one does not exist and to move back and forth between property keyframes.

Graph   The Motion Editor provides a graph of what the motion looks like for a given property.

When you first start working with Flash, you'll most likely *not* spend a lot of time working with the Motion Editor because its advanced capabilities, while useful for fine-tuning and detailing, can be confusing to the neophyte. That said, you'll consider the Motion Editor one more time when I talk about easing in the next section.

Making Animations More Realistic with Easing

Certification Objective

In the real world, things don't usually start moving and instantaneously come up to speed: they take some time to start up, and to slow down. To make your motion tweens more realistic, you can apply *eases* to them. There are two types: ease in (start up slowly) and ease out (slow down at the end). You have control over which type of ease to apply and the speed with which the ease moves. Using the Motion Editor, you can create custom eases as well. You do not have to use the Motion Editor to introduce easing, however.

1. Open the Basketball.fla file.

2. Click the motion tween you created.

3. In the Property Inspector, key in the easing value you desire (−100 to +100) or drag to the right or left to select the value. A value of −100 means the motion tween will ease in, starting slowly, coming up to speed over time (see Figure 8.21).

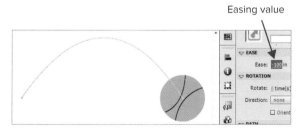

Easing value

FIGURE 8.21 An ease in applied to the motion tween

As soon as you do this, the Motion Editor shows the new addition in the Eases section (Figure 8.22). Looking at the graph, you can see more dots at the beginning of the motion. If you had created an ease out, you would see more dots at the end of the motion. Flash calls this new introduction a Simple (Slow) ease—the most basic of eases. Note that when Flash applied this ease, the Transformation section of the Motion Editor was updated to show its application: You can see that for each segment of the Transformation, the Ease section now says Simple (Slow), denoting that this ease has been applied to all directions of the tween (which, in this case, is only in the X direction).

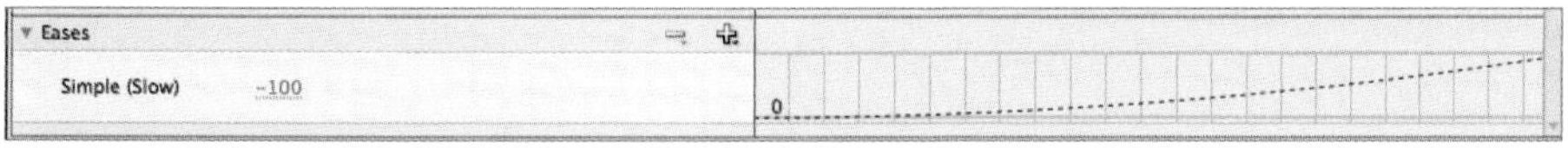

FIGURE 8.22 The new ease in as it appears in the Motion Editor

You are not limited to Simple (Slow) eases: You can apply a variety of different types using the Motion Editor. There are two steps:

1. Navigate to the Eases section in the Motion Editor and click the large plus sign to bring up the list of ease types you can create (Figure 8.23).

2. Navigate to the property in which you want to apply the easing (for example, Basic Motion), and then in the easing drop-down, select your new custom ease to apply it. Note that you have the ability to add the ease to a single property or multiple properties at once.

Simple (Slow)
Simple (Medium)
Simple (Fast)
Simple (Fastest)
Stop and Start (Slow)
Stop and Start (Medium)
Stop and Start (Fast)
Stop and Start (Fastest)
Bounce
Bounce In
Spring
Sine Wave
Sawtooth Wave
Square Wave
Random
Damped Wave
Custom

FIGURE 8.23 Available ease types

Once you've added an ease to a motion tween, you should play the movie to see how it looks, making adjustments as required.

Using Motion Presets

Flash comes with more than two dozen prebuilt motion paths you can apply to your motion tweens. The process is relatively straightforward.

1. While still in the Basketball.fla file, click the Timeline tab to move back to the timeline.

2. With the Basketball motion path highlighted, in the panel grouping immediately to the right of the stage, select the Motion Presets panel (second from bottom) or click Window ➤ Motion Presets. This brings up the list of available motion presets you can apply.

3. Click the arrow next to Default Presets to show the list of available presets.

4. Click the Bounce-In-3D preset. Note that Flash shows you what the motion will look like once applied.

5. Click Apply.

6. Flash notes that you currently have a motion applied and asks you if you want to replace it with the motion preset you've selected (Figure 8.24).

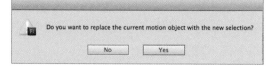

Do you want to replace the current motion object with the new selection?

No   Yes

FIGURE 8.24 Applying a motion preset to an already existing motion path

7. Click Yes. Flash creates the new motion path for you. Afterward, you can make movement or scaling adjustments as necessary.

8. Flash alerts you that to apply 3D effects to this object, you need to convert it to a movie clip in order to tween it correctly (Figure 8.25). Click OK.

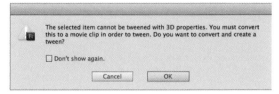

The selected item cannot be tweened with 3D properties. You must convert this to a movie clip in order to tween. Do you want to convert and create a tween?

☐ Don't show again.

Cancel   OK

FIGURE 8.25 Warning that object must be converted to movie clip to proceed

9. Press Enter to view the tween. Depending on where you placed your basketball originally, the bouncing ball effect will probably be somewhere offstage.

10. Click frame 1.

11. Find the first dot in the motion preset. This dot will be inside your basketball object.

12. Drag the dot so it's somewhere in the upper-left corner of the screen.

13. Flash moves the object into place. Minor adjustments to the motion path dot may need to be applied to get the object correctly displayed in the upper-left corner of the screen.

14. You can use the Free Transform tool to resize the object if desired.

15. Click the last frame of the motion path.

16. Repeat steps 13 and 14, except this time move the last dot of the motion path so it's aligned with the lower-right corner of the screen. Note that the basketball in the first frame is smaller than the one in the last. You're trying to accomplish the impression that the basketball is bouncing toward the viewer.

17. Press Enter to view the motion. Make adjustments as necessary.

18. View the Motion Editor to see the alterations that were applied.

19. Save the file and close.

You do not have to have a motion tween built to apply a motion preset. Simply click the object, bring up the Motion Presets window, select the motion preset you want to apply, and click OK. Flash asks you if you want to convert the object to a symbol and create a tween. If you select Yes, Flash carries out the operation.

If you've worked hard to create a motion path you like and you know you want to be able to reuse it, you can save your work as a custom motion preset. Just click Window ≻ Motion Presets and select the Custom Presets folder. Click the Save Selection As Preset button at the bottom left of the screen to save your preset (Figure 8.26).

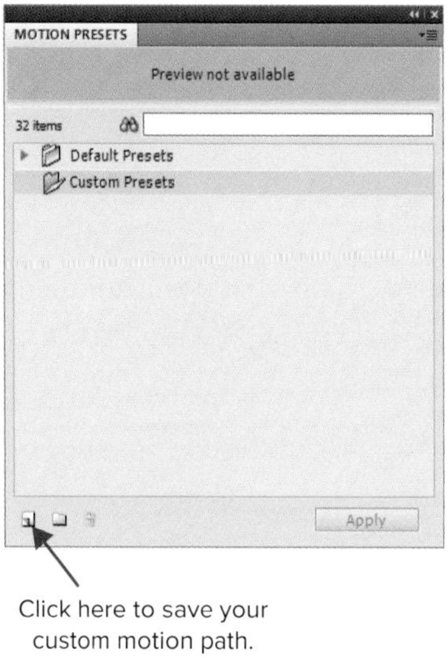

Click here to save your
custom motion path.

FIGURE 8.26 Saving a custom motion path

Understanding Classic Tweens

Certification
Objective

Before Creative Suite 4, all tweens were created using one tween methodology. As the suite was enhanced and improved and new versions came out, Adobe elected to keep the CS3 tween, calling it a *classic tween*.

Classic tweens have their place in the Flash world, and there may be times when you opt to use them. Here are a few reasons you would elect to use a classic tween over a motion tween:

▶ Because classic tweens use keyframes and not property keyframes, you have the ability to switch symbols in various frames of the tween.

▶ You can apply an ActionScript script to a classic tween, but you are not allowed to do so with a motion tween.

▶ Eases can be applied to a group of frames in the tween. With motion tweens, eases are applied only across the entire motion path and a custom ease is required when working with specific frames.

▶ With classic tweens, you can apply two color effects, whereas with motion tweens you're limited to one.

▶ If you're working on a legacy document that contains classic tweens, you may wish to retain them rather than go through the rebuilding effort required to make them into motion tweens.

As a general rule of thumb, you'll likely not go to a classic tween as your first selection. You'll usually opt instead for a motion tween in most cases.

Getting used to tweens requires practice. Remember that Ctrl+Z (Command+Z on the Mac) is your friend: if you make a mistake, just Ctrl+Z (or Command+Z) it to get back your previous work and start anew. Don't try to complicate a tween by introducing too many elements. Better to split your work up into more tweens than try to force a tween to do something too complicated.

For more information on the difference between motion and classic tweens, see `http://tinyurl.com/3aqyd3y`.

FURTHER RESOURCES

Between movie clips and tweens, you have some extremely sophisticated animation capabilities at your disposal. Because Flash is so popular, you can easily Google lots of examples of movie clips and tweens that have been done by the pros to get more advice and experience in jacking your own work up several notches. Best Google search queries would include things like the Flash version number (for example, "CS6") and the thing you're trying to accomplish (for example, "clock ticking"). There are some excellent pay-for-play (that is, subscription service) resources that any designer would find extremely useful and worth every penny. Among them I like www.Lynda.com and www.DigitalTutors.com. Lynda.com has specific product training that takes you from soup to nuts with a lot of one-off training series in between for special subjects (such as animation or design). DigitalTutors is a specialist in the game development and 2D/3D spaces. I like them because they like to mix products, and they have many, many specialized videos that help you dig deeply into new technologies. There are not a lot of Flash videos on DigitalTutors, but the ones that are there are excellent. I'm also a big fan of tv.adobe.com and labs.adobe.com. As you probe the Web for animation and AS3 advice, you'll find that there are some good and bad resources. I would love to hear from you if you run across some jewels that are worth viewing.

THE ESSENTIALS AND BEYOND

Now you'll use your newfound knowledge of motion tweens to create some 3D text.

1. Fire up Flash and create a new ActionScript 3.0 document.

2. Expand to a 400% view.

3. In the upper-left corner of the stage, create a rectangle, any color of your choosing, no stroke.

4. Using Classic Text, create a static text field and write a sentence in a tiny (for example, 8 pt. or smaller) font. In the example you see here I chose the classic palindrome "Able was I ere I saw Elba." Palindromes, of course, read the same way backward as they do forward.

5. Move the text object over the rectangle object.

6. With the Selection tool activated, marquee the two objects and press Ctrl+G (Command+G on the Mac) to group them.

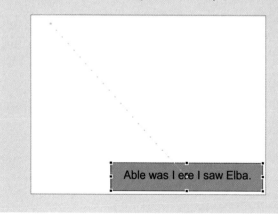

7. Go back to a 100% view of the stage.

8. Right-click frame 1 and select Create Motion Tween from the context menu.

9. Flash prompts you that you must convert the selection to a symbol. This is okay.

10. Click frame 24 to move the playhead to that frame.

11. Right-click frame 24 and select Insert Keyframe ➤ Scale.

12. While still in frame 24, move the symbol to the lower-right corner of the stage.

13. Activate the Free Transform tool and, while holding down the Shift key, resize the symbol so it's much larger than the object on frame 1.

14. Press V to activate the Selection tool and drag the motion path from the middle down and to the left a little so it makes an arc.

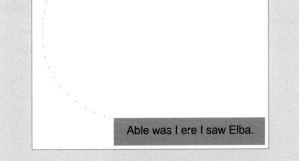

Able was I ere I saw Elba.

15. Play the movie. Voilà! A dynamically resizing text field moving across the stage in an arc. Very cool.

16. Click frame 1.

17. Activate the Selection tool and make sure the object on frame 1 is active.

18. In the Property Inspector, click Color Effect and select Alpha from the Style drop-down. Set frame 1's alpha value to 0 (completely transparent). This has the effect of setting both frame 1's and frame 24's value to 0.

19. Click frame 24 and make sure the object is active.

20. In the Property Inspector, click Color Effect and select Alpha from the Style drop-down (it will probably already be selected). Change frame 24's value to 100%.

21. Play the movie. Now you have a sign appearing out of nowhere, becoming more visible as it enlarges and moves to the lower-right side of the screen.

ANSWER TO ADDITIONAL EXERCISE

CHAPTER 9

Techniques for Creating More Technical Animations

In the past few chapters, you read about basic animation techniques, with some mention of more complex animation ideas. You even tried your hand at a basic parallax scrolling animation in Chapter 8. Now let's go into more technical detail with regard to these techniques, gathering a little more information and some more practice.

▶ **Creating a bicycle with rotating wheels**

▶ **Setting different speeds using parallax scrolling**

▶ **Creating a bouncing ball with color gradients, motion presets, and eases**

▶ **Adding perspective to the basketball scene with 3D tools**

Creating a Bicycle with Rotating Wheels

Flash provides some built-in tools to help you make the assets you create rotate, which is useful for wheels and other spinning things you desire to put in your content. But there are some issues that arise. Suppose, for example, you want to create a bicycle or unicycle. Think about the components: Not only is there a wheel rotating around an axle, there is also a chain sprocket and the pedals. So, there are at least three things spinning, two of which will most likely rotate differently than the others.

Drawing the Crank Arms

Certification
Objective

To start, let's draw the crank arms, which are the steel rods that come out of the main sprocket and connect to the pedals (for a picture of one, see http:// en.wikipedia.org/wiki/Crankset):

1. Open a new ActionScript 3.0 document and name it Bicycle.

2. Create a movie clip called mcBicycle. This movie clip will have several elements in it that make up the moving parts of a bicycle.

3. Select the Rectangle tool.

4. Select a silver gradient color, no stroke.

5. In the Rectangle Options section, set the corner radii to 25%.

6. Draw a relatively long, thin crank arm segment on layer 1.

7. Select the Oval tool, using the same silver gradient fill color and no stroke.

8. Draw an oval on the stage that will fit inside the right side of the crank arm. Think of this oval as a place where the crank arm connects to the sprocket.

9. Move the oval up onto the crank arm (see Figure 9.1).

10. Rename this layer Right Crank Arm.

F I G U R E 9 . 1 Creating a bicycle crank arm

11. Right-click frame 1 and select Create Motion Tween from the context menu. Flash notifies you that to create a motion tween you must first convert it into a symbol. Click OK to this prompt. Flash inserts a 24-frame motion tween and gives the new symbol a default name Symbol x, where x is a number that increments based upon how many symbols you ask Flash to insert. You are free to navigate to the library and rename this symbol to something more meaningful if you like.

12. Click frame 1 to make sure the playhead is positioned at the start of the motion tween.

13. Look up in the Property Inspector. You'll see a section called Rotation. (This section will not show up unless you've clicked frame 1 of the motion tween!)

14. Set a rotation of 1, and select the direction to be counterclockwise (CCW).

15. Press Enter to play the motion tween. You'll see that the crank arm rotates around its middle—not what you want. The crank arm must rotate around its end, not its middle.

16. Activate the Free Transform tool by pressing Q on the keyboard.

17. In the middle of the crank arm you'll see a tiny white circle: This is called the *registration point*. When you point your Free Transform tool mouse cursor to the registration point, the cursor turns into a black arrow with a tiny white circle beside it. This means you can move the registration point. Move it so it sits atop the knob you created.

18. Play the motion tween again. This time you'll note that the crank arm rotates around its end. This is the movement you're looking for.

19. Make a new layer above the Right Crank Arm layer and name it Left Crank Arm.

20. Go to the library.

21. Activate the Selection tool with the V key.

22. Drag a copy of Symbol 1 (or whatever you named it) to the stage, placing it to the left of the right crank arm.

23. Activate the Free Transform tool with the Q key.

24. Rotate the object 180 degrees so its knob is immediately adjacent to the right crank arm knob.

25. Adjust this crank arm's registration so it's on top of the knob you've created as well.

26. Using your mouse and/or arrow keys, nudge the left crank arm into place so its knob is immediately atop the right crank arm's knob (see Figure 9.2).

FIGURE 9.2 Adding a left crank arm

27. Right-click frame 1 of the Left Crank Arm layer and select Create Motion Tween from the context menu. Flash inserts a motion tween the same length as the right crank arm.

28. Set a rotation of 1 and a direction of CCW.

29. When you play the two motion tweens by pressing Enter, you should see a nice even rotation, just as a real bicycle's crank arms rotate. The reason you see this is that you have moved the registration points of each crank arm so they're over one another.

30. Insert a new layer called Sprocket in between the two crank arms. We'll make the sprocket later.

Creating the Pedals

Certification
Objective

Now that you have the crank arms built, you can begin to create the pedals. In thinking about the pedals, you realize they are generally held level as the bicycle goes down the road. This presents a little bit of a challenge. We'll need some sort of trick to help you accomplish the task.

1. Create a layer above the Left Crank Arm layer and name it Left Pedal.

2. Create another layer called Pedal Guide. This layer will be deleted later. It's simply going to be used as a guide for our pedal work.

3. On the Pedal Guide layer, draw a circle that consists of an oval with no fill and a regular black stroke. A cool trick you can use is to hold down the Alt and Shift keys (Option+Shift on the Mac) while beginning to draw your circle. Start your drawing from the middle of the crank arms and the circle will inflate outward until it lines up with the width of the two crank arms (see Figure 9.3).

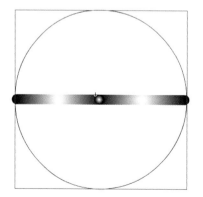

FIGURE 9.3 Drawing a circular guide

4. Lock the Pedal Guide layer. Now you're ready to create the pedals.

5. On the Left Pedal layer, select the Rectangle tool by pressing R on the keyboard.

6. Select a black fill and no stroke.

7. You previously set a 25% radii curve on all corners of any rectangles you drew. You don't want that now, so set it back to zero.

8. Draw a rectangle that matches the size of a pedal attached to a crank arm. Move the pedal so it's positioned over the left crank arm. (Note that you're still on the Left Pedal layer, but it will appear to you that you're placing the pedal on the left crank arm.)

9. Right-click frame 1 and select Create Motion Tween from the context menu. Flash draws a default 24-frame motion tween.

10. Flash prompts you that you need to save the pedal as a symbol in the library. Click OK.

11. You don't want the motion tween that long, so you'll need to shorten it. Instead you want to make four tweens of the bike pedal, each of which is six frames long, ultimately meeting the circle at frame 24. Pointing to the right-hand edge of the motion tween, you'll see a double-headed black arrow. Drag the right-hand edge of the movie clip left to frame 6.

12. The playhead should be on frame 6 as a result of the previous step. The crank arms should have moved into the position they occupy on frame 6, so they're no longer level. Drag the pedal down to meet the bottom crank arm. Flash creates a motion path pointing straight between frame 1 and frame 6 (see Figure 9.4).

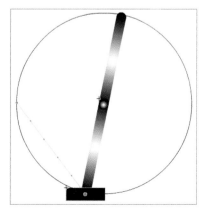

FIGURE 9.4 Motion path between pedal on frame 1 and pedal on frame 6

13. Note that Flash places a dot in the center of the pedal. This is pretty handy because you can use your arrow keys to nudge the pedal into position in alignment with the bottom crank arm.

14. Click away so that both the motion path and pedal are deselected.

15. Make sure the Selection tool is active by pressing V on the keyboard.

16. Point to the center of the motion path. The mouse cursor turns to a black arrow with a curve under it (I call it a smile). This means you can drag the motion path. Drag it so it lines up with the curve of the arc of the circle (see Figure 9.5).

FIGURE 9.5 Dragging the motion path into alignment with the arc of the circle

17. Click frame 1 of the motion tween to reposition the playhead.

18. In the Rotation section in the Property Inspector, set the rotation from 0 to 1.

Repeating the Process for the Three Arcs

Certification Objective

Now you have to repeat the process for the next three arcs, so you wind up with a complete circle.

1. Click frame 6 of the motion tween.

2. Click away to deselect all objects.

3. Click the pedal to make it active.

4. Press Ctrl+C (Command+C on the Mac) to copy the pedal object.

5. Right-click frame 7 and select Insert Blank Keyframe from the context menu (or press F6).

6. Press Ctrl+V (Command+V on the Mac) to put a copy of the pedal on the frame.

7. Use your Selection and Free Transform tools and arrow keys to place the pedal at the bottom of the crank arm.

8. Right-click and select Create Motion Tween from the context menu. Flash creates a motion tween, but it's only one frame long!

9. Drag the motion tween to the right to frame 12.

10. Drag the pedal up to meet the repositioned crank arm, keeping the pedal level. A new motion path appears.

11. Click away to deactivate the objects.

12. Press the V key to activate the Selection tool.

13. Move the motion path down to fit the second arc.

14. Repeat steps 5 through 13 for the next two arcs, making motion tweens six frames long each time. You'll extend the new motion tweens to frames 18 and 24, respectively.

15. When you're finished, press the Enter key. If everything went well, the pedals will revolve around with the crank arms, all the while staying level.

16. Create a new layer called Right Pedal.

17. Repeat steps 1 through 16, this time starting on the right crank arm and moving around the circle in a counterclockwise direction.

18. Now you can right-click the Pedal Guide layer and select Delete Layers.

Now you have two crank arms and two pedals in one movie clip (Figure 9.6). The arms and pedals go smoothly around in a circle.

FIGURE 9.6 A movie clip consisting of the combination of two crank arms and two pedals

Creating the Sprocket

Now we'll concentrate on the sprocket.

1. Click the Sprocket layer and unlock it. Make sure all other layers are locked.

2. Click the drawing tools button drop-down and select the PolyStar tool.

3. In the Tool Settings section in the Property Inspector, click the Options button.

4. In the Style drop-down, select star.

5. Set Number Of Sides to 24.

6. Set Star Point Size to 1 (see Figure 9.7).

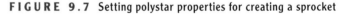

FIGURE 9.7 Setting polystar properties for creating a sprocket

7. Select the silver gradient for your fill color, with no stroke.

8. Hold down Alt+Shift and drag out from the center of your crank arms to draw the sprocket.

9. Right-click frame 1 of the sprocket and select Create Motion Tween, telling Flash it's okay to create a new symbol.

10. Click frame 1 of the motion tween.

11. In the Rotation section of the property inspector, set up a rotation value of 1 and a direction of counterclockwise (CCW, as shown in Figure 9.8.

12. Save the document with Ctrl+S (Command+S on the Mac).

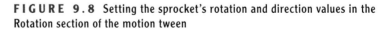

FIGURE 9.8 Setting the sprocket's rotation and direction values in the Rotation section of the motion tween

When you set up a motion tween so that the sprocket rotates one time counterclockwise (CCW), this results in a very slow rotation of the sprocket. The question is, When the sprocket is blended with the crank arms and pedals, will it look
natural? In the case of a bicycle, it will appear as though the bike is set to a very
high gear in which the big sprocket rotates slowly. It will look lifelike, but you can
easily ramp up the number of rotations to change the sprocket rotation speed.

Certification
Objective

Creating the Tires

Now it's time to make the tires. This time we'll use a different movie clip.

1. Click Scene 1 to move back to the stage.

2. From the Flash menu, click Insert ➤ New Symbol. The Create New
   Symbol dialog appears.

3. Create a new movie clip, giving it the name mcTire.

4. Select the PolyStar tool.

5. Click the Options button.

6. Set Number Of Sides to 32 and Start Point Size to 0.01; then click OK.

7. Select any fill color you like.

8. Hold down Alt+Shift (Option+Shift on the Mac), and click and draw
   to form the tire's spokes (see Figure 9.9).

FIGURE 9.9 Creating the tire's spokes

Now we'll make use of some of Flash's oval options to create the
wheel and tire.

9. Press O to activate the Oval tool.

10. Select a white or gray fill color.

11. In the Oval Options section of the Property Inspector, change the inner radius setting to 95.

12. Holding down Alt+Shift (Option+Shift on the Mac) and from the center of the spokes, draw outward until the wheel is at the edge of the spokes (see Figure 9.10). If you need to resize the wheel slightly using the Free Transform tool, you can hold down Alt+Shift while resizing.

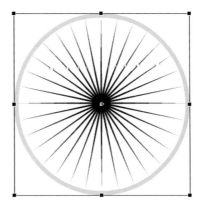

FIGURE 9.10 Creating the wheel

13. Repeat steps10 and 11 for the tire, using a black fill color and an inner radius setting of 85. Your completed tire should look like Figure 9.11.

FIGURE 9.11 Completed tire

14. Click the Scene 1 link to go back to the stage. There's no need to create a second tire.

15. Press Ctrl+S (Command+S on the Mac) to save your changes.

Creating the Bike Frame

The bicycle frame is easy to create. All you need are various combinations of the shape tools you're already familiar with. There are a handful of items you'll need to put together to create a bike frame (see http://en.wikipedia.org/wiki/Bicycle_frame for more information on the components of a bicycle frame):

Certification
Objective

▶ Forks

▶ Top tube

▶ Down tube

▶ Seat tube

▶ Seat stays

▶ Chain stays

▶ Seat

▶ Stem

▶ Handlebars

The shape of the bike frame you make can vary. You can take a photo of your own bike if you like or work from photos you find using Google. The important thing is to *not* exactly duplicate bike frames you're viewing. It's more like you're an artist who's trying to sketch what you see. Remember, when you're using the Free Transform tool, you can move the registration point so that you can make an object rotate around a different point. This will come in handy when you want to create the bike frame. So let's jump in and start building.

1. In the Bicycle file, create a new movie clip by clicking Insert ➤ New Symbol from the flash main menu, or press Ctrl+F8 (fn+Command+F8 keys on the Mac).

2. Name the movie clip mcBikeFrame.

3. The down, seat, and top tubes essentially form a triangle consisting of three semi-thick rectangles put together. Use the Rectangle tool to create the tubes. I recommend that you do this in Object Drawing mode because once you move the rectangles into place, if you're in Merge Drawing mode they melt together when you click away (if they're the same color) or a piece gets eaten away (if they're not the same color). Your pipes should look similar to Figure 9.12.

FIGURE 9.12 Bike frame tubes put together

4. The seat and chain stays form another triangle; however, the rectangle for the seat stay is a little smaller than the rectangles for the three previous tubes and the chain stay is an even smaller rectangle (see Figure 9.13).

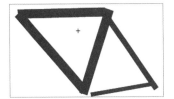

FIGURE 9.13 Adding more tubes to the frame

5. Use the various settings in the Oval tool to accommodate the place where the tires attach to the forks and the hole through which the sprocket mechanism connects to the frame.

6. Use a different color for the handlebars and seat riser, and even a different color for the seat.

7. Your finished product should look like a complete bike frame, sans wheels and sprocket mechanism (see Figure 9.14).

FIGURE 9.14 Completed bike frame

8. If you have any decorations you'd like to add, go ahead. Make the bike frame as colorful and cool as you like.

9. When you're done, use the Selection tool to marquee all objects and press Ctrl+G (Command+G on the Mac) to group them together. Your bike frame is done!

Assembling the Bike

Now you're ready to assemble your bicycle on the stage. When you create art assets that are movie clips, one advantage you get is the ability to reuse them in other files. When two or more Flash files are open, their respective libraries are available in the other's file. This library-sharing capability brings a cool thing to you: reusable assets. No need to reinvent the (ahem) wheel.

Certification Objective

1. In the Bicycle file, on the stage, create a layer called Bicycle. This is where your fully assembled bicycle will appear.

2. From the Flash main menu, click Insert ➤ New Symbol.

3. Create a movie clip called mcMovingBike. You are taken to the mcMovingBike movie clip editing section.

4. From the library, drag an instance of mcBikeFrame to the editing screen.

5. Drag one instance of mcTire onto the scene, resizing accordingly and positioning it into place beneath the bike frame's forks.

6. Make sure the tire instance is still active and then press Ctrl+D (Command+D on the Mac) to duplicate it.

7. Drag the duplicate to the rear of the bike and move into place.

8. Drag an instance of mcBicycle out onto the scene, resizing it and fitting it into place (see Figure 9.15).

FIGURE 9.15 The completed bike

9. If the wheels appear to be in front of the forks, you can right-click each one and select Arrange ➤ Send To Back from the context menu to move them backward. Alternatively, you can use layers in your movie clip to move objects behind or in front of one another.

10. Activate the Selection tool and marquee all of the bicycle objects.

11. Press Ctrl+G (Command+G on the Mac) to group them.

12. In Frame 4, right-click and select Create Motion Tween.

13. Flash tells you it will convert the group to a symbol for this purpose. Click OK. Flash creates a 24-frame motion tween.

14. The bike will move too quickly with a 24-frame motion tween. Click to extend the end of the motion tween to frame 60.

15. Right-click frame 60 and select Insert Keyframe ➤ Position to insert a property keyframe.

16. Drag the bicycle to the left a moderate distance. The bike can go in a straight line.

17. Press Enter to play the motion tween. Your bicycle's wheels, pedals, crank arms, and sprocket should look relatively close to those on a real-life bike. The movie plays over and over because you have not yet put in some ActionScript to stop it. This is fine for now because you have some more work to do.

Remember, when one object is in front of another and they're both on the same layer and you want to reverse the order—like the tire and the bike frame, for example—you can right-click an object and select Arrange ➤ Send To Back. You should remember that you can separate objects using layers. The lower a layer is, the more to the back it is.

The bike's chain is a much more complicated object more suitable for an advanced animator. The chain rotates around two sprockets of uneven size and sags when it's not under tension. Additionally, with multiple-speed bikes, the chain changes size on each end as the gear settings change. While making the chain is not a requirement for the ACA test or this book, if you were thinking about moving forward to make the chain, perhaps the best way to start such an animation would be to make a single chain link, assemble them together till you have a loop, group the objects, then work on a motion tween and rotation property keyframes to make the chain rotate properly. This work is left up to you if you so desire.

Setting Different Speeds Using Parallax Scrolling

As mentioned in the previous chapter, the idea behind parallax scrolling is to show one thing moving more slowly than another. Using separate motion tweens to create each of the segments involved in the scrolling effort and then adjusting the length of time each tween takes to play gives you the results you're looking for.

Creating the Buildings

Reconsidering the bike scene from the previous example, imagine you wanted to show the bike going along a city street. Because buildings are much bigger than a bicycle, if you wanted to be more accurate in your animation you would want to show the various buildings moving slower than the bike. Parallax scrolling is a great technique to use for this motion.

While showing a bicycle rolling along a picturesque small downtown scene replete with old shops and buildings is quite possible to do, it'll be easier right now if you create buildings in a movie clip using the Deco tool equipped with the Building brush and then drag the movie clip onto your bicycle scene at assembly time.

1. Working in the same bicycle file from the previous exercise, change the stage color to a nice sky blue.

2. From the Flash main menu, choose Insert ➢ New Symbol, or press Ctrl+F8 (fn+Command+F8 on the Mac).

3. Create a new movie clip with the name mcBuildings. You are taken to the mcBuildings movie clip editing screen.

4. Press U on the keyboard to activate the Deco tool.

5. From the Drawing Effect drop-down, select the Building brush (see Figure 9.16).

◀ If the bike is pointed to the left, everything moves counterclockwise (CCW). If it's pointed to the right, everything moves clockwise (CW).

Certification Objective

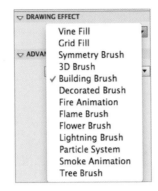

FIGURE 9.16 Setting a deco tool brush option

6. In the Advanced Options area, set the building size to 10.

7. Name the layer Buildings.

8. Click frame 1 of the Buildings layer.

9. Using the Building brush, just begin to draw big rectangles, clicking down on the bottom left, dragging right, then finishing by dragging up and letting go (see Figure 9.17). Because you want the buildings to appear in the bicycle scene, you might want to draw several buildings so different buildings appear to come on stage once you create a movie clip for them.

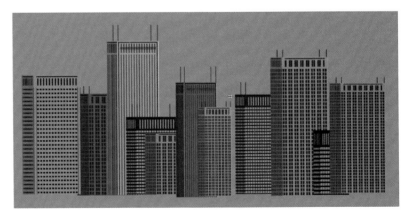

FIGURE 9.17 Drawing buildings in a movie clip

10. Group the buildings by marqueeing around them and pressing Ctrl+G (Command+G on the Mac).

11. Right-click frame 1 and select Create Motion Tween from the context menu, clicking OK to accept symbol creation.

12. Extend the motion tween to frame 240. Ultimately you'll want the buildings to scroll slowly across the screen once the movie clip is placed on the stage.

13. On frame 240, right-click and select Insert Keyframe ➤ Position.

14. Move the buildings to the right. Flash creates a motion path between the buildings on frame 1 and frame 240.

15. Play the motion tween by pressing the Enter key, taking note of its speed.

16. Click the Scene 1 link to go back to the stage.

Adding Some Clouds

Now you'll create a movie clip to show some moving clouds.

1. From the Flash main menu, click Insert ➤ New Symbol, or press Ctrl+F8.

2. Create a new movie clip called mcClouds. You are taken to the mcClouds movie clip editing screen.

3. Create a layer called Clouds.

4. Using the Oval tool in merge-draing mode, draw a few fluffy clouds on the stage. Try to make it so some of the clouds will appear offstage on both sides and they are not too similar (see Figure 9.18). You can switch back and forth between stage and movie clip editing to make adjustments if need be.

FIGURE 9.18 Drawing the clouds

5. With the Selection tool activated, marquee all of the clouds and group them with Ctrl+G (Command+G on the Mac).

6. Right-click the Clouds layer and select Create Motion Tween, allowing Flash to create a new symbol. Flash should create a 240-frame motion tween. If not, just extend the tween out to frame 240.

7. Move the clouds to the left. You can extend them fairly far offscreen, but leave at least a few clouds on the stage.

8. Navigate to frame 240.

9. You want the clouds to move even more slowly than the buildings. Extend the motion tween to frame 360.

10. Right-click frame 360 and select Insert Keyframe ➤ Position.

11. Drag the clouds to the right side of the screen, keeping a few on the screen.

12. Click the Scene 1 link to return to the stage.

Assembling the Scene

Now you'll assemble the entire bicycle scene.

1. Create new layers in your Bicycle scene called Bicycle, Road, Buildings, and Clouds, in that order from top to bottom.

2. With the Bicycle layer selected and the others locked, drag mcMovingBike onto the stage.

3. Using the Free Transform tool, resize the movie clip as required. The bike's height should take up about one-third of the screen size.

4. Unlock and select the Buildings layer and lock all the others.

5. Drag the mcBuildings movie clip onto the stage.

6. Use your Free Transform tool to resize as needed. The buildings should take up about two-thirds of the height of the stage and all of the stage plus some more. It's okay if the buildings extend out over the right and left sides of the stage (Figure 9.19).

7. Unlock the Clouds layer and lock all the others.

8. Drag the mcClouds movie clip onto your scene.

9. Use the Free Transform tool to resize and position the clouds as you desire.

10. Play the movie with Ctrl+Enter (Command+Enter on the Mac).

11. If you need to make adjustments to the durations of the movie clips, you'll have to double-click their icons in the library to go back into editing mode for each particular movie clip.

FIGURE 9.19 Building the completed bicycle scene

Adding a Highway

Use a black rectangle to create a highway, keeping it proportional in size. This means you have a couple of choices: You can show the bike close to the full size you drew it on the stage at first, making it closer to the eye than the city scene, which means the road must be bigger. Or you can scale the bike down so it is roughly proportional to the size of the buildings, which might make it difficult to see.

1. Continue working in the bicycle file from earlier exercises.

2. Create a black rectangle that covers the bottom of the buildings, about one-tenth of the total screen height or so.

3. Create a white rectangle to represent the road stripe. You only need one: You can use Ctrl+D (Command+D on the Mac) to duplicate it.

4. Duplicate the road stripe over and over again until the road is covered (see Figure 9.20). Another option would be to convert the stripe into a graphic, which would then allow you to drag new copies of it out from the library onto the stage.

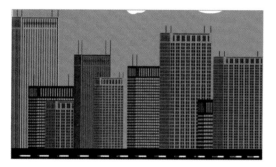

FIGURE 9.20 Making the road stripes

The only thing missing is a rider. You could certainly use Flash tools to draw a rider on the screen but you'll need inverse kinematics (IK) to rig the character so he looks like he's actually riding the bike. We'll talk about IK in the next chapter. You can check the file `Bicycle.fla` on www.sybex.com/go/ flashessentials if you need assistance.

EMBEDDED MOVIE CLIP CAUTIONS

You may frequently be torn by the question of whether to leave each separate motion animation as an individual movie clip or combine everything together into one, regardless of how many separate motion animations you might wind up with inside one movie clip. There are a couple of reasons to keep animations separate:

► First, you may want to reuse an animation. If it is embedded in another, more complex movie clip, it may be difficult or confusing to retrieve—might even screw up the original movie clip if you make a wrong step.

► Second, it is much easier to edit movie clips that have been dragged to the stage but have been kept isolated in their own layers. You still get the original look and feel as though they had been grouped together into a single movie clip.

Remember, you can always group all of your layers that contain motion into a layer folder so you know where everything is.

Creating a Bouncing Ball with Color Gradients, Motion Presets, and Eases

Suppose you have a desire to animate a basketball going up and through the hoop and net and then hitting the floor with a nice rubbery bounce.

Creating the Basketball Court's Floor

Certification
Objective
The place to start is with the floor.

1. Open a new ActionScript 3.0 file and save it with the name Basketball.

2. To create a basketball floor, navigate to http://images.google
    .com and search for "basketball floor." Google will return hundreds
    of photos. Pick one you like. (You won't actually be saving the photo
    or importing it; you'll just be using it as a model to create your own
    floor.)

3. The planks in a basketball floor are all the same width, but may
    vary in length. However, you can use one rectangle to do all of the
    work in creating the floor. Activate the Rectangle tool by pressing R
    on the keyboard.

4. Pick a stroke and fill color for your plank. If you have trouble picking
    colors, try hex value 96541A for the stroke and C36326 for the fill.
    You'll use these hex values to create a custom gradient that you'll
    ultimately use for your plank.

Because the rectangle is supposed to look like a floorboard, it should have
more color tones in it than simple fill and stroke colors. You could opt to have
several different rectangles showing other colors for a little more accuracy. But
in the interest of simplicity, you can use a custom color gradient to add a little
more zest to the board and just copy and duplicate it to make an entire floor.

Adding Pizzazz with Custom Color Gradients

Now you can create a custom gradient with some pizzazz for your basketball
floor.

1. Click the Color panel (found in the panel grouping just to the right of
    the stage); then click the color drop-down to select something other
    than a solid color. As you learned in Chapter 3, you have your choice
    of Linear Gradient, Radial Gradient, or Bitmap Fill.

    With a linear gradient, Flash draws the colors you select *across*
    an object. This gives the image of light falling on one side or the
    other of an object. In a radial fill, the colors are applied in a *circular*
    fashion. For example, if you used black at the edges and white in the
    center, Flash would draw a target-like gradient, smoothly meshing
    the colors together in between. This gives the effect of a light directly
    falling down on each edge of the object. You can use the Gradient
    Transform tool (nestled under the Free Transform tool) to modify
    either your linear or radial gradient.

    With a bitmap fill, you simply tell Flash to use a picture you've
    imported as the fill for an object: sometimes useful, but often a crutch
    that replaces creating the object yourself using Flash drawing tools.

Because lights generally shine down on a basketball floor, you might decide to pick the radial gradient as the best option for your floorboard.

2. With the original fill color in your floorboard selected, click the Color panel and choose Radial Gradient from the color drop-down. You're presented with a variety of options for adjusting the colors in your gradient (see Figure 9.21).

FIGURE 9.21   Radial gradient choices

Note that the default colors are black on the left and white on the right (provided you have not selected another color in a previous gradient). Note too that a black arrow shows up over the black block. This means it is the currently active color and you can modify it. Click the white color block and it now becomes the active block. (Linear gradient settings are similar.)

3. With the black block selected, type in the hex number you used earlier for the stroke color.

4. Now click the white block to make it active. You'll know it's active because Flash puts a black triangle above it.

5. Key in the hex number for the lighter color.

6. This new color is probably very similar to the first one you keyed in. To correct that, just click and drag anywhere in the middle of your custom gradient. Flash inserts a new block with the same color as the last one you entered.

7. Now you can move the color sliders up and down to get a slightly darker color. Note that while you're performing this activity, Flash

alters the hex, HSB, and RGBA numbers. You now have a three-color custom radial gradient.

8. Click the drop-down in the upper-right corner of the gradient panel and select Add Swatch from the context menu (see Figure 9.22).

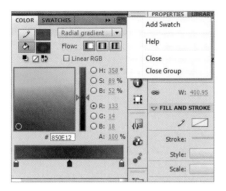

FIGURE 9.22 Adding a custom gradient as a swatch

9. Back at the stage, activate your Selection tool.

10. Click the floorboard fill to activate it.

11. Click the fill color section of the toolbar to bring up the Color Picker.

12. Your new swatch shows up at the bottom of the Color Picker. Select it to fill your board in with your custom gradient colors.

13. Now you can use the Free Transform tool to resize, skew, and move the board into place. Because you want the floor to have a three-dimensional effect, you can use the skew operation to tilt the boards slightly.

14. Use Ctrl+D (Command+D on the Mac) to duplicate the board, moving it into place next to the original.

15. Use the Free Transform tool to resize the board.

16. Repeat steps 14 and 15 to complete your basketball floor (see Figure 9.23). Be sure to stagger the board widths. The boards should be made narrower as they move into the scene.

17. Finish off the scene with a rectangle, 3-point stroke, no fill, to resemble the line typically drawn around the perimeter of a basketball floor.

FIGURE 9.23 Finished basketball floor

Creating a Backboard by Combining Motion Tweens

Certification Objective

It's easy to create a backboard using various rectangles that have different fill and stroke colors, lines that can be bent to form a net, and an oval that represents the hoop itself. The amount of work you want to go through is directly proportional to the realism your object denotes. For example, your scene might be so small that it wouldn't be worth the time to make sure the basketball looks dimpled like a real basketball. Creating highly lifelike animations takes time!

Figure 9.24 shows a completed basketball court, with the basketball on its own layer in the air ready to fly into the hoop. Now what's needed is a motion tween, right? Well, actually *two* tweens are required: one to get the basketball to the hoop in a nice believable arc, the other to allow the ball to fall to the ground with a nice ball-like repeated bounce. The first tween is easy to create, and the second is as easy, but you must recognize that it requires a motion preset.

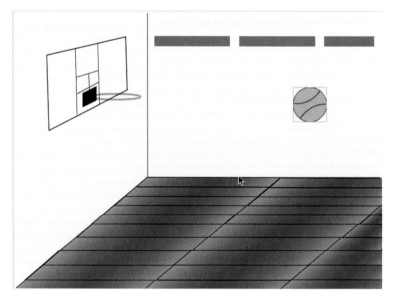

FIGURE 9.24 Completed basketball court with basketball ready for tweens

1. Create a layer for the basketball.

2. Create a basketball using an orange oval with black stroke.

3. Using the Line tool, draw two lines through the basketball.

4. Switch to the Selection tool.

5. Drag each of the lines so they arc toward one another.

6. Marquee all of the elements making up the basketball and press Ctrl+G (Command+G on the Mac) to group them.

7. Right-click frame 1 and select Create Motion Tween. Flash creates a 24-frame motion tween (provided you have not lengthened any other layers longer than 24 frames).

8. Right-click frame 24 and select Insert Keyframe ➤ All from the context menu.

9. Drag the basketball to the inside of the hoop. (The hoop must be on the layer above the basketball so it looks like the basketball is inside the hoop.)

10. Drag the resulting motion path upward into an arc.

11. Press Enter to play the motion tween to make sure it looks like the basketball is going up and into the hoop (see Figure 9.25). You can always extend or decrease the timelines if you're not happy with the speed of the movement.

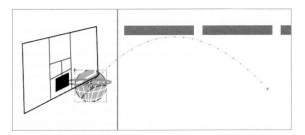
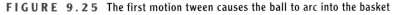

FIGURE 9.25 The first motion tween causes the ball to arc into the basket

12. Move to the frame just past the end of the motion tween you just created.

13. Right-click and select Insert Blank Keyframe, or press F7.

14. Click frame 24 again.

15. Click the basketball to make it the active object.

16. Press Ctrl+C (Command+C on the Mac) to copy the basketball.

17. Move to frame 25 again.

18. Press Ctrl+Shift+V (Command+Shift+V on the Mac) to paste the basketball exactly in the same place it was on frame 24.

19. With the second instance of the basketball selected, click Window ➢ Motion Presets.

20. Select Large-Bounce" from the list and click Apply. Flash builds the motion tween on the basketball, extending the number of frames out to accommodate the motion preset.

21. Navigate out to the end of the motion preset.

22. For all other layers in your scene, click the same frame as the ending frame of the preset and press F5 to extend that layer's frames out so the scene is consistent.

In Figure 9.26 you can see that the motion preset Flash builds is longer than the scene is wide (as denoted by the bounding rectangle and control boxes). To remedy this, just click on the end point of the preset and drag it back into the scene. Flash recalculates the preset accordingly.

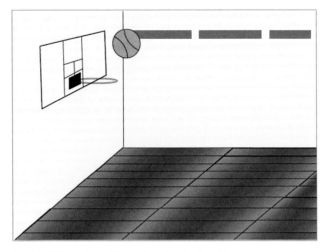

FIGURE 9.26 The end of the motion preset needs to be repositioned

Tweaking the Animation

Playing the movie will reveal any places where you might need to tweak the position of the ball, but once you're done, the ball should go up the air in an arc, drop into the hoop, and then come back out with a nice bounce. You'll notice when the ball bounces it squishes a little bit: a nice added benefit of the motion preset.

The following are the two last things you need to do to complete the scene:

1. The motion preset doesn't have a rotation associated with it. So the ball rotates when it goes into the basket but stays straight when it comes out and goes through the motion preset. To fix this, just click anywhere in the motion preset tween and change the rotate setting from zero to one time in the Rotation section of the Property Inspector. This makes the basketball continue spinning while it's going through its motion path.

2. Also, because a basketball is thrown with some vigor, it approaches the net faster at first and winds down as it falls into the net. To provide a slightly more realistic look you can select the first motion tween, and in the Property Inspector change the Ease section to +50, which is an ease out. This will make the ball spin a little faster at first but slow down as it hits the net.

Adding Perspective to the Basketball Scene with 3D Tools

Suppose you decide you'd like to have a school pennant in your basketball scene. If you create a pennant movie clip, you can use the 3D Rotation (hotkey W) and Translation (hotkey G) tools to rotate and translate the movie clip not just in the x- and y-axis but in the z-axis as well.

1. Create a new layer called Banner. Make sure this layer is at the top.

2. In the Banner layer, create a pennant by using the Rectangle tool and the Ctrl+Shift (Command+Shift on the Mac) trick to squish one end down while using the Free Transform tool.

3. Decorate your pennant with any shapes or text you'd like.

4. Group the objects together with Ctrl+G (Command+G on the Mac).

5. Convert the objects to a movie clip.

6. Turn on the 3D Rotation tool.

Figure 9.27 shows an example pennant movie clip with the 3D Rotation tool turned on. Each of the three circles has a different color—easy to remember the order: red = x, green = y, blue = z. Get it? RGB = XYZ.

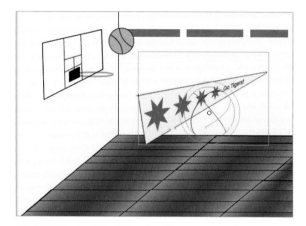

FIGURE 9.27   Using the 3D rotation tool to set a movie clip's x, y and z rotation

You can use the rotation and translation tools with the movie clip on the stage, or you can use the tools to alter an object's X, Y, and Z rotation and position at each property keyframe in the movie clip itself.

THE ESSENTIALS AND BEYOND

This chapter dealt with creating animations using more complex techniques such as rotation and parallax scrolling of objects with different motion speeds. You also worked with the 3D motion tool in Flash. You learned that there may be times when you want to create separate motion tweens, combining them together to create a more complex animation but leaving each part separate for other work you want to do in later animations.

For an additional exercise, you will create a moving sun arcing over a blue sky surface. You'll create a main timeline animation when you do this work.

1. Start a new ActionScript 3.0 document.

2. Set the stage color to a nice sky blue.

3. Name the first layer Background.

4. Create a second layer called Sun.

5. Create a third layer called Clouds.

6. From the main Flash menu, select Insert ➤ New Symbol.

7. Make your new symbol a graphic and call it grSun. You are taken to the grSun editing screen.

8. Using the PolyStar tool create a yellow star with no stroke, 32 sides, and a star point size of 0.50.

9. Draw a sun on the stage (of the grSun editing screen).

10. Use the Align tool to align the left edge and the top edge.

11. Now draw a yellow circle on the stage. Make the circle somewhat smaller than the tips of the sun points.

12. Drag the circle over the top of the star.

13. Using black and red brushes, draw some eyes and a mouth on the sun. Use your artistic, creative bent and embellish as you like.

(Continues)

THE ESSENTIALS AND BEYOND *(Continued)*

14. Drag the sun onto the stage on the Sun layer.

15. Using the Free Transform tool, reposition and resize the sun as required. You can have it start on the upper-left side of the screen or the upper right; it matters not.

16. Right-click frame 1 of the Sun layer and select Insert Motion Tween.

17. Extend the motion tween to frame 72. (Note that as soon as you do that, the playhead moves to frame 72.)

18. Right-click frame 72 and select Insert Keyframe ➢ All.

19. Drag grSun to the right side of the screen.

20. Activate the Selection tool.

21. Change the motion path so it is a nice gentle arc.

22. Lock the Sun and Background layers and click the Cloud layer.

23. Using the Oval tool in Merge Drawing mode, make a few clouds. It's okay if the clouds go beyond the stage on both sides.

24. Activate the Selection tool.

25. Marquee all of the clouds.

26. Press Ctrl+G (Command+G on the Mac) to group the clouds.

27. Right-click frame 1 of the Clouds layer and select Insert Motion Tween.

28. When prompted to convert the clouds to a symbol, click OK. Flash creates a motion tween the same length as the Sun (72 frames).

29. Extend the clouds' motion tween to frame 144. Note that the playhead is on frame 144.

30. Move the clouds to the left so they're nearly off the stage.

31. Go back to frame 1 of the Clouds layer.

32. Move the clouds to the right so they're nearly off the stage.

33. Play the movie with Ctrl+Enter (Command+Enter on the Mac). The sun's arc ends too soon.

34. Extend the sun's tween to frame 144.

35. Play the movie again. This time the sun should arc across at the same time as the clouds. The clouds should be in front of the sun—thus the reason the Clouds layer is above the Sun layer.

ANSWER FOR ADDITIONAL EXERCISE

See included file Sun.fla on this book's website at www.sybex.com/go/flashessentials.

CHAPTER 10

Creating Characters with Inverse Kinematics

Inverse kinematics (IK) is an animation technique in which you add *bones* to a character at specific joint locations and then use animation to make the character move along the joint lines. Knowing how to use Flash's IK tools will serve you well in your rich media development.

When you use Flash's IK tools to put bones in a character, you are said to be *rigging* the character.

▶ **Boning a character**

▶ **Constricting animations**

▶ **Animating IK'd objects**

Boning a Character

In the previous chapter, you created a riderless bicycle. Now it's time to fix that issue. You'll use a picture of yourself or someone else to make a relatively lifelike character and then use the Flash IK tools to rig it.

Snapping a Photo as a Base

Certification Objective

Follow these steps to start:

1. Have someone take a digital picture of you. The picture needs to be a side view of you. Hold your camera-side arm out from you a bit and curl your fingers as though you're holding onto a bicycle's handgrip.

2. After you have a picture you like, copy it to the folder in which you're keeping your bicycle file. You'll import the picture into Flash from there. See Figure 10.1 for a picture my wife took of me.

FIGURE 10.1 Side view required for Flash cartooning

3. Open the Bicycle document.

4. Create a new movie clip called mcRider. This movie clip will contain the tracing you make of your picture along with the rigging. The movie clip editing screen retains the same color as the stage, which is set to sky blue.

5. In the mcRider movie clip, create two layers: Rider Picture and Rider. The Rider Picture layer will hold the picture you took of yourself. The Rider layer will hold the tracing work you do on your picture. When you're done, you'll delete the Rider Picture layer.

6. Make sure the Rider layer is locked and you're positioned on the Rider Picture layer.

7. From the Flash main menu, click File ➤ Import ➤ Import To Stage, or press Ctrl+R (Command+R on the Mac).

8. Find your picture, select it, and click Open. Your picture appears on the movie clip editing surface.

9. Use the Free Transform tool to rotate and resize the picture as needed so you can see the entire picture.

Tracing Your Picture

Remember when you were a child and you traced a picture? This is the activity you'll engage in to "cartoonize" yourself. You'll need to use the enlargement drop-down or the Zoom tool to shift back and forth between different sizes of your picture.

Before you begin, take a look at your picture. Try to figure out the various sections of your body that make up one unit: for example, your head and neck, your upper arm, lower arm, hand, and so forth. Think about your cartoonized self riding a bicycle. What parts need to move? The following might be a list you would create:

Certification Objective

▶ Head able to rotate back and forth where head is connected to neck

▶ Neck able to rotate back and forth where neck is connected to body

▶ Upper arm rotates at shoulder

▶ Lower arm rotates at upper arm

▶ Hand rotates at lower arm

▶ Upper leg rotates at torso

▶ Lower leg rotates at upper leg

▶ Foot rotates at lower leg

▶ Lower pant leg rotates at pant seat (for shorts, or lower pant leg rotates at upper pant leg, which rotates at pant seat for regular jeans or slacks)

▶ Shirt sleeve rotates at shirt

Depending on how many sections you think need to move, you'll have to trace and color in the parts of your photo as individual sections. For example, if you want the head to be able to turn on the neck, the neck and head have to be two independent sections that will be brought together when you get ready to do your rigging.

You'll probably want to zoom in on sections of your body so you can trace them. Make sure you complete an *entire loop* of a section. In other words, as you trace, come back to the place where you started so that the loop is closed. In this way, you will be able to fill in the colors you need once the tracing is done.

1. Lock the Rider Picture layer and move to the Rider layer, making sure you unlock it.

2. Using the enlargement drop-down or Zoom tool (hotkey Z), zoom in on a segment of your picture that you wish to trace.

3. Select the Brush tool (hotkey B).

4. When you click the tool's fill color to bring up the Color Picker, you are shown a dropper icon. This means you can sample a color from your picture. Sample a portion of flesh color.

5. Begin tracing the segment that makes up your head, avoiding the hairline (for example, you want only the flesh that makes up your face).

6. Trace clear around until you've closed the loop for that segment (see Figure 10.2). You can unclick your mouse at a good stopping point, reclick, and begin working again. Flash calculates the corrections needed to smooth out the brush stroke. If you have a drawing tablet, the work will be a little bit easier than with a mouse.

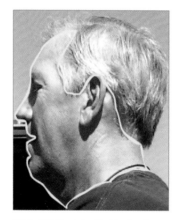

FIGURE 10.2 Beginning to trace the face by outlining it with a sampled flesh tone

7. Now you'll fill in some of the detail of the face before applying the final fill color. Pick out a part of your face that has a different color.

8. Sample the color and then trace the face component.

9. Activate the Paint Bucket tool (hotkey K). No need to change the fill color: the Paint Bucket tool will use the currently sampled color, the one you used to trace the face segment.

10. Click inside the segment you just traced. The segment should now completely fill in with that color. Hint: If it doesn't fill in, activate the Selection tool and click the outline. It should show as a complete loop.

11. If it does not, press Ctrl+Z (Command+Z on the Mac) to undo the fill, enlarge the section so you can see the tracing, use the Brush tool to close in any unclosed lines, then try the fill again.

12. You can click the Show or Hide All Layers button on the Rider Picture layer to examine how well your tracing is going (see Figure 10.3).

FIGURE 10.3 Filling in portions of the face; viewing with Rider Picture visibility turned off

13. Continue working like this, picking out different segments of the face, sampling their color, and tracing and filling in the outline of the segments.

14. When you have all the inside facial segments created, activate the paint bucket tool one more time.

15. In the fill Color Picker, sample the flesh tone you used to outline the face.

16. Fill in all sections of the face that do not yet have a color, hiding the Rider Picture layer occasionally to check your work.

17. Using the Selection tool, marquee all of the face components.

18. Group the face components with Ctrl+G (Command+G on the Mac).

19. Right-click the grouped facial components and select Insert Symbol, or press Ctrl+F8 (Command+F8 on the Mac).

20. Create a movie clip symbol called mcFace.

21. Repeat the preceding steps to sketch the rest of your picture, grouping and naming each of the body components you want to bone into individual movie clip objects (for example, mcUpperArm, mcLowerLeg). The upper and lower arms and hand should be separate components; ditto for the upper and lower leg and foot, the shirt sleeve on the shirt, the pant leg on the pant seat (for shorts; lower pant leg, upper pant leg and pant seat for regular dungarees).

22. Right-click the Rider Picture layer and select Delete Layers.

23. Navigate back to the stage.

24. Press Ctrl+S (Command+S on the Mac) to save your work.

TRACING TIPS

Here are some basic pointers to think about when doing this tracing work:

▶ Work from the inside out—focus on internal parts, and then move outward.

▶ As you draw a part of the body, create a rounded curve on each end of the body component. A rounded curve is best because once you join the components together and bone them, if you have sharp or squared edges in a component as the boned elements are moved, you'll see a separation of the elements that does not look natural. Rounded ends rotate around, keeping the color and movement more natural.

▶ Enlarge the area where you're working as required so you can more clearly see what you're tracing

▶ Use the Eraser tool (hotkey E) to get rid of any errant lines.

▶ Don't overdo it! Excessive detail isn't necessary. Put the detail in that describes the basic elements of what you're tracing, but don't fret about every nuance. At the scale your bike rider is going to appear on the stage, viewers will not likely observe the incredible detail you put into the colors in their iris.

▶ If a segment has heavy shadows on it, there's really no need to use very dark shadow colors if you don't want. Just sample a color that's a little lighter than the shadow.

▶ Allow yourself plenty of time. The tracing process may take hours, even days, to complete.

▶ If you're not happy with the current picture and you have another in the library, you can easily use Swap Symbol to substitute the picture.

Once you're done creating a cartoon version of yourself, you can delete the Rider Picture layer. It is no longer needed.

There's an easier way than all the cartooning, but it may not produce exactly the results you're looking for. Just take your photo, import it to the stage (or import it to the library then drag it out on the stage), highlight it and select Modify ➤ Bitmap ➤ Trace Bitmap from the Flash main menu. Stick with the default settings of Color threshold 100 and Minimum area 8 pixels and press OK. Don't like the results? Hit Ctrl+Z (Command+Z on the Mac) and try again with different settings. Repeat until you get the desired results.

Inserting Bones into Your Character

So you can insert the bones in your character, each of the graphic elements that are going to be rigged must be brought together into a movie clip. In your case, you'll have the upper and lower arms and hand as separate movie clips and the upper and lower legs and foot as separate movie clips as well. When done, you'll combine all of the elements in the arm (hand, lower arm and upper arm) into the bicycle movie clip and animate them. Movie clips within movie clips within movie clips—it's important to keep in mind what you're doing and where you're at during each step.

Certification Objective

1. From the Flash main menu, click Insert ➤ New Symbol, or press Ctrl+F8 (Command+F8 on the Mac).

2. Create a new movie clip called mcArmBones.

3. In the mcArmBones movie clip editing screen, use the up/down scrollbar to scroll the center X up toward the top of the screen. The X will help you align the items in your rigging.

4. From the library, drag mcUpperArm out onto the editing screen.

5. Activate the Free Transform tool.

6. Rotate mcUpperArm so it's straight up and down.

7. Move the mcUpperArm registration point to the top, where the shoulder is (see Figure 10.4).

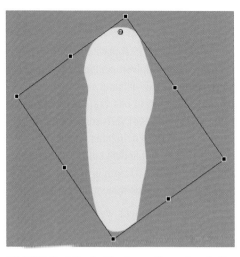

FIGURE 10.4 Placing mcUpperArm in the movie clip. Move the registration point to the top of the arm.

8. Repeat the previous process, dragging mcLowerArm out onto the editing screen, moving it into place, and adjusting its registration point as well.

9. Repeat the previous process, this time dragging mcHand onto the editing screen, moving it into place, and adjusting its registration point as well (see Figure 10.5).

FIGURE 10.5 Complete assemblage of upper and lower arms and hand

Now you're ready to put the bones on the arms and hand:

1. In the Tools panel, click the Bone tool ![bone tool icon] or press the hotkey M.

2. Starting with the shoulder, click and drag the first bone from the shoulder to the elbow. The bone color is the same as the outline color for the layer the asset is currently on.

3. Click the elbow and drag to the hand (see Figure 10.6).

FIGURE 10.6 Bones added to the arm

4. Look down at the timeline for mcArm. Note that Flash created a layer called Armature_x (where x is the next number in the sequence of armatures that have been created) when you inserted the bones. You cannot delete the Armature layer: It is required for the bones to work.

5. Activate the Selection tool.

6. If you've correctly boned the arm, you should be able to click and drag the hand and the arm, rotating them around the bone connection areas (see Figure 10.7).

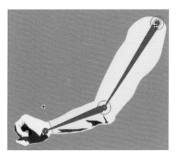

FIGURE 10.7 Moving the arm bones around to check their fluidity

7. Repeat the preceding steps to create movie clips for the boned legs (mcLegBones), head (mcHead), neck and shoulders (mcNeckAnd-Shoulders), pant leg and pant seat (mcPantLegsAndSeat), and sleeve and shirt (mcShirtAndSleeves).

Once you're done, you should have one movie clip that handles all of the arm rigging, another for the legs, and so on.

Constricting Animations

If you think about your arm and hand, there are certain positions into which they cannot be moved. For example, you likely cannot rotate your arm back behind you in a 180-degree circle.

Certification
Objective

When you're rigging characters, you have to be cognizant of the limitations of the limbs and constrain accordingly. Flash provides constraint options for this purpose.

1. Open the mcLegBones movie clip.

2. Resize the screen so all of the leg fits on the screen.

3. Click the upper leg bone. An IK bone property sheet appears in the Property Inspector (see Figure 10.8).

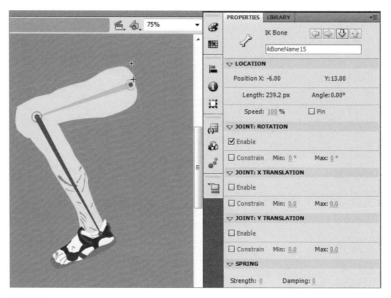

FIGURE 10.8 Getting ready to constrain a bone's movement (Joint: Rotation section in the Property Inspector)

4. Click the Constrain button and set the upper leg bone with -45 and +135 degrees, respectively. This means the upper leg can move up 135 degrees (consider a football kicker) and behind 45 degrees, for a total of 180 degrees of freedom of movement. The constraint indicator 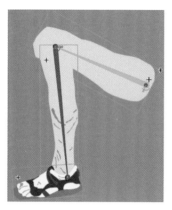 shows up on the bone as a little scale.

5. Move the leg up into a position that looks as though it is coming up to the top of a bicycle's pedal rotation (the foot is at 12:00 noon, to use a clock metaphor). See Figure 10.9.

FIGURE 10.9 Getting the leg ready: Set it as though it's on the upper part of the pedal rotation.

6. Right-click frame 2 of the Armature layer and select Insert Pose. This makes a copy of the original pose.

7. Move the upper and lower legs down slightly so it appears as though the foot and the pedal are at 9:00.

8. Repeat the process, inserting two more poses, each of which has the leg positioned at 6:00 and 3:00, respectively.

9. Finish off with one more pose, this time with the leg back at 12:00 again.

10. Scrub the playhead or press Enter to observe the pedaling motion.

11. While still in the mcLegBones movie clip, create a new layer called Pants.

12. Lock all other layers.

13. On the Pants layer, bring in the pant segments.

14. Using the Bone tool, bone the pant segments.

15. Using the process of inserting poses, make the pants behave the same way the leg behaves.

Repeat the previous steps for the arm bones and shirt. The shirt presents an interesting problem because the main part of the shirt really doesn't move much, but the arms do.

When working with IK, there is the concept of parent and child bones. Each bone can be separately enabled for rotation, x or y translation (moving in a particular coordinate), and constraints. The trick with the shirt will be to disable its ability to rotate *but* make it the parent bone to the sleeve(s). That is, when you start dragging your first bone out, start at the shirt and move into the first sleeve part. This makes the shirt the parent. Click on the bone to see its properties. Use the arrow keys IK Bone ⬅️➡️⬇️⬆️ to move back and forth or up and down between parent and child.

Animating IK'd Objects

Certification Objective You can animate IK'd objects and then use movie clips to show natural-looking movement. In the following sections, you'll place your cartoonized and IK'd self on the bike you created earlier and then match up the two so you have natural-looking motion.

Creating the Bicycle Animation

Certification Objective Reference the file `Bicycle.fla` in the book's website at www.sybex.com/go/flashessentials. Now it's time to put the completed parts onto the mcMovingBike movie clip.

1. Open the mcMovingBike movie clip.

2. Press Enter to observe the motion tween in play. Note the pedal movements. You will almost certainly need to make some adjustments to the mcLegBones movie clip to make the leg movement match the pedal movement. But for now let's get the legs moving with the bike.

3. Create a new layer called Rider's Legs.

4. Lock the Bicycle layer.

5. Drag the mcLegBones movie clip onto frame 1 of the new layer (see Figure 10.10). (Note that I did not include the rest of the body for illustration purposes.)

FIGURE 10.10 Placing the mcLegBones movie clip onto the bicycle

6. Use the Free Transform tool to move the rider onto the bicycle, and resize accordingly.

7. In frame 1 of the Rider's Legs layer, right-click and select Create Motion Tween. The new tween extends itself to match the tween on the Bicycle layer.

8. In the Rider's Legs layer, navigate to the end of the tween.

9. Right-click and select Insert Keyframe ➤ All.

10. Drag the legs so they are on top of the bike, which has moved to the left in the last frame of the tween.

11. Because you've updated mcMovingBike with the rider and you have an instance of mcMovingBike on the stage, the drawing is updated automatically (see Figure 10.11).

FIGURE 10.11 Rider finds its way onto the main stage.

12. Now you enter into an adjustment process. The leg strokes you've assembled in your IK work probably won't match the pedal strokes of the bike. You must make tiny edits to the poses in your IK movie clip—mcLegBones—working to the point where you match the pedal movement. This may mean you have to add additional poses, lengthening out the movement over time to get the two to match up.

13. Repeat the previous process for the rest of the body parts. Fortunately, you do not need to do any pedal matching with these remaining parts. But you do need to make the hand look as though it's gripping the handlebars. You may also want to make the head bob up and down a bit so it looks more realistic.

YOUR OTHER OPTIONS

There are several ways you could tackle the previous IK project. For example, you could have made the bicycle and the rider all in one movie clip. Or you could have made the bicycle in one movie clip, the rider in another. It's not absolutely necessary to make a bunch of movie clips for different animation features. However, creating objects you can reuse is a time-saver and something to think about. If you have a library of previously created objects—an arm, a hand, a head—you can reuse those objects in other projects. Thus, boiling your work down to a variety of smaller objects might be a smart idea.

Keep in mind that drawing symbols independently and then scaling within Flash adds a little more to the calculations Flash must perform, albeit minute.

Creating Bouncing Movement Using IK Springs

When you're not necessarily interested in things rotating around pivot points but you want to show things exploding or bouncing in and out, you can use the Spring setting of IK when working with Flash. For example, maybe you want to draw an exploding view of the way several parts fit together for a widget. You can reference Spring_IK.fla on the book's website as you work through this chapter.

One of the advantages of the spring setting is that you can set it so viewers are able to manipulate the object, which is called *runtime*, versus you manipulating it, which is called *authortime*.

Certification
Objective

1. Open a new ActionScript 3.0 file and name it Spring IK.

2. On the stage, create a new perfect square. Make it small, with a colorful fill and a black stroke.

3. Activate the Selection tool by pressing the V key on the keyboard.

4. Marquee the square.

5. Press Ctrl+D (Command+D on the Mac) to duplicate the object.

6. Drag the duplicated object so it's immediately below the first one.

7. Change the new object's fill color.

8. Repeat steps 5 through 7 another three times until you have a total of five blocks on the stage.

9. Activate the Oval tool by pressing O on the keyboard.

10. Pick a colorful fill and a black stroke.

11. Hold down the Shift key and draw a perfect circle on the stage immediately below the five squares (see Figure 10.12).

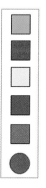

FIGURE 10.12 Preparing five blocks and an oval for setting up a spring IK

12. Activate the Selection tool.

13. Marquee the top square, making sure to get its stroke and fill.

14. Right-click the object and select Convert To Symbol from the context menu.

15. Make a movie clip, naming it mcSquare1.

16. Repeat steps 12 through 15 for the remaining squares, giving them consecutive numbers (e.g. mcSquare2, mcSquare3, etc.).

17. Marquee the oval.

18. Convert it into a move clip, giving it the name mcOval.

19. Your library should now have mcSquare1, mcSquare2, mcSquare3, mcSquare4, mcSquare5, and mcOval. The stage looks the same as before except you now know the objects on the stage are movie clips, not shapes.

20. Activate the Free Transform tool with the keyboard shortcut Q.

21. Click each movie clip in order, starting from the top and working your way down, and move the registration point to the top.

22. Activate the Bone tool with the keyboard shortcut B.

23. Starting at the top, draw a bone from the first block to the second.

24. Repeat until all blocks and the oval have a bone on them (see Figure 10.13).

FIGURE 10.13 All five blocks and oval have a bone connecting them

25. Activate the Selection tool. The cursor should continue to show a small bone on the lower-right corner.

26. Click the parent (top) bone.

27. In the Property Inspector for the parent bone, in the Joint: Rotation section, uncheck the Enable check box.

28. In the Joint: Y Translation section, check the Enable check box.

29. In the Spring section, enter a strength of 1 (see Figure 10.14).

FIGURE 10.14 Setting the Y translation and spring strength for the parent bone

30. In the IK Bone section at the top of the Property Inspector, click the down arrow to move to the next child.

31. Repeat steps 27 through 29 for each succeeding child bone.

32. The spring is now built. Click the oval and drag the spring up and down.

33. Play the movie with Ctrl+Enter (Command+Enter on the Mac). Note that nothing happens. You cannot move the spring.

34. Close the movie window.

35. Click the Armature_*x* layer name.

36. In the Property Inspector for the armature, in the Options section, click the Type drop-down and change it from Authortime to Runtime.

37. Play the movie again.

38. This time you can click the oval to move the spring up and down.

39. Play with the strength setting to see the difference between a light strength of 1 and a heavy strength of 100.

Showing a spring in runtime is handy for a variety of uses, such as illustrating how parts go together to form a more complex object.

Certification
Objective

For more information, tutorials, and other content regarding Flash IK, see http:// tv.adobe.com.

THE ESSENTIALS AND BEYOND

In this chapter you learned how to create and add bones to movie clips, thus giving them movement. This technique, called inverse kinematics (IK), can be useful for creating realistic movement in living things. You also learned how to use the Flash IK infrastructure to create spring-like movement.

ADDITIONAL EXERCISE

Use the file BigHead.fla on the book's website (www.sybex.com/go/flashessentials) for your work. In this exercise, you'll attach the head (a movie clip called mcBigHead) to various colored balls that are boned one to another. When you swing the head around, the string of balls should follow it.

1. Draw a blue ball on the stage below the head.

2. Turn the blue ball into a movie clip called mcBlueBall.

3. Repeat steps 1 and 2 to create yellow, red, and green balls, each of which is a separate movie clip with a similar name (e.g., mcGreenBall).

4. Using the Free Transform tool, move the registration point of the head to the bottom. It's okay to leave the registration point of the blue ball intact.

5. Using the Bone tool, connect mcBigHead and mcBlueBall together.

6. Repeat step 5, this time connecting mcBlueBall to mcYellowBall and so forth, adding a bone between each ball and the next one below it.

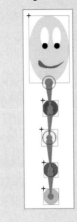

7. Press the Selection tool.

8. Try rotating mcBigHead. What happens? You should see that none of the boned objects below it move at all; they simply follow the path around BigHead's rotation.

9. Now move one of the balls. You should see that the array of balls and BigHead become disrupted.

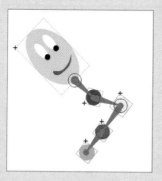

10. The key to making the balls flow smoothly around mcBigHead is to click the bottom ball and begin dragging around. You'll see that mcBigHead follows obediently around.

ANSWER TO ADDITIONAL EXERCISE

The answer to this exercise can be found in the download file `Bighead.fla`

CHAPTER 11

Working with Audio

A huge *component of* the way people communicate today involves audio. Working with Flash to include audio files is very easy to do. This chapter will walk you through the basics of including these kinds of files in your rich media work.

▶ **Creating a rich media project with audio**

▶ **Creating the drum set**

▶ **Creating the cymbals and cymbal stands**

▶ **Adding sounds to the drums**

▶ **Compressing audio**

▶ **Using the sounds supplied with Flash**

▶ **Putting a sound on the stage**

▶ **Controlling a sound with a code snippet**

Creating a Rich Media Project with Audio

When you think about audio, most likely your thoughts immediately turn to music and the things that make music happen. In this chapter, you'll create a set of drums, each of which when hit plays its correct sound. Never played the drums before? Well, this will be a great educational exercise for you because it will teach you about the equipment needed to do so. If you're a drummer, you will probably never have created a rich media document representing your passion before. It's a win-win situation.

A standard drum set consists of at least two but usually more drums, some cymbals of different types, and the associated hardware needed to keep the assemblage of drums manageable and reachable by the drummer. When drummers talk about drum sets, they often refer to how many drums they have, and they often use the word *kit* in place of the more proper term *drum set*. For example, someone with a kit that has five drums will say they have a *five-piece kit*. They don't count the cymbals in their description of the kit.

Drum kits usually consist of one or more of the following drums:

▶ Snare drum

▶ Bass drum

▶ Tom-toms (referred to singularly as a *tom*)

A drum kit also has one or more cymbals:

▶ Ride cymbal (usually used for keeping time)

▶ Crash cymbal (usually used for emphasis)

▶ High-hat cymbals (two cymbals mounted facing one another on a pedal-actuated stand that allows them to crash together)

Drum kits also have some required hardware:

▶ Cymbal stands

▶ High-hat stand

▶ Bass drum pedal

▶ Tom-tom stand in some kits

Certification Objective   Good designers who don't know a lot about the subject for which they're being contracted to create rich media will likely do some research before they begin crafting their work. In this first exercise, you will perform some of this research.

1. Open up your web browser and navigate to images.google.com.

2. Type in the search string **drum set**, **drumset**, or **drum kit**. You'll be presented with literally millions of pictures of various drum sets.

3. Select a picture of a kit you really like.

4. Count the number of drums (not the cymbals!). How many pieces does your favorite kit have?

5. Continuing to browse through the photos, see if you can figure out who the top drum manufacturers are. (Hint: Ringo Starr, formerly of the Beatles, plays Ludwig drums.) List at least three major drum manufacturers. (Ludwig's URL is www.ludwig-drums.com.)

6. Visit the website of the three manufacturers you chose.

7. Research how drum manufacturers make their drums. What wood(s) do they use for the shells?

8. What colors are available for the shells?

9. Repeat step 5, this time trying to figure out who the top cymbal manufacturers are. (Hint: Lots of drummers—myself included—believe Zildjian cymbals are at the top of the cymbal food chain.)

10. Visit the website of one of the cymbal manufacturers you chose. (Zildjian's URL is `http://zildjian.com`)

11. Research what material(s) are used to create cymbals.

12. Do some research to find out what a standard drum set made by a top-level manufacturer will cost. You'll be surprised to find that drummers have thousands of dollars tied up in their equipment.

13. Finally, pick out the drum set that you really like: number of drums and cymbals, and color of shells. Make sure you have a picture of the kit because you'll be using this information to create your Flash drum set.

NOT ALL DRUM KIT LAYOUTS ARE ALIKE

The kits you've just researched work for 99 percent of drummers, but because music is such a creative endeavor, drummers often resort to unusual layouts that include other drums or even non-drum objects that are used as drums. A great example of this kind of drummer is Will Champion from the band Coldplay. Champion plays a standard kit a lot of the time, but he will use unusual assemblages of drum objects for a kit as well.

Creating the Drum Set

Now that you've done your research, you can begin creating your Flash drum set. Because you want to show the drums' depth—giving the viewer some perspective of the entire kit—you'll draw the set as though it were rotated about 45 degrees away from you. You'll also need to think about the light source illuminating the drums: Where is the light coming from? For this exercise, the light source will appear to be coming from the upper-left side of the screen.

Drawing the Bass Drum

Most of the drums consist of four basic parts: hoops, shells, connectors (lugs and rods), and drumheads. The hoops are used to hold the drumheads down on the shells. The lugs are bolt assemblages that fasten the hoops fast to the shell. Once you've got the technique down when you build the bass drum, you can repeat it with the other drums.

1. Open up a new ActionScript 3.0 document, and name it Drums. (You may also reference the file Drums.fla on this book's website at www.sybex.com/go/flashessentials.)

2. Each component of the drum set will occupy its own layer. Name your first layer Bass Drum.

3. Begin by using Merge Drawing mode to draw two relatively large circles on the stage. These will represent one of the hoops that hold down the drumhead. Use a 1-pixel black stroke with no fill. Position the circles over one another with a slight overlap (see Figure 11.1).

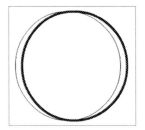

FIGURE 11.1 Drawing the bass drum hoops

Drawing the Bass Drum Hoops

Follow these steps:

1. The overlap of the two circles creates two crescent-shaped areas where you can fill in a color. Because your imaginary light is shining from the top-left side of the screen, use the Paint Bucket tool to fill in the left section with a lighter color than the right section, but keep

the color the same and only slightly vary the tint. In the example shown in Figure 11.2, I used the standard red color (hex #FF0000, RGB 255 000 000) for the left hoop section and Flash's canned red gradient for the right half. This gives the effect of light completely shining on the left section but only partially hitting the right one.

FIGURE 11.2 Filling in the bass drum hoop colors

2. Using the Selection tool, marquee the hoops.

3. Press Ctrl+D (Command+D on the Mac) to duplicate the hoops.

4. Use the Selection tool or the Free Transform tool to move the duplicated hoop temporarily out of the way.

5. Marquee each hoop in turn and convert them to graphic symbols named grHoop1 and grHoop2.

Making the Drum Head

Most drumheads come in white, clear, and black and are made from a tough plastic called Mylar. You'll put a drumhead in the oval described by the front hoop.

1. Using the Color tool, create a radial gradient that uses two or three colors for your drumhead. If you go with a black color, for example, then you want a deep blue or purple light somewhere in the middle of the gradient representing the light shining on the head.

2. Using the Oval tool, fill in the white circle resulting from the previous step.

3. Use the Gradient Transform tool to rotate and stretch the color blend, thinking about what the light will look like reflecting off of the head (see Figure 11.3).

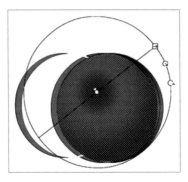

FIGURE 11.3 Filling in the drumhead with a reflective color

4. Right-click the drumhead and convert it to a graphic symbol called grBassDrumHead.

Moving the Back Hoop into the Back of the Front Hoop

Now you want to move the back hoop into place behind the front hoop. You're striving for a 3D look, paying attention to the perspective view of your photograph. Look at the nuances of the photo: What size is the back hoop relative to the front?

1. Activate the Free Transform tool.

2. Resize grHoop1 so it's slightly smaller than grHoop2. Because you're striving for a perspective effect, the back hoop will naturally appear to be slightly smaller than the front.

3. Move the grBackHoop into place so it's slightly behind the front hoop.

4. With grBackHoop still active, right-click and select Arrange ≻ Send To Back. This places the part of grBackHoop that was over grFront-Hoop behind it (see Figure 11.4).

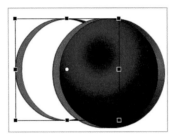

FIGURE 11.4 Positioning the back hoop behind the front hoop and drumhead

Creating the Drum Shell

Now you need a shell that fills in the depth between the front and back hoops. Real drums are made of a complex shell created from layers of birch or walnut wood glued together. The drum is then wrapped with its shell overlay. In your case, you'll simply make a circle, tucking it in between the front and back hoops. This will almost get you where you want to go, but there will be two triangles—one on top, one on bottom—that need to be filled in to complete the effect.

1. Using the Oval tool with a black stroke and red gradient fill, draw a circle the same size as the inside of the back hoop (see Figure 11.5).

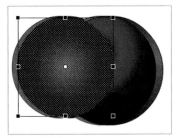

FIGURE 11.5 Creating the shell using basic shape tools and color gradients

2. Use the Gradient Transform tool to position the gradient so it too is properly reflecting light from the upper-left corner of the screen.

3. Activate the Free Transform tool and move the circle into place adjacent to the edge of the back hoop (see Figure 11.6).

FIGURE 11.6 Using Merge Drawing mode and circles to fashion the drum's shell

4. Using the Pencil tool, draw two black lines—one on the top, and one on the bottom—to connect the front and back hoops.

5. Using the Paintbrush tool, sample the darker color in the red gradient and then paint in the area between the lines you just drew and the area where the shell does not meet them.

Drawing and Placing the Lugs and Rods

The front and back drum hoops go over the front and back drumheads, which in turn fit over the drum shell. Everything is held together using some combination of lugs, threaded rods, and screws. In the case of your drum, there's no need to show extreme detail. Just showing rectangles representing the lugs and small, narrow rectangles representing the rods will work.

1. Use the Rectangle tool with no stroke and a silver gradient radial fill to draw a rectangle somewhere on the stage to represent a lug.

2. Right-click the new object and create a new graphic symbol called grLug.

3. Using the Rectangle tool again, still with no stroke and a silver gradient, draw a thin rectangle and turn it into a graphic symbol called grRod. The rods can also be used for the bass-drum support legs (called *spurs*).

4. Activate the Selection tool.

5. Click grLug and duplicate it.

6. Move it into place somewhere on the front hoop (see Figure 11.7).

7. Use the Free Transform tool to skew, resize, and rotate the lug so it fits onto the front hoop.

8. Repeat the process for the back lug.

9. Duplicate grRod and move the duplicate into place between the two lugs you just put on the drum.

10. If the rod appears to be above the two lugs, right-click it and select Move Backward. This causes the rod to move under the lugs but does not completely hide it under the other objects (see Figure 11.7).

Rod   Lug   Front hoop

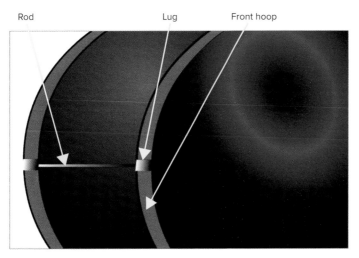

FIGURE 11.7 Lugs and rods connecting drum heads and shell together

11. If you group the two lugs and the rod, you can easily duplicate them and move them into the next place on the drum. However, you will need to break apart the group so that you can use the Free Transform tool to resize each of the lugs and the rod so the duplicate fits into its new position.

12. Put lugs on the right side of the drum.

13. Use grRod to make the drum spurs (the legs of the bass drum).

14. When you're done, marquee all of the objects, group them, and create a new graphic symbol called grBassDrum (see Figure 11.8).

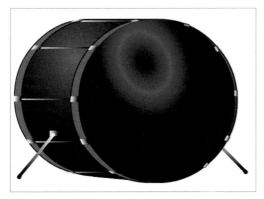

FIGURE 11.8 Completed bass drum

15. Save your work.

Creating the Tom-Toms and Snare

Now that you understand the basic components that make up a drum—front and rear hoops, front and rear or top and bottom drumheads, drum shell, and lugs and rods—you can repeat the process for each of the tom-toms and the snare drum.

Before you begin, take a look at your picture. You should note that at least one tom-tom, and usually two, are mounted to the top of the bass drum via two tubes, one of which comes out of the bass drum, the second of which connects to the tom-tom. The two tubes are connected together with a ratchet system that locks down with the twist of a knob. The previously described mechanism probably isn't necessary to include in your rich media document: Only drummers will notice. Just make it look similar to the actual mechanism by drawing the tubes (in your case, silver rectangles with a linear gradient) and you'll be fine. Tom-toms that connect to the top of the bass drum are often called *ride toms*.

The bigger tom-toms that sit on the floor are called *floor toms* and usually have steel rods called *legs* coming out of them that allow them to sit on the floor. In some cases, floor toms mount to a stand that looks somewhat like a cymbal stand, only a little more heftily constructed. Many newer kits have a tom-tom that's not as small as the ride toms and not as big as the floor tom(s): it's called a *mid-tom*. These mid-toms usually mount to a stand, whether alone or with a cymbal. All toms can be tuned to specific pitches.

The snare drum is a unique animal. It's not as tall as the other drums but very often as wide if not wider than the ride toms. Snare drums are generally constructed from metal, not wood, but some more expensive snare drums are constructed from very fine wood. Snare drums can be quite expensive and drummers pride themselves on the purchase of an upscale snare drum. The snare drum has its own stand: The upper half supports the snare drum with some rubber finger-like grips that can be tightened down on the rim, and the lower part swings out on a scissor-type system.

To get a better look at the detail of these objects, you can simply go to `images.google.com` and key in search terms such as "snare stand," "snare drum," "mid-tom," and "floor tom."

WHY IT'S IMPORTANT TO CONVERT OBJECTS INTO SYMBOLS

After you are finished with each drum, marquee it, right-click, and convert it into a movie clip symbol. Save the drums with names such as, for example, mcRideTom1, mcRideTom2, and so forth. Do the same with the cymbals and stands, and when all are completed and saved as movie clip symbols, you can pull them out of the library to put them together as a whole kit on the stage. Remember that with movie clip symbols, you have the ability to right-click an object and send it to the back, which allows you to arrange your kit so that some drums are behind one another—providing you with the perspective view you're looking for.

Making the Cymbals and Cymbal Stands

Non-drummers are not aware of this, but very often a drummer will have more money tied up in their cymbals than in the actual kit itself. Cymbals—especially Turkish hand-hammered cymbals from companies like Zildjian—can be very costly.

With most kits drummers have at least one ride cymbal, which sits to their right (there is such a thing as a left-handed drummer, and in that case the entire layout of the kit is reversed, so the ride cymbal would be on that person's left), a crash cymbal on their left, and a special set of cymbals called high-hat cymbals. High-hat cymbals face one another and crash together when the drummer steps on the high-hat pedal.

In the following sections, you will create a cymbal stand and a cymbal. As with the toms and bass drum, you will learn the techniques needed to repeat the process.

Drawing the Cymbal Stand

Cymbal stands are typically built out of strong steel tubes that have been chromed and that telescope inside one another. Cymbal stands have a scissor-like system that swing outward so they can stand on the floor. Atop the cymbal stand there is a wing nut and a rod that allows the cymbal to be attached to the cymbal stand.

1. Check your picture to get an idea of what a cymbal stand looks like. You'll be re-referencing this picture as you draw your stand.

2. With the Drums.fla file still open, use the Selection tool to click and delete the bass drum. Don't worry! You turned it into a graphic symbol, so you're deleting only an instance of it off of the stage. The actual symbol is still nicely tucked away in the library.

3. Activate the Rectangle tool with no stroke and the silver linear gradient fill .

4. Draw a long, narrow rectangle.

5. Draw a second long, narrow rectangle, this one slightly thinner than the rectangle you drew in step 4.

6. Draw a third long, narrow rectangle, this one slightly thinner than the one you drew in step 5.

7. Position the rectangles over one another: the widest on the bottom, the thinnest on the top (see Figure 11.9).

FIGURE 11.9 The three cymbal stand tubes

8. Each of the tubes has a connector at its top with a wing nut that tightens down on the smaller tube inside it. Near the top of the lower and middle tube, draw a rectangle to mimic the connector.

9. Using the Oval tool with the same silver linear gradient fill and no stroke, draw an oval on the stage.

10. Press Ctrl+D (Command+D on the Mac) to duplicate the oval.

11. Move the second oval a little out of the way.

12. Using the Free Transform tool, rotate the second oval 180 degrees. You're doing this because you're going to combine the two ovals to look like a wing nut and the linear gradient will cause a light-colored line to run through the center of the wing nut if you don't.

13. Join the two ovals.

14. Draw a small rectangle.

15. Move the small rectangle over one of the connectors you created in steps 8 through 13, positioning it so it appears as though it's a screw coming out of the connector.

16. Rotate the two ovals so they're vertical.

17. Move the ovals into place adjacent to the small rectangle you placed in step 15 (see Figure 11.10).

FIGURE 11.10 Creating the cymbal stand tube connectors

18. Repeat steps 8 through 17 to create a second connector for the middle and top tube. While you are simply creating an art asset on the stage during these steps and *not* converting them to symbols, one consideration you might have is to convert them to symbols as well. Doing so allows you to reuse just one symbol at all spots on the cymbal stand. One of the points of this exercise is to show you that raw art assets can commingle with symbols on the stage.

19. Activate the Selection tool, marquee all of your work, right-click, and save the objects as a graphic symbol named grCymbalStandTubes.

20. Save your work.

Drawing the Scissor-Style Brace for the Cymbal Stand Legs

Cymbal stands must be folded up and stored for easy transport from gig to gig. The legs for the cymbal stand are ingenious. Three legs connect on a round connector and are tightened down with a wing nut. There are three supports, one for each leg. They are riveted to each leg with a free-moving rivet and swing out when the legs are spread apart.

1. With the cymbal stand tubes still on the stage, drag a copy of grRod onto the stage.

2. Use your Free Transform tool to resize and manipulate grRod so it angles out near the top of the bottom tube.

3. Duplicate the instance of grRod and move the new copy to the opposite side of the tube.

4. Duplicate the on-stage instance of grRod one more time, moving it backward so it appears in perspective—that is, as though you are looking at the cymbal stand legs on the stage. This rectangle is behind the bottom tube and you can only barely see it. The other two are more fully visible to the viewer (see Figure 11.11).

FIGURE 11.11 Creating and positioning the cymbal stand legs

5. To make all of the graphic instances on the stage look real, you'll have to work with the Arrange ➤ Send To Back and Arrange ➤ Send To Front commands to position all objects correctly.

6. Now repeat steps 1 through 5 with slightly smaller rectangles connected at the opposite angle of the legs (see Figure 11.12).

FIGURE 11.12 Creating and positioning the cymbal stand leg supports

7. To create realistic-looking rubber tips for each of the legs, start by creating a small black rectangle, with 25 percent curve on the bottom and 15 percent curve on the top (see Figure 11.13).

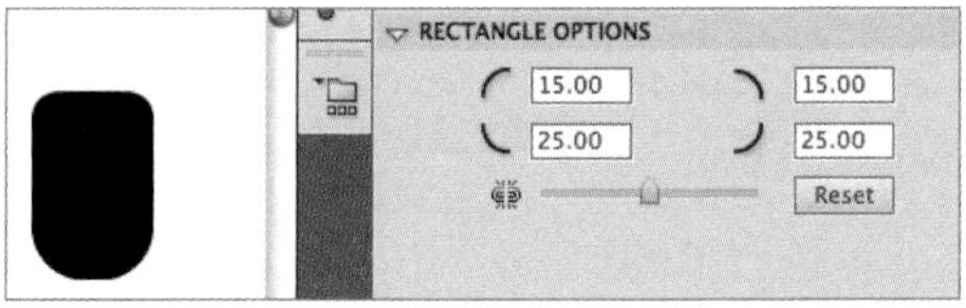

FIGURE 11.13 Creating realistic-looking rubber tips for the legs

8. Activate the Free Transform tool, and then, using the Ctrl+Shift (Command+Shift on the Mac) trick, click the corner of the top and bottom of the rubber tips, widening out the bottom and narrowing in the top.

9. Right-click and convert to a graphic symbol called grRubberTip.

10. Resize the instance of grRubberTip and move it into place at the bottom of one of the legs.

11. Duplicate the grRubberTip instance twice and place each of the duplicates into their respective positions in the remaining legs.

12. At the top of the cymbal stand, draw a round circle with no border fill and a radial gradient. The circle should be about 1.5 times larger than the small tube.

13. On top of the circle you just drew, place a small rectangle, no border fill, linear silver gradient.

14. Marquee all objects, and save the collection as a graphic symbol called grCymbalStand (see Figure 11.14).

FIGURE 11.14 Completed cymbal stand

15. Save your work

16. Delete the instance of grCymbalStand from the stage.

Creating the Cymbal

Cymbals are very interesting-looking instruments. They are slightly rounded, with a middle part called the *bell* that's more rounded. There's a hole in the middle of the cymbal that mounts it to the cymbal stand. The cymbal sits atop a thick wool cushion to keep it from rattling against the steel of the cymbal stand.

1. Take a look at the photo of your drum set, paying attention to the colors in the cymbal.

2. Open the Color panel.

3. Create a custom radial gradient that has the mixture of colors in it that you see in the photo.

4. Using Merge Drawing mode, draw a narrow oval on the stage using your custom gradient.

5. Activate the Selection tool.

6. Marquee the bottom half of the oval and delete it.

7. Repeat steps 4 through 6, this time making a smaller, fatter oval and cutting off its bottom half. Make sure you keep the objects separate until you are ready to join them together.

8. Marquee the two objects, right-click, and convert them to a movie clip symbol called mcCymbal (see Figure 11.15).

FIGURE 11.15 Completed cymbal

9. Delete the instance of mcCymbal from the stage.

10. Save your work.

Creating the High-Hat Stand and Cymbals

The high-hat represents a little more complicated rendition of the cymbal stand you just created because it has a pedal that, when pressed, moves a steel rod up and down through the middle of the cymbal stand tubes. There are not one but two cymbals on a high-hat, each one facing the other. Typically the bottom cymbal is heavier than the top. Drummers buy cymbals that are specially designed for high-hats in pairs.

The concept is that when the drummer presses the pedal, the two cymbals clash together. The drummer can also hold the pedal slightly down, keeping the cymbals slightly apart, giving them a nice *sssssttt* sound.

The high-hat is used primarily for time keeping but also for emphasis in songs.

You have all of the information you need to create a high-stand and cymbals. You may want to create some additional hardware components such as washers and wing nuts as graphic symbols (see the Drums.fla file on this book's website for reference). Remember that if you convert a symbol such as a drum to a movie clip, you have the ability to use the 3D Rotation Tool to give your drum a slight inward curve to produce a more 3D-like feel.

My completed drum kit is shown in Figure 11.16.

FIGURE 11.16   Completed drum set

Adding Sounds to the Drums

You went through all of that development just so you could add some sounds to your rich media on-stage assets. But that's one of the points that surfaces so easily when discussing design context: The assets come first, and the sounds are easy to add afterward.

Now that you have your drum kit made, you'll convert each of the drum and cymbal movie clip instances on the stage to a button. When the user clicks one of the buttons, the drum or cymbal makes its appropriate sound. You'll make use of the Code Snippets panel and modify the Click To Play/Stop Sound audio event snippet to accomplish your work. When sounds are played through Flash, they are said to be a sound stream and there is a sound event that handles the stream.

You'll start with the first ride tom-tom (the one on your right as you're looking at your kit).

Certification
Objective

Importing the Sounds and Preparing for ActionScript

Next you need to import the sounds for the drums (see the files in the Sounds folder on the book's website.) and prepare each individual sound for ActionScript. Flash can work with a variety of audio file formats, including files created with Adobe Soundbooth (now called Adobe Audition) (.asnd), Wave (.wav), Audio Interchange File Format (.aiff, Mac OS only), and MP3 (.mp3). Optionally, you can just drag sounds to the stage and adjust in the timeline. This is discouraged for all but short sounds. Best to programmatically manage sounds.

1. From the Flash main menu, click File ➢ Import To Stage.

2. From the Sounds folder, select all of the sounds to import.

3. Click OK.

4. Flash imports the sound files into the library. They are ready for use.

5. In the library, for each sound, right-click it. Select Properties, then in the ActionScript tab of the Properties window check Export for ActionScript. You will be prompted that a class definition could not be found for that file and one will be created for you. That's OK. Select OK and proceed to the next sound, repeating the process until all of the drum sounds have been linked for ActionScript.

Creating the Buttons

You'll use the techniques you used earlier to create a button, and then you'll add glow filters to the different button states.

1. Right-click the first ride tom-tom and select Convert To Symbol from the context menu.

2. Create a button called btnRideTom1.

3. Double-click btnRideTom1 to go into button-editing mode.

4. Right-click the Over frame and select Insert Keyframe.

5. Create a glow filter with an orange color and 35-pixel BlurX and BlurY.

6. Right-click the Down frame and select Insert Keyframe. Flash copies the assets from the Over frame, including the application of the glow filter.

7. Change the Down frame's glow filter to a yellow color (see Figure 11.17).

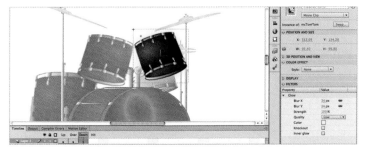

FIGURE 11.17 Adding Over and Down frames and glow filters to btnRideTom1

8. While still in button-editing mode, insert a new layer called Sound.

9. In the Sound layer, click the Down frame.

10. Right-click the Down frame of the Sound layer and select Insert Blank Keyframe.

11. With the blank keyframe in the Sound layer highlighted, look over at the Property Inspector. There you'll see a new section called Sound. Click the Name drop-down and select RideTom1.wav (Figure 11.18). Flash inserts an icon in the Down frame of the Sound layer, showing you that it has inserted the RideTom1 sound.

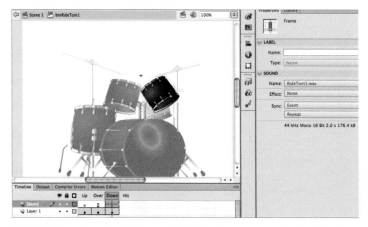

FIGURE 11.18 Adding the **RideTom1.wav** sound to btnRideTom1

12. Make any other adjustments you'd like. For example, if you like you can make the sound play in the left channel or right or fade from one to the other by clicking the Effect drop-down. You should leave the Sync drop-down set to Event and the Repeat drop-down's set to Repeat.

13. Navigate back to the stage.

14. Repeat steps 1 through 12 for the remaining drums and cymbals.

MOVIE CLIP EXTRAS

While you worked, you may have wondered why you made the drums and cymbals movie clip symbols and the stands graphic symbols? The simple answer is that movie clip symbols can have a filter applied to them and graphic symbols cannot. Therefore, when you were ready to create your buttons and you knew you wanted glow filters on each of them, movie clips were the appropriate choice. You could always use graphic symbols instead for your buttons and simply alter the tint of the object on each of the Over and Down frames, essentially accomplishing the same goal.

Adding a Hit Zone to the Cymbals

The cymbals are a little too narrow to easily hit. This is a time when you can use a button's Hit frame to help out.

1. Double-click one of the cymbal buttons to enter button-editing mode.

2. In the bottom layer, click the Hit frame.

3. Right-click the Hit frame and select Insert Keyframe.

4. Activate the Oval tool, selecting no frame and a yellow fill.

5. Draw an oval over the cymbal, sizing it so it roughly covers the cymbal (see Figure 11.19). Note that the color does not matter: as with a mask layer, you're simply describing a shape by which Flash will determine the zone in which a button is active.

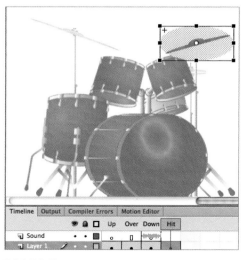

FIGURE 11.19 Drawing an oval to describe the hit zone

6. Click the Sound layer.

7. Right-click and select Insert Blank Keyframe.

8. Insert the same cymbal sound that you inserted in the Over frame.

9. Click Scene 1 to exit to the stage.

10. Press Ctrl+Enter (Command+Return on the Mac) to test the movie. The hand icon indicating a button should show up as you veer closely but do not touch the cymbal. This indicates that the Hit area is

working. Note that the hit area does not have to be anywhere in proximity to the cymbal. You could put it clear across the stage in another place and it would work equally as well.

Compressing Audio

In addition to audio compression, Flash document quality can be enhanced by controlling JPEG quality.

Flash audio can be compressed using various presupplied algorithms. You should be aware that if you do not choose a different algorithm, when you play the movie (thus creating a .swf file), Flash compresses your audio in MP3 format, which is usually fine because it produces a low file size with reasonably good quality. In addition to audio compression Flash document quality can be enhanced by controlling JPEG quality. You have the following algorithm compression choices:

▶ Default: MP3, mono, 16 kilobits per second (16 Kbps).

▶ ADPCM: Use this selection for small sounds (of which your drum sounds are a great example). Sample and bit rates are selectable, and Flash shows you the expected file size reduction (see Figure 11.20). When you use this algorithm, by default stereo sounds are converted to mono.

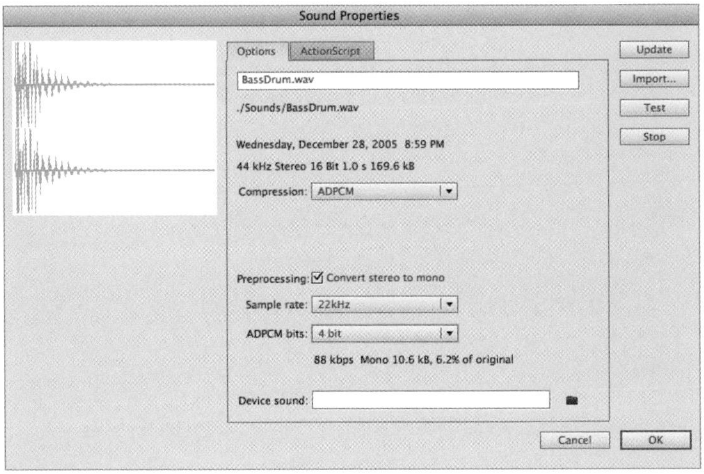

FIGURE 11.20 Projected file size reduction using ADPCM compression algorithm

▶ MP3: Even though the default compression is already MP3, this selection allows you to set the bit rate and quality of the compression, reducing the file size even further or increasing the quality of the output.

▶ RAW: No compression is applied. However, you are able to convert from stereo to mono using this feature.

▶ Speech: Useful for voice.

One of the sounds you used in your drum scene is in stereo. You'll use this exercise to set a conversion algorithm that converts it to mono.

1. Navigate to the library.

2. Right-click the BassDrum.wav sound and select Properties.

3. Note that it was recorded in 44 kilohertz (kHz) stereo in 16-bit, it is 1 second long, and it's relatively large at 169.6 Kilobits (Kb).

4. In the Compression drop-down select ADPCM.

5. Go with the default sample rate of 22 kHz and the number of bits at four. Keep the Convert Stereo To Mono check box checked. Note that the file size is only 6.2 percent of normal—a significant reduction. Click OK.

<aside>Although you have some basic sound-editing capabilities in Flash, most sounds are created using more robust sound-editing software. A good free example is Audacity.</aside>

Using the Sounds Supplied with Flash

If you don't want to go to the effort of supplying your own sounds, Flash comes with a ton of canned sounds. Use this exercise to access them.

1. With the Drums.fla file still open, from the Flash main menu click Window ➤ Common Libraries ➤ Sounds (see Figure 11.21).

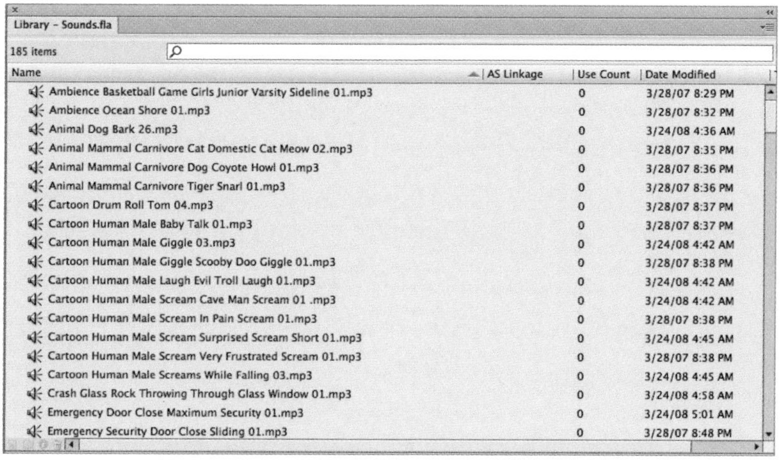

FIGURE 11.21 The Flash Sounds library

2. Scroll through the list of sounds.

3. Right-click any sound you're interested in and click Play on the context menu. Flash plays the sound.

Putting a Sound on the Stage

Sometimes you want a background sound that plays continuously. For example, maybe you have a beach scene in which you want the ocean waves to be an active part of your rich media. Flash allows you to drag and drop a sound right onto the stage for such purposes.

1. With the Drums.fla file still open, create a new layer called Background Sound.

2. Make sure the Background Sound layer is active.

3. Open the Flash Sounds library.

4. Select a sound you like and drag it to the stage. Human Crowd Hooray 04.mp3 might be a good choice because it's short and optimistic.

5. Note that Flash puts a line over the keyframe to note there's a sound on the layer.

6. Play the movie.

7. Don't like the sound? Delete the layer.

Controlling a Sound with a Code Snippet

Flash provides a Click To Play/Stop Sound code snippet you can use to play and stop sounds whenever a button is pressed. In this exercise, you will create a sign button to encourage the drummer to play a sound.

1. With the Drums.fla file still open, create a new layer called Encouragement Sign.

2. Make sure the Encouragement Sign layer is active and all the other layers are locked.

3. Create a sign that has as its text *Encourage the Drummer!* Use your own creative skills to design a sign of your choice. Put the sign somewhere in the upper-right corner of the stage.

4. Right-click the sign and convert it to a button called btnETDSign (see Figure 11.22).

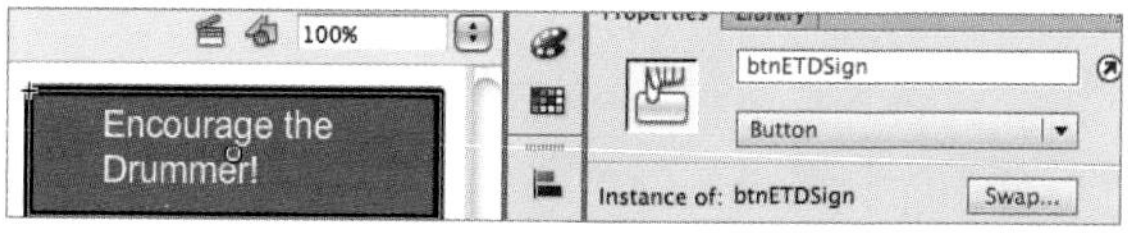

FIGURE 11.22 Encourage the Drummer! button

5. Highlight btnETDSign and give it the instance name of btnETDSign, the same name as the button. The button must have an instance name tied to it to be used with ActionScript.

6. Make sure the library is visible.

7. Open the Flash Sounds library.

8. Drag the file Human Crowd Ooos 02.mp3 to the library.

9. Right-click the file and select Properties. The Sound Properties window for the sound opens.

10. Click the ActionScript tab.

11. Click the Export For ActionScript check box. Flash puts the name of the file in the Class box.

12. Delete the 02.mp3 section of the name (see Figure 11.23).

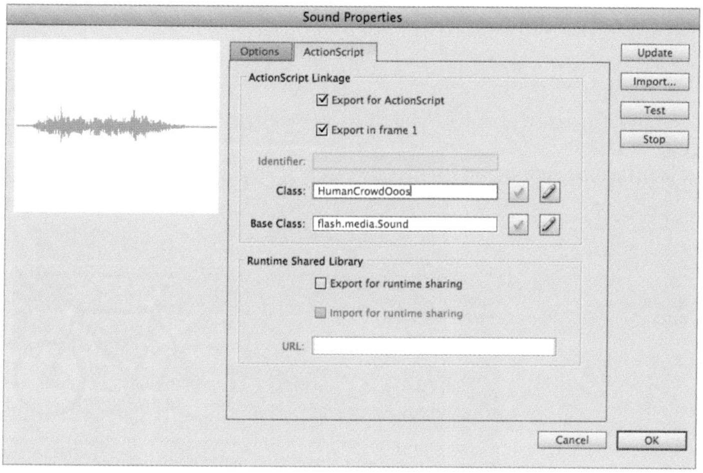

FIGURE 11.23 Linking the sound for ActionScript

13. Click OK.

14. Flash puts up a classpath box. Click OK.

15. Open the Code Snippets panel.

16. Make sure btnETDSign is selected, and then, in the Audio And Video section of the Code Snippets panel, double-click the Click To Play/Stop Sound snippet. Flash creates an Actions layer (if one doesn't already exist), opens the Actions panel, and copies the Click To Play/Stop Sound code (see Figure 11.24).

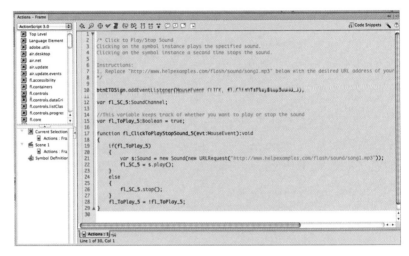

FIGURE 11.24 The Click To Play/Stop Sound code in the Actions panel

17. In line 21 of the script, replace the Sound(new URLRequest(www .helpexamples.com/flash/sound/song1.mp3)) with HumanCrowdOoos. This action ties the sound you put in the library and linked for ActionScript to the button (see Figure 11.25).

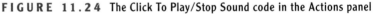

FIGURE 11.25 Replacing the URL with the name of your sound file

18. Press Ctrl+Enter (Command+Return on the Mac) to play the movie. If you have an error, Flash will switch to the Compiler Errors panel and give you a description of the error. Double-click it to be taken to the source of the problem. Check your spelling (especially the number of *o*'s in the phrase).

19. If the movie is successful, you should be able to click the button to encourage the drummer. Try clicking once to start the sound, then clicking it right away to stop it.

THE ESSENTIALS AND BEYOND

In this chapter you have created an active rich media document and attached sounds to each of the elements in it. You also learned about the sound compression selections in Flash. You learned how to put a sound on the stage and how to set up a button to play and stop the sound when clicked repeatedly. Now use the following exercise to create a cool background for your drum set.

1. Create a new layer called Background and move it to the bottom.

2. Make sure all the other layers are locked.

3. Hide the Drums and Encouragement Sign layers.

4. Draw a dark-blue or dark-purple rectangle to fit the stage.

5. Use the Align panel to precisely fit the rectangle to the stage.

6. Enlarge the stage to 800%.

7. Draw a small white star with nine points.

8. Right-click the star and turn it into a graphic symbol with the name grStar.

9. Open the Spray Brush tool.

10. Click the Edit button and add the grStar graphic.

11. Spray the background with tiny stars.

12. Unhide the Drums and Encouragement Sign layers to reveal a beautiful background for your drums.

ANSWER TO ADDITIONAL EXERCISE

CHAPTER 12

Working with Video

Because video is such an intrinsic element in our lives, any rich media document must be able to support videos that tell all or part of your story. The developers of Flash have made it amazingly easy to incorporate your videos into your rich media documents.

▶ **Understanding supported Flash video file types**

▶ **Setting up ActionScript cue points**

Understanding Supported Flash Video File Types

Humans are *analog* creatures. When you talk, your voice creates nice round undulating waves of sound, and when you listen, your ears receive waves of sound. When you smell, you receive waves of smell. When you feel warmth on your body, you are receiving waves of heat. Humans and all other life forms live in an analog—in other words, streams of waves—environment. Figure 12.1 shows what the analog waveform for the sentence "Hello, my name is Bill" looks like.

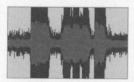

FIGURE 12.1 What the sentence "Hello, my name is Bill" looks like in analog waveform

Video represents the same kind of waves. Creatures typically move in a smooth analog kind of way. When someone shoots a video of the real world, they are capturing analog signals.

But computers are *digital*. They like to have nice sawed-off square waves (see Figure 12.2) because the waves represent sequences of ons and offs. In the end, that's all a computer really knows about: 0s or 1s, which signify on or off, respectively.

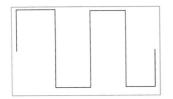

FIGURE 12.2 Digital waves: on/off

So, the problem becomes how to take an analog sound or video and convert it into something computers can understand and yet still have realistic sound and video—in other words, maintain that *fidelity* to the ears and eyes.

This is a job for a *codec*. Codecs are simply software applications that do two jobs: convert analog signals to digital while at the same time compressing what would otherwise be a huge file size into something more manageable. The level of compression, hence the fidelity of the file, is relative to the kind of codec chosen.

When you want to include video files in Flash, you must use one of three different file formats:

▶ FLV, which uses the Sorenson Spark codec (see http://en.wikipedia.org/wiki/Sorenson_codec) or the On2 VP6 codec (see http://en.wikipedia.org/wiki/VP6). (Sorenson Spark is the older of the two codecs.) FLV files are embedded directly into Flash Player. They're great when you have a quick little video you want to embed into the timeline. These are intended for smaller videos—you'll want to consider the F4V file type, which is a file that sits alongside your SWF, for larger videos. There's nothing wrong with embedded videos, but go carefully! For larger files you'll want to use the F4V format instead.

▶ F4V, which uses the H.264 codec (see http://en.wikipedia.org/wiki/H.264). F4V files sit alongside the SWF file and are consumed by the Flash Player a little bit at a time. The F4V format is useful for larger videos.

▶ MP4, which also uses the H.264 codec.

You should also be aware that Flash also supports server-side streaming video, and as a matter of fact, Adobe manufactures video streaming software. See www.adobe.com/products/flashmediaserver/ for more details. This is a topic that's beyond the scope of this book, so just be aware there is a hierarchy of video-serving capability via Flash. In most cases, you'll likely use the FLV format and occasionally use F4V. There are many benefits for using FLV for Adobe

AIR apps including popular file format, good audio and video quality, good compression, ease of editing, and copyright protection among others.

Converting Non-supported File Types

Fortunately for you, the folks at Adobe have included two different programs that can help you get your videos into Flash:

▶ The Flash Media Encoder utility

▶ The Flash Import Video Wizard

First, there is a nifty little utility called the Adobe Media Encoder that will take your video in an unsupported file type and convert it to one Flash can use. This is a separate program from Flash Pro and is invoked the same way you start any program. If you lack a video to convert, feel free to use RaymondLeeTheDrummerDude.wmv on this book's website at www.sybex.com/go/flashessentials.

1. Start the Adobe Media Encoder program (Figure 12.3). (You'll find this program in the Applications folder on your Mac or by clicking Start ➢ Adobe Create Suite in Windows.)

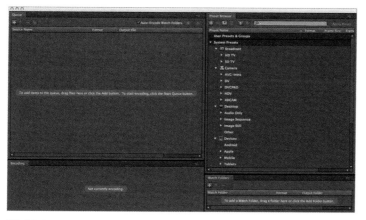

FIGURE 12.3 The Adobe Media Encoder 6.0 program screen

2. Click the plus sign underneath the Queues tab at the top of the window. This brings up a file browser window.

3. Navigate to the video you want to convert and select it.

4. In the Preset Browser pane on the right side of the Media Encoder program, select the Flash drop-down in the Web Video section (Figure 12.4).

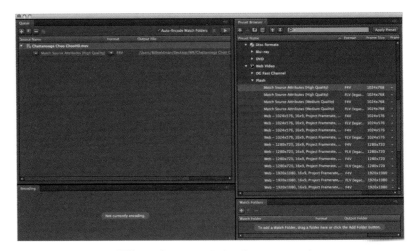

ΓIGURE 12.4 With movie now loaded, select a conversion type.

5. Select the conversion type you're interested in. For example, maybe you have a larger-format movie you want to convert to a smaller format. In most cases, F4V will be a better choice than FLV because F4V is the newer of the two Flash video formats.

6. Click the Start Queue button ▶ or press Enter (Return on the Mac) to begin the conversion.

The process can take a bit of time and will show you each frame as it is processed.

You can also launch the Adobe Media Encoder when you use the Import Video Wizard (see the next section).

Using the Import Video Wizard

Unless you're interested in converting your movie to a different size or frame rate, you will usually want to use the Flash Import Video Wizard in place of the Media Encoder program. When you use the Flash Import Video Wizard, you will have a choice between two ways Flash will import the video for you:

▶ Load external video with playback component.

▶ Embed FLV in SWF and play in timeline.

Certification Objective

Generally speaking, the first option (the default in the Flash Import Video Wizard) is the best because the movie stays separate from the Flash SWF file. You should be aware that when FLVs are placed on the timeline, their frame rate *must* match the frame rate of the SWF (24 fps by default). Also, it's important to point out again that using longer videos on the timeline may produce syncing bugs. And, you *cannot* import video to a Flash document when the publish style is HTML.

ASSURING FILE LOCATION FIDELITY

Before you begin using the Import Video Wizard, you'll want to make sure the video is in the same location it will be when it's uploaded to the web server. Suppose, for example, you keep your audio files in a folder called Audio and now you want to upload a video and use Flash's movie capabilities to play it. You create a Video folder on your development computer, copy the movie to that folder, and then use Flash to do the video preparation work. To make things simple, when you're ready to upload the video you should create a Video folder on the web server and copy the video there as well. When Flash runs the video, it will consult the *relative* directory path—in this case, the Video folder—and play the movie there. If your website folder structure matches your development machine's structure, you won't have to do any modifications to get the movie to play successfully once it's on the Web.

In this exercise you will use the movie RaymondLeeTheDrummerDude.f4v that's included on the book's website. This is a movie of a drummer rehearsing various songs with a big band jazz group.

1. Open a new ActionScript 3.0 document.

2. From the Flash main menu, click File ➤ Import ➤ Import Video selection to bring up the Import Video Wizard (Figure 12.5).

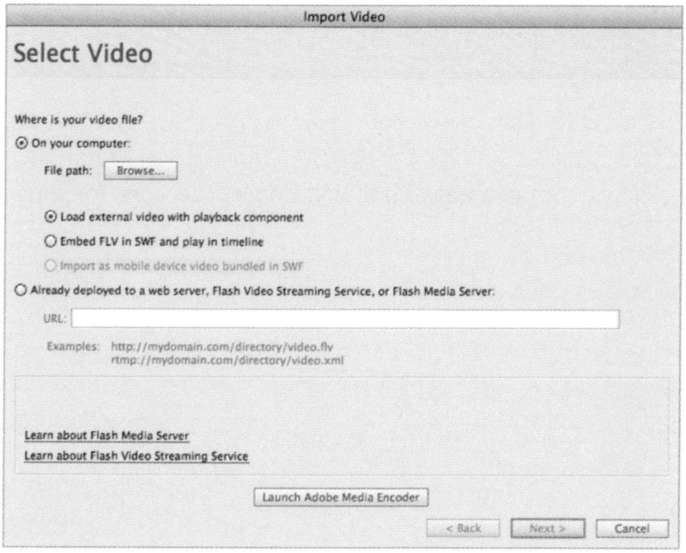

FIGURE 12.5 The Flash Import Video Wizard

3. Click the Browse button, navigate to the movie you want to import, and select it.

4. Assure that the Load External Video With Playback Component radio button is selected and click the Next button.

5. You are presented with a Skinning screen (Figure 12.6), in which you can determine what tools you want to include with the playback component as well as its color. Stick with the default `MinimalFlatCustomColorPlayBackSeekCounterVolMuteFull.swf` file (Figure 12.7). The list of prepared SWF files that provide playback capability is substantial, providing you with a variety of canned choices. The wizard also provides the ability to create your own if you do not find any of these choices satisfactory.

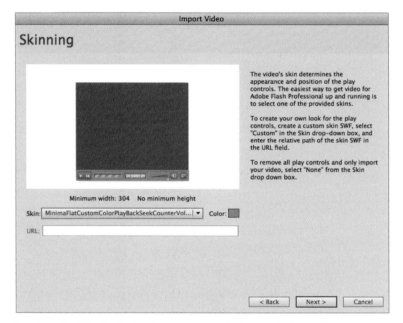

FIGURE 12.6 The Flash Import Video Wizard Skinning dialog

None
MinimaFlatCustomColorAll.swf
MinimaFlatCustomColorPlayBackSeekCounterVolMute.swf
✓ MinimaFlatCustomColorPlayBackSeekCounterVolMuteFull.swf
MinimaFlatCustomColorPlayBackSeekMute.swf
MinimaSilverAll.swf
MinimaSilverPlayBackSeekCounterVolMute.swf
MinimaSilverPlayBackSeekCounterVolMuteFull.swf
MinimaSilverPlayBackSeekMute.swf
MinimaUnderPlayBackSeekCounterVolMuteFull.swf
MinimaUnderPlayBackSeekCounterVolMuteNoFull.swf
SkinOverAll.swf
SkinOverAllNoCaption.swf
SkinOverAllNoFullNoCaption.swf
SkinOverAllNoFullscreen.swf
SkinOverAllNoVolNoCaptionNoFull.swf
SkinOverPlay.swf
SkinOverPlayCaption.swf
SkinOverPlayFullscreen.swf
SkinOverPlayMute.swf
SkinOverPlayMuteCaptionFull.swf
SkinOverPlaySeekCaption.swf
SkinOverPlaySeekFullscreen.swf
SkinOverPlaySeekMute.swf
SkinOverPlaySeekStop.swf
SkinOverPlayStopSeekCaptionVol.swf
SkinOverPlayStopSeekFullVol.swf
SkinOverPlayStopSeekMuteVol.swf
SkinUnderAll.swf
SkinUnderAllNoCaption.swf
SkinUnderAllNoFullNoCaption.swf
SkinUnderAllNoFullscreen.swf
SkinUnderAllNoVolNoCaptionNoFull.swf
SkinUnderPlay.swf
SkinUnderPlayCaption.swf
SkinUnderPlayFullscreen.swf

FIGURE 12.7 The list of playback component styles from which you can choose when in the Flash Import Video Wizard

6. You can choose to stick with the default dark-gray color or pick a new color from the Color Picker. Once you have chosen a color, click the Next button.

7. The Finish Video Import screen (Figure 12.8) provides you with a summary of the work the Import Video Wizard is going to do. Click the Finish button.

Import Video

Finish Video Import

The video you are using is located at:

/Users/BillHeldman/Documents/Writing/Sybex/ACA Study Guide/Chapter 12/video/WRDrumVideo.f4v

The video will be located at: (relative paths are relative to your .swf)
WRDrumVideo.f4v

A Flash Video component will be created on the stage and configured for local playback.

The video component uses a skin that has been copied next to your .fla. This file will need to be deployed to your server.

Before exporting and deploying your .swf, you may need to update the URL in the Property Inspector to refer to the video's final location on your web or Flash Media server.

☐ After importing video, view video topics in Flash Help

[< Back]   [Finish]   [Cancel]

FIGURE 12.8 The Finish Video Import summary report

8. If the video imports a bit larger than the stage area, use the Align panel to match the height and width of the stage and to center the movie on the stage (Figure 12.9). Note that there is some room at the top utilized by the FLVPlayback component. Make sure the movie and controls appear on the stage: it's okay if the FLVPlayback component appears above the stage (that is, in the pasteboard).

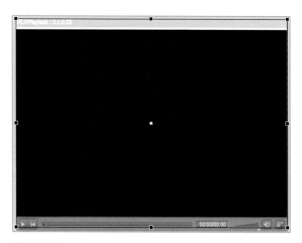

FIGURE 12.9 Aligning the movie to the size of the stage

9. Play the movie with Ctrl+Enter (Command+Return on the Mac).

10. While the movie is playing, test all of the control elements: stop and start the movie, change the volume, mute the volume, and so forth. The FLVPlayback component handles all of the playback elements for you.

11. Save the file.

TIP   Images and movies can also be exported using File ≻ Export from the main Flash menu.

Once you have a movie on the stage, Flash notes in the Property Inspector that your movie is an instance of FLVPlayback and provides you with several different control elements for adjusting your movie (Figure 12.10) in the Component Parameters section. Additionally, the library has an FLVPlayback component in it.

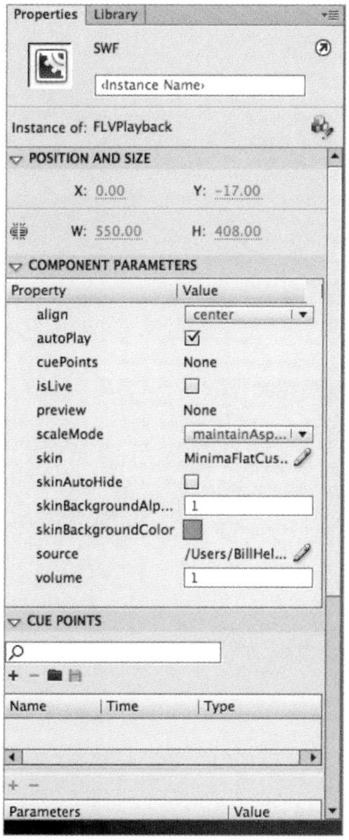

FIGURE 12.10   The **FLVPlayback** Component Parameters section in the Property Inspector

The following list includes brief explanations of the FLVPlayback component parameters, some of which are directly adjustable within the Property Inspector; others must be managed via code:

▶ align: Determines the alignment of the video within the FLVPlayback component bounds.

▶ autoPlay: A Boolean (true/false) value that determines if the video will immediately begin playing when the Flash movie is launched.

▶ cuePoints: If cue points are used in the video (more on that in the next section), the points are noted here.

▶ isLive: If the video is being served up by Flash Media Server, this check box should be checked.

▶ preview: Provides a preview Image that will appear before the video plays. The viewer sees the playback controls and the preview image.

▶ scaleMode: This dropdown allows you to select aspect ratios for the video should you resize the playback screen. The default is to maintain the vertical and horizontal aspect ratio.

▶ skin: This is the skin you picked when you ran the Import Video Wizard.

▶ skinAutoHide: Hides the skin when the mouse cursor is not over the video.

▶ skinBackgroundAlpha: Sets the transparency value (0: 1) of the skin. This is a percentage value. Zero is no alpha—completely transparent, whereas one means completely opaque. Think of this the same way you would express a percentage without using the percent sign (e.g., 50% = 0.50). Thus a 50% alpha value would be expressed as 0.5 in this field.

▶ skinBackgroundColor: Sets the background color of the skin.

▶ source: The relative path to the video. *Relative* means that you don't include a drive letter; you use slashes (/) and folder names to point to the video file. This is hugely important when you're ready to install the video on a web server. Flash needs to know the path to the video.

▶ volume: Sets the volume (0: 1). See note above about how this number setting works.

FLASH MEDIA SERVER AND MOVIE EDITING PRODUCTS

Adobe has a variety of Flash Media Server products for businesses of any size and professional requirement. See www.adobe.com/products/ flashmediaserver/. Also, Adobe has a professional video editing product called AfterEffects. See www.adobe.com/products/ aftereffects.html.

Setting Up ActionScript Cue Points

The drummer in the movie—Raymond Lee—plays drums for a big band jazz and swing group in the Denver area called William and the Romantics. This video was shot during a rehearsal session. Ray used his video editing software to chop out various sections of his playing to reduce the video down to a few short segments. There are two songs he is rehearsing with the band: Louis Prima's famous "Sing, Sing, Sing" and Glen Miller's "I've Got a Gal in Kalamazoo." The video switches between the two songs several times.

As you watch the video, you'll see that there are distinct places where the video changes somehow. These would be ideal locations to introduce *cue points* (provided, that is, you would like to have places to which viewers can jump in the video).

Adding ActionScript Cue Points to Your Video

In this exercise, you will use the FLVPlayback component you created in the previous exercise and add some ActionScript cue points. Additionally, you will include some buttons on the stage so that viewers can navigate to the various sections of the video using the ActionScript cue points. (Reference the file RayTheDrummerDude2.fla on this book's website if needed.) As you do this work, pay attention to the location in which the video is located. This path must match the path you use on the web server at the time you decide to publish the movie and the SWF file or the cue point data will be erased.

1. If the video you created in the previous exercise is not open, open it.

2. Click the video player (in reality you are clicking the FLVPlayback component).

3. In the Property Inspector, click the arrow next to the Component Parameters section to minimize it. The Cue Points section beneath it is expanded (Figure 12.11).

FIGURE 12.11 The Cue Points section of the FLVPlayback properties

4. Using the Free Transform tool, resize the video so it takes up about two-thirds of the stage.

5. Change the stage color to match the video player's skin color (Figure 12.12).

FIGURE 12.12 Making the FLVPlayback component smaller, getting ready for buttons

6. Click the FLVPlayback component to activate it.

7. Give the component an instance name of RTDD (realizing that the acronym stands for Ray the Drummer Dude). In order to tie the ActionScript cue points you'll be creating to the buttons you'll be creating, you must have an instance name for your video.

8. Activate the Selection tool.

9. In the Cue Points section of the Property Inspector, click the plus sign to add a new ActionScript cue point.

10. Click the name section and give this new ActionScript cue point the name Start (see Figure 12.13).

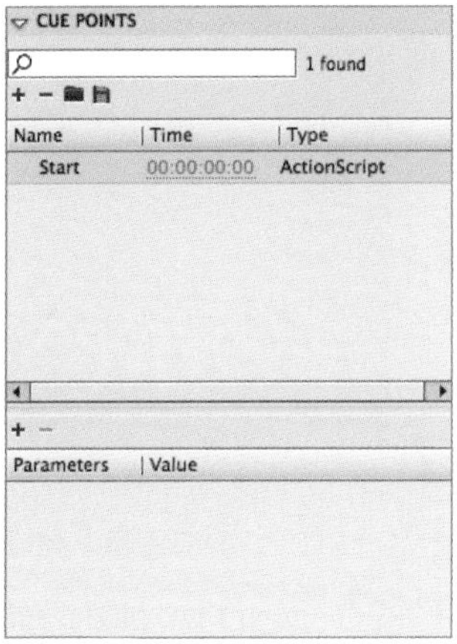

FIGURE 12.13 Giving an ActionScript cue point a name

11. Click the slider on the FLVPlayback component that allows you to move ahead or back in the video—it's called the seek bar—and slide to 00:16:01:54.

12. Repeat steps 9 and 10, giving this new ActionScript cue point the name Kalamazoo.

13. Drag the seek bar to 00:25:01:54.

14. Repeat steps 9 and 10, giving this new ActionScript cue point the name KalamazooBW (see Figure 12.14).

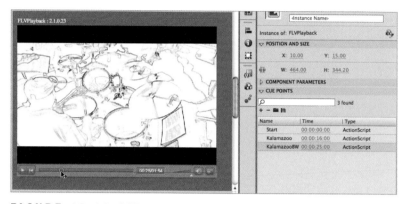

FIGURE 12.14 Adding additional ActionScript cue points

15. Drag the seek bar to 00:42:01:54.

16. Repeat steps 9 and 10, giving this new ActionScript cue point the name Sing_Sing_Sing.

17. Drag the seek bar to 00:55:01:54.

18. Repeat steps 9 and 10, giving this new ActionScript cue point the name Kalamazoo_Reprise.

19. Save your work.

Adding Parameters to Cue Points

Now that you have some cue points set up, you can add parameters to them. Parameters are simply data points that describe more about a specific cue point. The parameters consist of two sections: parameter and value. In the Parameters part, you type the name of the parameter. In the Value section, you type the data you'd like to store. The data can be anything, but if you type words, you need to use underscores to separate them: no spaces!

In this exercise you'll add some parameters to a couple of your cue points.

1. In the same video you were working with in the previous exercise, click the Start cue point.

2. In the Parameters section, click the plus sign to add a parameter.

3. In the Parameters area, click and type the name **RTDD**.

4. In the Value area, type **Ray_At_Rehearsal** (see Figure 12.15).

FIGURE 12.15 Giving an ActionScript cue point a parameter

5. Click the Kalamazoo cue point.

6. Repeat steps 3 and 4 using the parameter name Kalamazoo_Info and the value Recorded_1942_In_film_Orchestra_Wives.

7. Add a second parameter with the name Singers and the value Tex_Beneky_Marion_Hutton_The_Modernaires.

8. Save your work.

You can assign as many parameters and values for each cue point as you like. Programmatically, you could access these values using ActionScript.

Adding the Buttons

Now all you have to do is add some buttons that, when pressed, navigate the user to a particular cue point. With the Flash Code Snippets panel, this job is easier than it sounds.

1. If the Flash file from the previous exercises isn't open, open it now.

2. Activate the Rectangle tool, select no stroke and a fill color that matches your stage background and video skin colors.

3. In the Rectangle Options section of the Property Inspector, set all four corners to 25.

4. Draw a rectangle on the pasteboard.

5. Activate the Text tool, and select a sans-serif font and an appropriate font color.

6. Make a text field on the pasteboard with the word *Start* in it and position it atop the rectangle you created.

7. Activate the Selection tool and marquee both objects.

8. Right-click the marqueed objects and select Convert To Symbol.

9. Make a button symbol named btnStart.

10. Double-click the new button symbol to enter button-editing mode.

11. Right-click the Over frame and select Insert Keyframe. Flash makes an exact copy of the asset on the Up frame.

12. Alter the button's look somehow (e.g., change its color or change the text color).

13. Repeat steps 11 and 12 for the Down frame.

14. Move the button into place (see Figure 12.16).

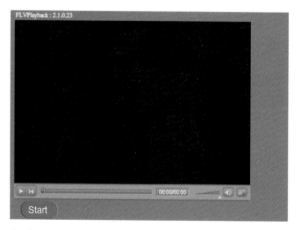

FIGURE 12.16 Placing the button on the screen

15. Repeat steps 2 through 14 for the remaining buttons, labeling them Kalamazoo, KalamazooBW, and SingSingSing.

16. Save your work.

Now it's time to add the code to the buttons.

1. Select the FLVPlayback component.

2. In the Property Inspector, uncheck the autoPlay property.

3. Give the video an instance name of videoJazz.

4. Select the Start button.

5. Give the symbol an instance name of btnStart.

6. Open the Code Snippets panel and navigate to the Audio And Video section.

7. Double-click the Click To Seek To Cue Point snippet. Flash creates an Actions layer at the top of the main timeline (if it does not already exist), opens the Actions panel, and copies the required code into the Actions panel at this frame.

8. In the Actions panel, there are two changes you need to make to the code: the video instance name and the cue point. Change them to videoJazz and Start, respectively. You'll need to key in the video instance name twice.

9. Add stop(); to the top of the Actions panel (see Figure 2.17).

```
1   stop();
2   /* Click to Seek to Cue Point (Requires FLVPlayback component)
3   Clicking on the specified symbol instance seeks to a cue point of the video in the
4
5   Instructions:
6   1. Replace video_instance_name below with the instance name of the FLVPlayback com
7   2. Replace "Cue Point 1" below with the name of the cue point to seek to. Keep the
8   */
9
10  btnStart.addEventListener(MouseEvent.CLICK, fl_ClickToSeekToCuePoint);
11
12  function fl_ClickToSeekToCuePoint(event:MouseEvent):void
13  {
14      // Replace video_instance_name with the instance name of the video component.
15      // Replace "Cue Point 1" with the name of the cue point to seek to.
16      var cuePointInstance:Object = videoJazz.findCuePoint("Start");
17      videoJazz.seek(cuePointInstance.time);
18  }
19
```

FIGURE 12.17 Adding ActionScript code to the button: two places where you change the video instance name and one place where you key in the cue point name

10. Test the movie.

FIGURE 12.18 Final video product running in a Flash movie

11. Repeat steps 4 through 10 for the remaining buttons.

12. When you play the movie, you should be presented with four active buttons that, when clicked, take you to the cue point you gave in the ActionScript code (see Figure 2.18). This is an exciting merger of code and rich media: code even the coding neophyte can manage!

13. Save the file.

THE ESSENTIALS AND BEYOND

In this chapter, you learned how easy it is to bring video into your Flash documents. You learned about the Flash Media Encoder utility and the Flash Import Video Wizard. You also learned how to create cue points and tie them to ActionScript events.

Let's polish this chapter off with one last video activity: attaching a video directly inside a Flash document on the main timeline. This is something you should *not* be frequently doing. It's better for most movies to live outside the Flash file and be referenced by the FLVPlayback component. This prevents you from having inordinately large Flash files. The video streaming mechanism in the FLVPlayback component will help regulate the opening and downloading of video frames by your viewers.

But there are occasional times when you just want to place a video right on the stage. Let's go through the exercise. You'll use the supplied video RayTheDrummerDudeLive .flv, a video of Raymond Lee playing "I've Got a Gal in Kalamazoo" at a wedding.

   1. Open a new ActionScript 3.0 document.

   2. Using Windows Explorer in Windows or a Finder window on the Mac, locate the file and drag it onto the stage. The Import Video Wizard launches (shown here).

Import Video

Select Video

Where is your video file?

⊙ On your computer:

    File path: [Browse...]

    /Users/BillHeldman/Desktop/Ray the Drummer Dude Live.mov

    ⊙ Load external video with playback component

    ○ Embed FLV in SWF and play in timeline

    ○ Import as mobile device video bundled in SWF

○ Already deployed to a web server, Flash Video Streaming Service, or Flash Media Server:

    URL: [   ]

    Examples: http://mydomain.com/directory/video.flv
               rtmp://mydomain.com/directory/video.xml

This video file does not appear to be encoded for Flash Professional. You can re-encode the video using Adobe Media Encoder.

Learn about Flash Media Server

Learn about Flash Video Streaming Service

[Launch Adobe Media Encoder]

[< Back]   [Next >]   [Cancel]

3. Click the Embed FLV In SWF And Play In Timeline button, then click Next. The Embedding window appears.

4. Make sure Embedded Video is the selection in the Symbol Type drop-down.

Import Video

Embedding

How would you like to embed the video?

Symbol type: [Embedded video ▾]

    ☑ Place instance on stage

    ☑ Expand timeline if needed

    ☑ Include audio

[< Back]   [Next >]   [Cancel]

5. Make sure the Place Instance On Stage, Expand Timeline If Needed, and Include Audio check boxes are checked. Click Next.

6. The Finish Video Import window appears. Click Finish.

THE ESSENTIALS AND BEYOND *(Continued)*

```
                              Import Video

Finish Video Import

    The video you are using is located at:

    /Users/BillHeldman/Documents/Writing/Sybex/ACA  Study Guide/Chapter 12/RayTheDrummerDudeLive.flv

    The video will be placed on the stage.

    The timeline will be expanded to accommodate the playback length.

          ☐ After importing video, view video topics in Flash Help




                                        < Back      Finish      Cancel
```

7. Launch the Align panel.

8. In the Match Size section, click the Match Width And Height button.

9. In the Align section, click the Align Horizontal Center and Align Vertical Center buttons to place the video directly on the stage.

10. Play the movie.

ANSWER TO ADDITIONAL EXERCISE

CHAPTER 13

Working with ActionScript

Good design is only half the battle when creating rich media documents. Often a program—code, if you will—is required to make some action happen within the document. Unfortunately, it is at this juncture that many designers quit because they're intimidated by or even afraid of code. But ActionScript is such a versatile and widely deployed language that there shouldn't be much to worry about in terms of assimilating the technology.

This chapter will introduce you to the basics of writing ActionScript code. ActionScript is a well-known and well-understood language, considered a dialect of JavaScript, one of the foundational web languages and widely used throughout the industry. If you have something you'd like to accomplish with ActionScript, there are likely several thousand examples on the Web for you to look at. Code snippets and reusable code have made coding so much more approachable for non-software-developer types. (Of course, as with everything else on the Web, it is important to remember that there is a lot of junk out there as well as good stuff. Just because you think you find a great snippet doesn't necessarily mean it is. Another important point is that some code words were *deprecated* by Adobe, meaning they should no longer be used.)

▶ **Getting started with ActionScript**

▶ **Programming ActionScript to calculate your BMI**

▶ **Publishing your work**

Getting Started with ActionScript

ActionScript is a compiled programming language that can be used directly in Flash documents or with an interactive development environment (IDE) called Flash Builder (see www.adobe.com/products/flash-builder

.html). It isn't just used for writing Flash code; it's also used to create what are called Adobe Interactive Runtime (AIR) applications—apps that go beyond the Flash platform and the Web and run on desktops or portable devices (see www.adobe.com/products/air.html). For your purposes (in other words, this book and the commensurate exam), you only need to know that ActionScript is used in Flash documents to make certain animated elements work.

What does the word *compiled* mean? When you are writing code using a compiled language, you must submit your code to a compiler that checks for syntax errors within your code, bundles any other code libraries that you call alongside your own code, and then outputs the whole thing as a *runtime executable*, which, in the case of Flash, plays inside your SWF file. You will no doubt make mistakes when writing your ActionScript code—mistakes you won't see until you run the movie for the first time. You'll discover possibly one reason Flash was named the way it was: Your movie rapidly jumps from one frame to the next and at the same time Flash displays the problem in the Compiler Errors panel, a window immediately adjacent to the timeline.

ActionScript Basics

As you've already learned, when writing ActionScript in Flash, you can use the Actions panel. Before you proceed further, there are just a few things you need to know as you're reading the ActionScript code in the Actions panel (to follow along with these descriptions, open the Flash file AS3Examples.fla available on this book's website at www.sybex.com/go/flashessentials):

Event listeners   ActionScript is tied to objects or events on the stage through what is called an *event listener.* The idea is this: You put a button on the stage and then set up some code that "listens" for activity on the button. How does Flash know which button is which? You assign the button a unique instance name and then refer to that instance name in code. In line 3 of Figure 13.1, you can see that ActionScript is listening to the button instance name btnGo (you can also see the actual button on the stage). What is ActionScript listening for? A mouse event. And to which mouse event is it listening? Why, the clicking of a mouse, of course! All of this is easily readable in Figure 13.1.

FIGURE 13.1 Actions panel showing code for a button and a variable declaration

You are not limited to tying an event listener to a button; there are a variety of activities in which ActionScript could be listening. For example, you could have a listener that listens for Flash to enter a given frame. This listener, called Event .ENTER_FRAME, is hugely useful for triggering actions that are not tied to any one object on the stage.

Functions   If the listener "hears" the activity it is looking for (such as a button click), it runs a function—a piece of code that performs some specific job for you. Referencing Figure 13.1, you recognize the button's instance name (btnGo). Now you can see that the code sets up an event listener, predicated on a mouse click. The last half of the section in parentheses is the function name (fl_ClickToGoToAndStopAtFrame).

You should be aware that there are two different times in which ActionScript refers to the function name: first, within the event listener declaration, and second, in the function declaration itself. When the event listener "hears" an event happen, we say that it *calls* the function. In almost all cases, the function definition follows immediately after the event listener, though it's not required (it's just good formatting).

Function definition   You can recognize AS3 functions because they are always formulated the same way. There is the keyword function, followed by a function name, followed by left and right parentheses, inside of which there may be one or more *arguments*, followed by a colon and a thing called the *return type*. (In Figure 13.1, the return type is void). After the function declaration, you'll see left and right curly braces. All function code *must* be written in between the two curly braces. If you forget to add a closing curly brace, you will run into a thing called a *compilation error* (also frequently referred to as a *compiler error*—which is what Flash calls them). Figure 13.2 shows what the compiler error looks like. Note that this particular error is meaningful, although you may run across a compiler error that is more cryptic. Half the fun of writing code is deciphering nebulous compiler errors (I'm joking).

Timeline	Compiler Errors	Motion Editor	
Location		Description	
Scene 1, Layer 'Actions', Frame 1		1084: Syntax error: expecting rightbrace before end of program.	

FIGURE 13.2 Compiler error in the Compilation Errors panel

You should also be aware that your program may be perfectly fine from a syntactic perspective—meaning you don't generate any compiler errors—but the program still does not run correctly. This is attributable to some kind of logic error you've inadvertently built into the code. In other words, the code is doing exactly what you told it to do, but what you told it to do isn't correct. These errors can be tremendously difficult to find because the compiler doesn't give you any hints.

Variables In the top line (line 1) of Figure 13.1 you also see what is a called a *variable declaration*. Variables are places in the computer's memory that the code sets aside to store working information. In line 1 of the figure, you can see that a variable called myText has been declared. This variable tells the computer to store information that is of the type TextField—just one of the many variable types ActionScript knows about. You don't really need to care about the technical details of what a text field is; just know that in some cases Flash needs to set up a text field so you can dynamically assign text. You'll use this in a moment.

You can and will use variables for a variety of work. Suppose, for example, that you want to calculate something. You need to store working numbers somewhere, so you declare a variable for each different element of the equation you're using. You can use variables to determine if something is true or false, for sound and video work, and much more. The primary idea you should have in your head at this point is that a variable is a piece of memory set aside for some work you want to do and the computer is expecting a certain type of data to be put into this memory. You can't put true/false data into a number variable, for example.

Class Your code doesn't have to be created in the Actions Panel. You can create separate ActionScript 3.0 class files that work alongside your .FLA file.

Working with Dynamic Text

You should be aware that many ActionScript programmers rarely visit the stage; nearly everything is done in code.

To get your feet wet working directly with code, you'll create a text field in code, put it on the stage, and then format it. (You can reference TextTest.fla on this book's website if you like.)

Before proceeding, it's important to note that you can always tell what size your SWF file is simply by looking in the SWF History section of the Property Inspector. As you change things and then run the movie, the SWF History section will show you the change in file size. As you go about writing the following code, check the SWF file's size to see how you're doing. Less is more!

Certification
Objective

1. Open a new ActionScript 3.0 document.

2. From the Flash main menu, choose Window ➢ Actions or press F9. The Actions panel opens, ready for you to write some code.

3. On line 1, type the line 1 text from Figure 13.1: `var myText:TextField = new TextField();`. As you type, you'll find that ActionScript brings up a code hints window that suggests possible code words you might want to use (a huge time-saver). Note also that all ActionScript key words are blue.

INTRODUCTION TO THE CONSTRUCTOR

When you see the keyword new and the name of the field type followed by parentheses (e.g., `TextField()`), you are looking at what we call a *constructor*. The point with a constructor is to build—or in programmer parlance, *instantiate*—a new object of a certain type. In this case you're instructing ActionScript to build you a new text field with the name myText.

4. Now you'll add some text to your new text field. On line 2, type `myText.text = "Hello World!";`. In this code you're addressing the text field's text property (one of many properties a text field has), assigning it the sentence (coders call sentences *strings*) "Hello World!" Don't forget that code statements must include a semicolon! Note that strings are highlighted in green.

5. On line 3, type the code `stage.addChild(myText);`. This code does exactly what it says: It adds the child text field called myText to the stage. Think of the stage itself as the parent and any objects being

placed on it as child objects and you'll have the right notion of what's going on.

6. Play the movie with Ctrl+Enter (Command+Enter on the Mac). If there are any errors, Flash will switch from the timeline to the Compiler Errors panel with a description of the error. Close the movie and double-click the error to go to that section of your AS3 code. At this basic level, if you encounter an error you've probably not included a semicolon at the end of a statement or you have mistyped something. Check your code against the figures. (See Figure 13.3.)

FIGURE 13.3 ActionScript code so far, and what it looks like when it runs in the movie

Certification
Objective
Programmatically Adjusting a Text Object's Coordinates and Formatting

Right now this is pretty boring, ordinary text, but hey, at least you've put something on the screen using code, right? Now you'll jazz the text up some more.

1. With the same Actions panel open, type the following code on line 4: **myText.x = 50;**. This code tells Flash to place the upper-left corner of the text field at 50 on the x-axis. In the Flash coordinate system, x moves from 0 on the left to positive numbers as you move farther right. Additionally, y moves from 0 on the top to positive numbers moving *down* the screen (quite different than the coordinate system you were taught in school in which the y-axis numbers were positive as they moved up).

2. On line 5, type **myText.y = 50;**.

3. Play the movie. You should see that Flash has adjusted the placement of the text field.

> Colons tell ActionScript what type of variable you want to use. Dots tell ActionScript what property you want to assign for a given object (e.g., myText's **y-axis**).

Now you'll add some formatting to the text object.

Certification
Objective

1. With the current Actions panel still open, on line 6 of the script type `var myFormat:TextFormat = new TextFormat();`. This line tells Flash that you want to set up a new type of text format, different from the default. Note that you've not yet used this format; you have just declared it. Note also that all code you write is case sensitive: an uppercase *A* is different than a lowercase *a*.

2. On line 7, you will assign a new text color by keying in the following: `myFormat.color = 0x0000FF;`.

DISASSEMBLING HEX COLOR CODES

Hex is easy to disassemble. Disregard the 0x component: this just tells you you're using hex. The following six numbers are the important ones: two for red, two for green, and two for blue. Each set of two numbers can vary from 0 through *F*—0 being fully off, *F* being fully on. Thus, 0000FF has 0 red, 0 green, and blue fully turned on.

3. On line 8, type the following: `myFormat.font = "Arial";`. Remember that Flash will prompt you to embed fonts, and you should probably heed its advice.

4. On line 9, key in this code: `myFormat.size = 48;`. Note that a font size is a number and not a string and therefore does not require any double quotes around it.

5. On line 10, type this code: `myFormat.bold = true;`. This is an example of what programmers call a *Boolean* (e.g., true or false) expression. Either the font is bolded or it's not.

6. On line 11, you'll tell ActionScript to use your new format with this code: `myText.setTextFormat(myFormat);`.

7. Play the movie with Ctrl+Enter (Command+Return on the Mac). Note that you may get mixed results with the output.

Testing Your Work

You have entered the twilight zone of text cutoff problems. If you examine your movie, it appears that the problem may be that line 3 of your code is executed before the rest of the code has a chance to run (see Figure 13.4). A text cutoff problem isn't necessarily a problem; it's just not aesthetically pleasing. Let's correct that.

FIGURE 13.4 ActionScript code so far, along with (bad) output

1. Using Ctrl+X and Ctrl+V (Command+X and Command+V on the Mac), move line 3 to the end of the script.

2. Rerun the movie. Oops, you still get the same chopped-off output. That's because the text field ActionScript generated is too small for your font size. To see this, you'll use some more code.

3. Cut line 3 (the line that says "stage.addChild(myText);" and paste it at the bottom of the script in line 12.

4. Click in the now-empty line 3 and hit the backspace key to delete it.

5. Add a new line after line 4 where the code says mytext.y = 50;.

6. Enter this new code on line 5: **myText.border = true;**. This allows the display of a border around the text field you're drawing on the stage.

7. Rerun the movie to see the border. It's now easy to see where the text field's borders are located.

8. After line 5, make a new line.

9. On line 6 key in this code: **myText.wordWrap = true;**. This Boolean expression allows Flash to wrap the string within the boundaries of the text field.

10. Rerun the movie to see how the latest changes have helped (or not). Hopefully it's clear to you how insufficient testing on your part could lead to a rather humorous result (see Figure 13.5).

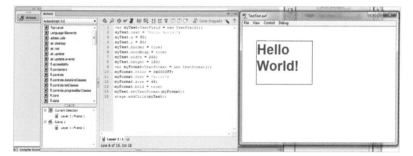

FIGURE 13.5 Further testing reveals more problems

The problem has to do with the fact that you've not instructed ActionScript what size your text field should be, so it went with the defaults. Computers are so darned obedient when it comes to this kind of thing!

1. With the Actions panel from the previous work still open, make a new line after line 6.

2. On the new line 7, type this code: `myText.width = 200;`.

3. Press Enter (Return on the Mac) and type another line of code: `myText.height = 150;`.

4. Run the movie. You have now corrected the problem (see Figure 13.6)!

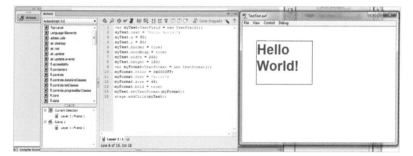

FIGURE 13.6 Success!

5. Save your work.

You must test and retest your rich media documents that include code to make sure they're working properly. In the case of the previously listed issue, they came from the TextField object. You can always find out more about the different properties by visiting

```
http://help.adobe.com/en_US/FlashPlatform/reference/actionscript/3/
flash/text/TextField.html
```

Programming ActionScript to Calculate Your BMI

Are you familiar with the body mass index (BMI)? The BMI is a measure of one's body fat. It is calculated using the person's weight and height. If your BMI is less than 18.5, you're skinny. If it's between 18.5 and 24.9, you're perfectly normal. If your BMI is 25 and 29.9, you're classified as overweight. And if your BMI is over 30, you're considered obese.

It turns out creating a BMI calculator is a pretty good way to learn ActionScript programming because it requires you to declare variables to use in your calculation. The formula for the BMI in imperial (i.e., US) measurements is BMI = (weight in pounds / height in inches^2) × 703. It's also great for learning how to take input from a user. (You can use the file BMI.fla on this book's website as a reference if you need to.)

1. Start a new ActionScript document.

2. Create a Classic Text static text field that says **Enter your height in inches:**.

3. Immediately to the right of the static text field, create a text field of type input text.

4. Give the input text field an instance name of tfldHeight.

5. In the Character section for the text field, select the Show Border Around Text button ▣. If you don't do this, the user will have no idea where to begin keying in their height data (see Figure 13.7).

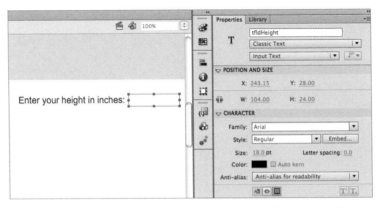

FIGURE 13.7 Setting up user guidance and user input text fields

6. Repeat steps 2 through 5. The new static text field should say **Enter your weight in pounds:** and the input text field should have the instance name of tfldWeight.

7. From the Flash main menu, click Text ➤ Font Embedding and embed the font you chose for your text fields.

8. Repeat steps 2 through 5 again, this time creating two dynamic text fields instead of static or input text fields. The leftmost dynamic text field should say **Your BMI is:** and its instance name should be tfldBMIText. Give the second dynamic text field the instance name tfldBMIData. You'll turn both boxes' visibility off until after the calculation is performed. Since static text fields cannot have an instance name assigned to them, you must use a dynamic text field for this work. The second text field won't require any user input, therefore you should make it a dynamic text field.

9. Repeat steps 2 through 5 again, this time creating two dynamic text fields. The first dynamic text field will have the text **Your BMI category is:** with the instance name tfldCategoryText. The second will have the instance name tfldCategoryData.

10. Make sure the all the text fields on the right nicely match. Better to have a little space between one instruction or label and its commensurate dynamic or input text field than to have a jagged look on the screen. In the case of Figure 13.8, each of the static or dynamic text fields is positioned at *x*-coordinate 260.

11. Create a button called btnCalcBMI on the stage, giving it the instance name btnCalcBMI (see Figure 13.8).

> ◄
>
> **Think about how you phrase instructions for users. Carelessly formed instructions may lead to user confusion about what you want them to do and result in diminished user satisfaction with your program.**

FIGURE 13.8 Completed user screen

You've already seen the code needed to programmatically create the text fields. For a beginner, it's easier to create the form assets on the stage and then programmatically access them with ActionScript.

12. On the main timeline, create a new layer and name it Actions. Make sure the Actions layer is at the top.

13. Name the layer with the text fields and button on it Form. Make sure the Form layer is locked and click the Actions layer to make it active.

14. Save your work.

Writing the Code to Declare Variables and Hide Dynamic Text Fields

Now that you have the interface built, it's time to write the code.

Certification
Objective

1. Click Window ➤ Actions or press the F9 key to open the Actions panel.

2. On line 1, type the command **stop();**. This command stops any stray executions from taking place.

RECOGNIZING METHODS

Any time you encounter a command word with parentheses after it, you are looking at what is called a *method*. Think of a method as a piece of helper code you use to perform some job for you. Methods are included in libraries that come with the programming environment. Once you become a more sophisticated coder, you will likely want to write your own methods to accomplish various jobs for you, but check first! There may already be a method that does what you want.

3. When you write lots of code, it's important to add comments at certain points so that others who need to maintain it (or you, months later when you no longer understand what you intended) understand your intent. On line 2 of the script, type **//Declare variables for user input and calculations**. No semicolon is required for this comment. The compiler ignores comments.

4. Next you will create some variables to hold the input data your user gives you. On line 3 of your script, type this: **var**.

`userHeight:Number = 0.0;`. This process simultaneously declares and *initializes* the variable to initially contain zero.

5. On line 4 of your script, key in this variable declaration: `var userWeight:Number = 0.0;`.

6. On line 5 of the script, type `var BMI:Number = 0.0;`.

DETERMINING WHETHER NUMBERS HAVE A FRACTIONAL COMPONENT

In the case of the BMI calculator, you'll more than likely end up with a number ending with a decimal. Thus, you used the variable type Number for your variables. However, if you expect all numbers to never have a fractional component you can use the variable type Int instead. Int stands for *integer*.

7. On line 6 of the script, type this comment: `//Hide the dynamic text fields`.

8. Line 7 will have the code that turns off the BMI label: `tfldBMIText .visible = false;`. You are working with the tfldBMIText object, and you're setting its visibility property to false (invisible).

9. Repeat step 8 on line 8 for the tfldBMIData text field. `tfldBMIData .visible = false;`.

10. On line 9, type the code `tfldCategoryText.visible = false;`.

11. One line 10, type the code `tfldCategoryData.visible = false;`.

12. Save our work. Your code should look similar to Figure 13.9.

```
1   stop();
2   //Declare variables for user input and calculations
3   var userHeight:Number = 0.0;
4   var userWeight:Number = 0.0;
5   var BMI:Number = 0.0;
6   //Hide the dynamic text fields
7   tfldBMIText.visible = false;
8   tfldBMIData.visible = false;
9   tfldCategoryText.visible = false;
10  tfldCategoryData.visible = false;
```

FIGURE 13.9 Your code so far

Garnering User Input

Now that you have the basic skeleton set up, it's time to deal with user input. Because everything is predicated on the calculation button being pressed, the calculation part will all happen between the two curly braces that make up the button press function.

You'll assume the user has already keyed their data into both input text fields. In reality, it's not quite that easy. In production environments, you will probably want to write code perform *error trapping*. For example, what would happen if the user didn't key in anything for their height? For the purpose of this exercise, however, we'll assume the user keyed in both pieces of information.

Also, you should know that the user thinks they're keying in numeric data, when in fact it is currently in text form. You'll have to call a Flash method that turns the text into a number.

**Certification
Objective**

1. Still working with the file from the previous exercise, on line 9, type this comment: **//Set up button listener and function**.

2. On line 11, type this event listener code: **btnCalcBMI
   .addEventListener(MouseEvent.CLICK, calcBMI);**. Note that the script is listening on button btnCalcBMI for a mouse click event. If the script hears that event, it runs function calcBMI. Note the "MouseEvent.CLICK" blurb. This is the event source, the thing that's driving the firing of the event - in this case a mouse click.

3. On line 12, type the start of the function code: **function
   calcBMI(event:MouseEvent):void**. Do *not* put a semicolon after this statement! It will generate a compiler error. The compiler reads the function statement, enters into the body of the function (which is roped in by curly braces), and then begins to read function statements, each of which does end in a semicolon.

4. On line 13, type a left curly brace.

5. On line 14, type the code needed to take the height the user keyed in, convert it to a number, and put it into your userHeight variable: **userHeight = Number(tfldHeight);**.

6. On line 15, type this code: **trace(userHeight);**. The trace method is useful for showing you the contents of various variables you have declared. Note that trace is a method that requires at least one argument. In this case, it is whatever the variable userHeight contains. The Output window in which the trace command puts its text is in a panel that sits next to the Timeline and Compiler Errors windows.

7. On line 16, type a right curly brace.

8. Play the movie, key in your height in inches, and note the contents of the Output window. (See Figure 13.10).

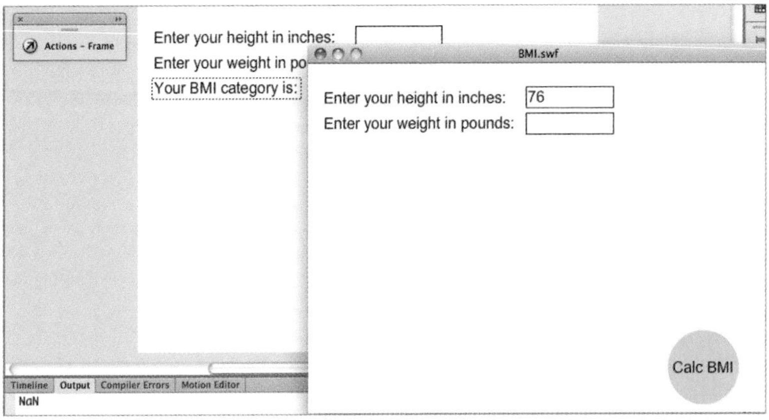

FIGURE 13.10 The program running in a movie, with trace command output showing up in the Output window

9. There's a problem. The Output window shows NaN, which, in compiler parlance, means "not a number." So you've done something wrong. The error lies in the fact that you asked Flash to output the text field itself, not the text field's properties. Change the line in step 5 to `userHeight = Number(tfldHeight.text);`. Adding .text to the code means that you're telling Flash to go to the tfldHeight object and get whatever's in the text field there.

10. Rerun the movie, again keying in your height in inches. This time you should see the correct output.

11. Now that you're sure the code works, erase line 16.

12. Enter a new line 16 with the following code: `userWeight = Number(tfldWeight.text);`.

13. Press Enter (Command on the Mac) to create a new line. There should now be a space between line 16 and the curly brace on line 18. Line 17 should be blank.

14. Save your work.

Calculating and Outputting the Results

You've handled the user input; now it's time to take care of calculating the results.

Certification
Objective

1. On line 17, key in the following code: **BMI = ((userWeight / (userHeight * userHeight)) * 703);**. This code calculates the user's BMI and puts the result into a variable called BMI. Note the order of operations. Enclosing a math operation in parentheses within a set of parentheses forces the inner parenthetic operation to happen first. Thus the height is squared first and then the division operation happens, then the multiplication.

2. Round the resulting BMI using this code on line 18: **BMI = Math .round(BMI);**.

3. Put the BMI calculation into the tfldBMIData text field on line 19: **tfldBMIData.text = String(BMI);**.

4. Make the BMI text appear with this code on line 20: **tfldBMIText .visible = true;**.

5. Make the BMI data appear with this code on line 21: **tfldBMIData .visible = true;**.

6. Make the Category text appear with this code on line 22: **tfldCat-egoryText.visible = true;**. (See Figure 13.11.)

7. Make the Category text appear with this code on line 23: **tfldCat-egoryData.visible = true;**.

```
1   stop();
2   //Declare variables for user input and calculations
3   var userHeight:Number = 0.0;
4   var userWeight:Number = 0.0;
5   var BMI:Number = 0.0;
6   //Hide the dynamic text fields
7   tfldBMIText.visible = false;
8   tfldBMIData.visible = false;
9   tfldCategoryText.visible = false;
10  tfldCategoryData.visible = false;
11  //Set up button listener and function
12  btnCalcBMI.addEventListener(MouseEvent.CLICK, calcBMI);
13  function calcBMI(event:MouseEvent):void
14  {
15      userHeight = Number(tfldHeight.text);
16      userWeight = Number(tfldWeight.text);
17      BMI = ( (userWeight / (userHeight * userHeight )) * 703);
18      BMI = Math.round(BMI);
19      tfldBMIData.text = String(BMI);
20      tfldBMIText.visible = true;
21      tfldBMIData.visible = true;
22      tfldCategoryText.visible = true;
23      tfldCategoryData.visible = true;
24  }
```

FIGURE 13.11 Your code so far

8. Run the movie to test your work. Make any corrections you need to.

9. Save your work.

Now that you have the program running, all you have to do is put in some logic that tests to determine what the user's BMI is and output a category into the `tfldCategoryData.text` property.

1. In the file you were working on in the previous exercise, on line 24 type this comment: **//Test to see what category the user's BMI falls into.**

2. On line 25, type this code: **if(BMI < 18.5)**. Note that there is no semicolon here.

3. On line 26, type a left curly brace.

4. On line 27, type this code: **tfldCategoryData.text = "Underweight";**. This code puts the string "underweight" in the tfld-CategoryData text field.

5. On line 28, type a right curly brace. (See Figure 13.12 for the code so far.)

```
1   stop();
2   //Declare variables for user input and calculations
3   var userHeight:Number = 0.0;
4   var userWeight:Number = 0.0;
5   var BMI:Number = 0.0;
6   //Hide the dynamic text fields
7   tfldBMIText.visible = false;
8   tfldBMIData.visible = false;
9   tfldCategoryText.visible = false;
10  tfldCategoryData.visible = false;
11  //Set up button listener and function
12  btnCalcBMI.addEventListener(MouseEvent.CLICK, calcBMI);
13  function calcBMI(event:MouseEvent):void
14  {
15      userHeight = Number(tfldHeight.text);
16      userWeight = Number(tfldWeight.text);
17      BMI = ( (userWeight / (userHeight * userHeight )) * 703);
18      BMI = Math.round(BMI);
19      tfldBMIData.text = String(BMI);
20      tfldBMIText.visible = true;
21      tfldBMIData.visible = true;
22      tfldCategoryText.visible = true;
23      tfldCategoryData.visible = true;
24      //Test to see what category the user's BMI falls into
25      if(BMI < 18.5)
26      {
27          tfldCategoryData.text = "Underweight";
28      }
29  }
```

FIGURE 13.12 Code with an **if** statement in it

6. On line 29, type this code: **else if (BMI >= 18.5 && BMI <= 24.9)**. (No semicolon.) The two ampersands (&&) represent a logical and. Both sides of the and have to be true in order for the whole statement to be true. A logical or is written with two "pipes" (||). A logical or means either side must evaluate to true for the statement itself to be true. But both sides of an or do not need to be true.

   7. On line 30, type a left curly brace.

   8. On line 31, type `tfldCategoryData.text = "Normal";`.

   9. On line 32, type a right curly brace.

   10. Repeat steps 7 through 10 for the next two category types: over-
      weight and obese. Overweight falls between 25 and 29.9, while obese
      is anything over 30. (See Figure 13.13 for the code).

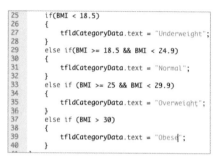

```
25      if(BMI < 18.5)
26      {
27          tfldCategoryData.text = "Underweight";
28      }
29      else if(BMI >= 18.5 && BMI < 24.9)
30      {
31          tfldCategoryData.text = "Normal";
32      }
33      else if (BMI >= 25 && BMI < 29.9)
34      {
35          tfldCategoryData.text = "Overweight";
36      }
37      else if (BMI > 30)
38      {
39          tfldCategoryData.text = "Obese";
40      }
```

FIGURE 13.13 Completed `if` statements for evaluating BMI and
outputting weight category

   11. Run your movie, fix any compiler errors, and test your work.

   12. Save your file.

   Figure 13.14 shows an example of the kind of output you should expect from a
successful run of your BMI app.

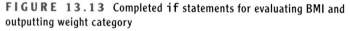

BMI.swf

Enter your height in inches: 72
Enter your weight in pounds: 180
Your BMI is: 24
Your BMI category is: Normal

Calc BMI

FIGURE 13.14 BMI app running

   ActionScript has all kinds of methods you can use. Three common ones are
gotoAndPlay(), navigateToURL(), and SoundMixer.stopAll()

Publishing Your Work

Once you have an application you like, you can publish it so that you can put it on a website. Remember that the SWF file resulting from simply running the completed movie can be copied to any computer that has Flash Player installed or can run in a browser with the Flash Player installed. But if you want the app to run in an HTML page, you need to publish it. In this exercise you'll publish your BMI app.

Certification Objective

1. With the application still open from previous exercises, from the Flash main menu, click File ➤ Publish Settings. The Publish Settings window opens (see Figure 13.15).

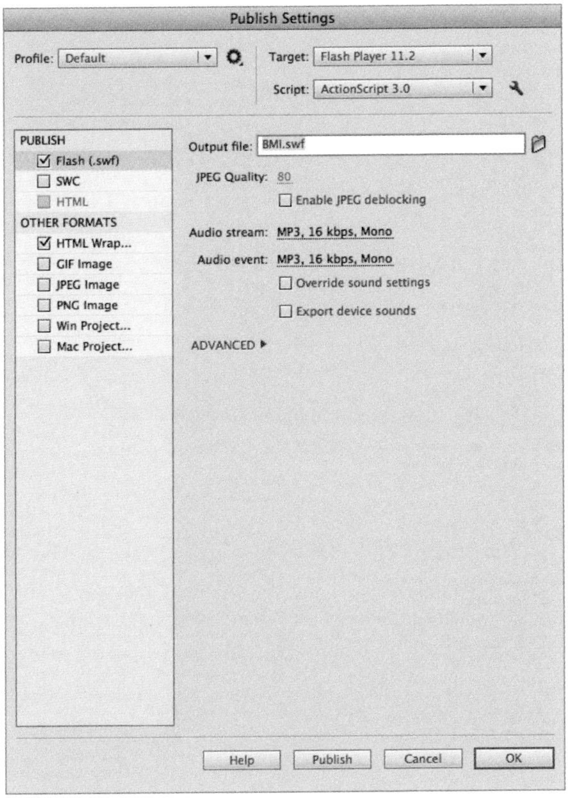

FIGURE 13.15 The Publish Settings window

The most important elements of the Publish Settings window are the level of Flash Player to which you intend to publish, the version of ActionScript to which you're publishing, and whether you're publishing to HTML or a different environment.

The Flash Player question is the most important because it addresses the number of users who'll be able to view your content. Generally speaking, the later the version of Flash Player you target, the fewer users there will be who'll be able to view your content. In the case of the BMI app, there are no bells and whistles in use that would require the latest and greatest Flash Player version.

The ActionScript version question is a subtler one. Some ActionScript code is version 3.0 only. The good news is that when you select a downscale version of ActionScript, Flash will alert you that you've used AS3-only syntax. In the case of the BMI app, you've properly formulated your syntax for ActionScript 3.0, but older Flash Player installations that know about only ActionScript 2.0 will not choke on the code and will successfully run the app. That said, AS3 has been around long enough that the upgrade cycle between AS2 and AS3 has likely run its duration. Thus, you'll be able to leave the Script drop-down set for ActionScript 3.0.

2. In the Target drop-down, select Flash Player 9.

3. Click OK.

4. From the Flash main menu, click File ➤ Publish.

While it appears that nothing really happened, in fact Flash has created an HTML file that you'll need to upload to your website for your new app to successfully run.

No Spaces!

The HTML file has the same name as your FLA file—which could cause concern if you have spaces in the filename. Remember that web servers don't like spaces in filenames and will replace them with the strange %20 (web-speak for "space") escape sequence. Rename your production HTML file to something that contains no spaces.

To publish your app, simply upload the HTML and SWF files; then link to the HTML file on the page in which you wish to reference the app. Other supported publish file types include Projector (EXE), SWC, Quicktime (MOV), GIF, JPEG, PNG, and HQX.

THE ESSENTIALS AND BEYOND

In this chapter you learned how to write some basic ActionScript code. You learned about event listeners, functions, and variables. You also learned how to programmatically change the text in text fields as well as how to convert text to a number. Additionally, you learned how to use ActionScript's math capabilities to run a calculation based upon user input.

Now let's add some (ahem) flash to your app. You will make it so that you start out with no background color in your tfldCategoryData, but you will programmatically change the text field's background color based upon the user's BMI outcome. This becomes a design question: What color resonates with a given weight category? For example, does the color pink symbolize underweight? Oh, maybe not, because pink is associated with breast cancer awareness and some users may take umbrage with pink being associated with underweight because it is brings up the reality that people lose weight when they're on chemotherapy. Do you see the kind of consideration you have to put into your designs? Let's go with blue for underweight, green for normal, orange for overweight, and red for obese.

1. Open your BMI file and open the Actions panel.

2. Navigate to the code section in which you do your if statement tests.

3. If the code enters the first if statement, it means the user is underweight. Add this comment beneath the existing line of code: **//Change Category Data text field background color to blue.** This should be new line 28.

4. On line 29, type this code: **tfldCategoryData.backgroundColor = 0x0000FF;**.

```
25    if(BMI < 18.5)
26    {
27        tfldCategoryData.text = "Underweight";
28        //Change Category Data text field background color to blue
29        tfldCategoryData.backgroundColor = 0x0000FF;
30    }
31    else if(BMI >= 18.5 && BMI < 24.9)
32    {
33        tfldCategoryData.text = "Normal";
34    }
35    else if (BMI >= 25 && BMI < 29.9)
36    {
37        tfldCategoryData.text = "Overweight";
38    }
39    else if (BMI > 30)
40    {
41        tfldCategoryData.text = "Obese";
42    }
```

5. Repeat steps 3 and 4 for the next three else if statements, inserting **0x00FF00** for green (normal weight), **0xFF6600** for orange (overweight), and **0xFF0000** for red (overweight).

(Continues)

```
25        if(BMI < 18.5)
26        {
27            tfldCategoryData.text = "Underweight";
28            //Change Category Data text field background color to blue
29            tfldCategoryData.backgroundColor = 0x0000FF;
30        }
31        else if(BMI >= 18.5 && BMI < 24.9)
32        {
33            tfldCategoryData.text = "Normal";
34            //Change Category Data text field background color to green
35            tfldCategoryData.backgroundColor = 0x00FF00;
36        }
37        else if (BMI >= 25 && BMI < 29.9)
38        {
39            tfldCategoryData.text = "Overweight";
40            //Change Category Data text field background color to orange
41            tfldCategoryData.backgroundColor = 0xFF6600;
42        }
43        else if (BMI > 30)
44        {
45            tfldCategoryData.text = "Obese";
46            //Change Category Data text field background color to red
47            tfldCategoryData.backgroundColor = 0xFF0000;
48        }
```

Be sure to test your work to make sure the colors accurately come up based upon a BMI. You may need to bring up your computer's calculator and manually calculate a few sample BMIs just so you have some data with which to validate the code. This is a highly important step: performing quality assurance testing before you deploy.

It's also important to know that this app is not yet production worthy. In other words, you would consider this a great prototype app, but you would not put it out there for users for several reasons:

▶ You don't have any error trapping in the code for bogus heights and weights. For example, you shouldn't be able to key in a height of 13 inches and a weight of 1500 pounds, or vice versa. What are the reasonable boundaries for an actual BMI calculation?

▶ You don't have a reset button. When the program is done calculating your BMI, you have to close the app and start over. This isn't good. What happens if a user fat-fingers their height or weight?

▶ You haven't done any error trapping in the event a user keys in nonnumeric characters. Try it yourself: Run the app and key in letters for both the height and width. The app will successfully run, displaying NaN in the BMI field. This means there's a logic error, not a computational problem. These are very sticky but important issues to resolve before pushing an app out to a runtime production environment.

ANSWER TO ADDITIONAL EXERCISE

```
○○○                    BMI.swf

Enter your height in inches:   [76        ]
Enter your weight in pounds:   [230       ]
Your BMI is:                   [28        ]
Your BMI category is:          [Overweight]




                                    Calc BMI
```

Also reference BMI.fla on this book's website if you need further assistance.

Adobe Rich Media Communication Using Flash Professional CS6 Objectives

The Adobe Certified Associate (ACA) certifications are industry-recognized credentials that can help you succeed in your design career—providing benefits to both you and your employer.

Getting certified is a reliable validation of skills and knowledge, and it can expand your career opportunities, improve your productivity, and help you stand apart from your peers.

This Adobe Approved Courseware for the ACA can be an effective component of your exam preparation. To prepare for certification, review the most current exam preparation roadmap available at www.adobe.com/support/certification, where you will find information on where you can take a test and how to promote your status once you've passed.

Certification Objective

To help you focus your studies on the skills you'll need for the exam, Table A.1 shows each objective and the chapter in which you can find information on that topic—and when you go to that chapter, you'll find certification icons like the one in the margin here.

These Adobe exam objectives were accurate at press time; please refer to www.adobe.com/support/certification for the most current exam roadmap and objectives.

Good luck preparing for your certification!

TABLE A.1: Adobe Rich Media Communication using Flash Professional CS6 objectives

Topic	Exam objectives	Adobe Flash Professional CS6 Essentials
Objective 1.0 Setting Project Requirements	1.1 Identify the purpose, audience, and audience needs for rich media content.	Chapter 1
	1.2 Identify rich media content that is relevant to the purpose of the media in which it will be used (websites, mobile devices, and so on).	Chapter 1
	1.3 Understand options for producing accessible rich media content.	Chapter 1
	1.4 Demonstrate knowledge of standard copyright rules (related terms, obtaining permission, and citing copyrighted material).	Chapter 1
	1.5 Understand project management tasks and responsibilities.	Chapter 1
	1.6 Communicate with others (such as peers and clients) about design and content plans.	Chapter 1
Objective 2.0 Identifying Rich Media Design Elements	2.1 Identify general and Flash-specific best practices for designing rich media content for the Web, mobile apps, and AIR applications.	Chapter 1, 2, 3, 6, 12
	2.2 Demonstrate knowledge of design elements and principles.	Chapter 1, 12
	2.3 Identify general and Flash-specific techniques to create rich media elements that are accessible and readable.	Chapter 1, 5
	2.4 Use a storyboard to design rich media elements.	Chapter 1, 7
	2.5 Organize a Flash document.	Chapter 4

Topic	Exam objectives	Adobe Flash Professional CS6 Essentials
Objective 3.0 Understanding Adobe Flash CS6 Interface	3.1 Identify elements of the Flash interface.	Chapter 1, 2
	3.2 Use the Property Inspector.	Chapter 2, 3, 4, 5, 6, 7, 8, 9, 10, 11, 12, 13
	3.3 Use the timeline.	Chapter 4, 7
	3.4 Adjust document properties.	Chapter 4
	3.5 Use Flash guides and rulers.	Chapter 4, 7
	3.6 Use the Motion Editor.	Chapter 3, 7, 9
	3.7 Understand Flash file types.	Chapter 2, 12
	3.8 Identify best practices for managing the file size of a published Flash document.	Chapter 2
Objective 4.0 Building Rich Media Elements by Using Flash CS6	4.1 Make rich media content development decisions based on your analysis and interpretation of design specifications.	Chapter 1
	4.2 Use tools on the Tools panel to select, create, and manipulate graphics and text.	Chapter 1, 2, 3, 9
	4.3 Import and modify graphics.	Chapter 1, 2, 6, 10
	4.4 Create text.	Chapter 5
	4.5 Adjust text properties.	Chapter 1, 4, 5
	4.6 Create objects and convert them to symbols, including graphics, movie clips, and buttons.	Chapter 1, 4, 6
	4.7 Understand symbols and the library.	Chapter 3, 6, 7
	4.8 Edit symbols and instances.	Chapter 6
	4.9 Create masks.	Chapter 4

(Continues)

TABLE A.1 *(Continued)*

Topic	Exam objectives	Adobe Flash Professional CS6 Essentials
	4.10 Create animations (changes in shape, position, size, color, and transparency).	Chapter 4, 7, 8, 9, 10
	4.11 Add simple controls through ActionScript 3.0.	Chapter 7, 13
	4.12 Import and use sound.	Chapter 11
	4.13 Add and export video.	Chapter 12
	4.14 Publish and export Flash documents.	Chapter 11, 12, 13
	4.15 Make a Flash document accessible.	Chapter 1
Objective 5.0 Evaluating Rich Media Elements by Using Flash CS6	5.1 Conduct basic technical tests.	Chapter 5, 7, 13
	5.2 Identify techniques for basic usability tests.	Chapter 13

Next Steps

So, you've read this book, practiced using Flash, and successfully passed the Rich Media Communication with Adobe Flash Professional Adobe Certified Associate (ACA) exam. Good for you!

What are your next steps? Fortunately for you, there are a myriad of areas for you to explore. Since its inception, Flash has been the go-to product for web-based animations, so there is an extensive body of knowledge that designers and developers have built around it. Simply garnering a web education in Flash will take up all of your waking moments. But what are some of the specifics you should be looking at?

Interaction of Animation and Code

A beginner's guide to Flash cannot begin to do justice to a comprehensive discussion of ActionScript. Many (most?) of the complex animations on the Web are actually the compilation of some great on-stage designs with solid AS3 code backing them up. Want to create a game spinner similar to the one in the child's game Chutes and Ladders? The design is relatively rudimentary, but the code is well beyond beginner level. Want to make things magically appear and reappear? While you can certainly leverage tweens to the hilt, at some point you'll likely rely on AS3 code.

The code's the thing, but the code has to have objects to manipulate or it's not worth anything.

In my classes I give students this advice all the time: We no longer live in a world where straight good design principles can get you where you need to go. You *must* develop a strong understanding of the technology, especially when it comes to code, so that you can leverage those design attributes. The people who have strong skills in *both* design and code but who live primarily at the sweet spot where those skills merge are the ones who find the most success in our disruptive, volcanic, web-centric world.

Determine to become a code wonk!

Oh, and by the way, garnering a huge body of knowledge in AS3 will be very good for you in other realms. For example, considering the powerful troika of HTML5, CSS3, and JavaScript, your AS3 skills will make you feel right at home in the JavaScript world because AS3 is simply a dialect of JavaScript. You've been learning it all along and didn't know it!

Also, gathering a solid body of knowledge with regard to AS3 will allow you to do more in code and less on the stage, which speeds up your rich media efforts. And as an added benefit, you might want to investigate developing Adobe AIR apps as a sideline to your rich media work.

Dispense with the Written Narrative

As a writer, it pains me to say this, but when it comes to text, less is more. As good as the information age has been, its one big downfall has been the flood of text one is invited to read. People are simply too busy to read (and more important, comprehend) all of the text they're faced with on a daily basis. Therefore, it's to your benefit to find ways to show what you want to say while at the same time using very little, if any, text. Flash is an ideal tool for this.

Big Bad Voodoo Daddy is a very good big band jazz and swing group of international acclaim. Consider their Flash-based site: `www.bbvd.com/theatre_home.html`. There's very little text on the main page, but you clearly understand what you're looking at: the door to some kind of theater with marquees on both sides of the theater entrance providing you with rich media information about who and what is involved. Investigate further, navigating to other pages, and you find the same kind of thinking. As you venture inside, you'll find that the designers have kept the theater analogy. You're seated at the Cab Calloway cocktail table, which in reality is a preview sampling of BBVD's tribute to the legendary big band leader.

Here's the thing the BBVD site does: It causes you think that you're going inside a theater, sitting at a table. You're actively engaged in the site, not simply reading some static text pages. That is the entire point of rich media.

So, put on your designer hat and take that viewer inside your experience. Instead of letting them read the menu, show them the goodies you have to offer.

Integrate Music and Video Into Your Work

Because you can so easily bring music and videos into your work, you now have lots of opportunities to decide when and where those elements are important to your rich media story.

Have you ever visited a site and were startled by some loud blaring music you didn't really care about? Have you become frustrated searching around on such a site for some sort of "Volume = Off" button only to find none?

The trick to integrating music and video into your work is to do it in such a way that it is timely for your viewers. Set the mood with your music, provide a video that instructs further, and you've enhanced the document. Stomp into the room with 76 trombones and you'll likely turn off your viewers.

You've invited someone into your environment. Now what music and video moments do you think are important to share with them?

Don't Think of Flash as the Be-All and End-All

I love Flash. I mean, I *really love* Flash. This is an amazing product. But it's not the end of the world. It's a tool—okay, a pretty cool tool—in your web development world.

The problem is that the smaller computers—the smartphones and tablets of the world—may not be able to run Flash. Adobe has recently announced it will no longer continue developing Flash Player for these devices.

When Steve Jobs came out on stage and declared that he would not allow Apple to run Flash on the iPhone and iPad, he also explained why: HTML5 can do the same thing.

What he meant was that the combination of HTML5, CSS3, and JavaScript can do the same thing.

And he was right.

But here's the thing: You have a huge, beautiful rich media development tool in front of you in the form of Flash. When you're doing web development for PCs, it's smart to think Flash because your time to product delivery is reduced.

However, when working on apps for smaller devices, you may want to consider the HTML5, CSS3, JavaScript alternative. Check out Adobe Edge as a tool that will assist you in developing rich media content using this troika.

In the end, it's safe to say you can trust Adobe—with its rich legacy of bringing forward industry-standard web development and rich media tools—to help you navigate through the changes into the next, new Internet developments.

INDEX

Note to the Reader: Throughout this index **boldfaced** page numbers indicate primary discussions of a topic. *Italicized* page numbers indicate illustrations.